T0285264

GAMBLING ON GREEN

GAMBLING ON GREEN

Uncovering the Balance Among Revenues, Reputations, and ESG

KEESA C. SCHREANE

WILEY

Published by John Wiley & Sons, Inc., Hoboken, New Jersey.
Published simultaneously in Canada.

For general information on our other products and services or for technical support, please contact our Customer Care Department within the United States at (800) 762-2974, outside the United States at (317) 572-3993 or fax (317) 572-4002.

Wiley also publishes its books in a variety of electronic formats. Some content that appears in print may not be available in electronic formats. For more information about Wiley products, visit our web site at www.wiley.com.

Library of Congress Cataloging-in-Publication Data is Available:

ISBN 9781119892090 (hardback)
ISBN 9781119892120 (epub)
ISBN 9781119892137 (ePDF)

Cover Design: Wiley
Cover Image: © Olha Filatova/Shutterstock

SKY10035643_080522

To Mom, Dad, and Tiffany: Your love, wisdom, humor, and support have given me a foundation and safe space to imagine and believe that all things are possible.

Contents

Contents

Acknowledgments

Thanks to my family and friends, whose support made the journey of this book a brighter one.

Much appreciation to my Wiley team: executive editor Sheck Cho, managing editor Susan Cerra, marketing leader Jean-Karl Martin, sales leader Paul Reese, and editorial assistant Sam Wu, as well as my editorial coaches Hilary Poole and Erika Winston, and content editors Alex Joseph and Shivani Rajpal.

Optilytics Media, thanks for the phenomenal support in bringing structure to my external messaging, resources to deliver that messaging, and excitement around my vision.

Thanks to my Ceres partners who provided a wealth of information and support! Thank you to CEO Mindy Lubber, as well as Siobhan Collins, Mary Ann Ormond, Susan Sayers, and Whitney Williams.

A special round of thanks to my London Stock Exchange Group team members and friends who provided encouragement at every turn.

I appreciate my kind, generous interviewees who graciously shared their stories, expertise, and intelligence.

I'm thankful for my parents, my sister Tiffany, and my amazing community of aunts, uncles, cousins, and extended family who give grace, provide prayers, and steadfast support.

Rawlston, I am so grateful for your partnership, perspective, and continued encouragement.

To the Spirit in which I live, move, and have my being.

About the Author

Keesa C. Schreane is a business strategist, commentator, and speaker. Her specialties include the ESG (environmental, social, and governance) space, as well as risk analysis and sustainable finance.

She is a founder, executive producer, and host of Refinitiv Sustainability Perspectives podcast. Recognized as an industry leader, the show discusses global ESG trends, regulations, and investment strategies with asset managers, asset owners, and C-suite sustainability and corporate officers.

She's also a broadcast television and livestream contributor and writer, who has appeared on numerous outlets including Black Enterprise, Cheddar News, CNBC, CBS, Essence, Latina, and Refinitiv Sustainability Perspectives.

Her expertise includes business development, commercial strategy, sales and marketing, employee resource group leadership, relationship management, and sustainable finance. She is a Fundamentals of Sustainability Accounting (FSA) credential holder and is a Certified Anti-Money Laundering Specialist (CAMS).

Keesa serves on numerous boards and committees, including Ceres President's Council where she and other members leverage their expertise to support transforming the economy to build a just and sustainable future for people and planet.

Connect with Keesa at www.keesaschreane.com.

Introduction

To be a good global citizen is to have a balanced perspective. I've found that identifying how different things interrelate helps me understand how people's actions can reduce the pain of recent events, from pandemics and climate degradation to financial inequity and war. Focusing on interconnectivity helps me to see beyond the devastation. It helps me dare to see glimmers of hope and possibility based on how humans can compassionately respond to these events.

Of course, those glimmers of hope don't negate the realities, tragedies, and impacts that persist.

The potential for a global health crisis loomed for decades and yet somehow still felt like a surprise. COVID-19 directly affected everyone in a manner that many of us had not experienced in our lifetimes. People lived through the illness and death of loved ones, severe business disruption, shutdowns, lockdowns, and of course a lingering sense of unease during travel and in social gatherings. The ways we interact with each other, as well as how we perceive how our health choices affect those around us, are forever altered.

Personal health choices continued to be the subject of scrutiny as the United States Supreme Court overturned *Roe vs. Wade* in June 2022. Although some corporations swiftly committed to covering costs for employees who need to travel out of state for reproductive healthcare, many Americans still feel vulnerable, angry, and violated at decisions surrounding our health and privacy.

Then there are tragedies resulting from invasions and natural disasters and the disastrous human conditions that result. Heart-wrenching images of men, women, and children fleeing for their lives or confined en masse to small sanctuaries of relative safety like subways or bunkers are all too common. Real-time commentary on social media puts horrific images and stories of war and disaster center stage.

Inevitably these events affect both the economy as a whole and individual financial circumstances. While market watchers marveled at how Wall Street rebounded from the pandemic crash, many of us—and our friends and family—were hit hard by layoffs, downsizings, or our own small businesses having to shut down. Supply-chain resources were stretched or nonexistent. The ranks of the unemployed swelled.

Even before the world could recover from the affects of the pandemic, Russia's war in the Ukraine caused a worldwide impact. Unfathomable brutality and carnage were nightmares fully manifest on our mobile phone screens. Rising oil prices and increasing food costs provided ongoing reminders of turmoil abroad—contributing to inflation fears, humanitarian emergencies, and food scarcity.

Those of us in the corporate world can no longer afford to ignore the volatility of the wider world. Just as other members of society, corporate leaders have an obligation to help fix what is broken. Environmental health, regional stability, social justice and ethical corporations are intricately tied to not just the performance of the economy and the market but the social fabric of communities themselves. Sustainability, social, and governance concerns intersect with both the private and public sectors. Climate-related devastation is already affecting vulnerable populations—it will not be long before we all are feeling the effects.

As a woman who focuses on creating and maintaining strong business partnerships, my view of these events focuses sharply on the interrelatedness between global phenomena and individuals. I often find myself asking, How can businesses, governments, and other organizations play a role in mitigating negative impacts? This is the lens through which I view the world—by focusing professionally on doing business in a way that strengthens communities and economically empowers employees, partners, and other stakeholders, I can attempt to find optimism and learning within these events, so as to work toward preventative measures and amplify resilience. During these times of political turmoil and instability, employees in different industries and regions began mobilizing to raise funds and deliver supplies to support people in need. This demonstrates that in times of social crises, humans react quickly to help their fellow humans.

Since the pandemic hit, many corporate managers have updated their workplace safety plans to ensure contractors, vendors, and employees are equipped with knowledge about protocols to keep each other safe—both today and as a precautionary measure for future health crises. Internal policy-setting and implementation shows that the heart of policy management and governance is about people-centered, ethical leadership.

The pandemic forced us to reckon with the ways low-income and underserved communities and demographics—such as those with underlying health conditions or who are located near toxin-producing industries and high traffic—are strongly affected by national and global crises. As a result, we saw the government injecting money into environmental and social justice initiatives. There has also been a corresponding drive for corporations to do their part to reduce bias and racial injustice within their companies.

As a result of broader conversations about environmental degradation, corporations have begun to commit to climate action plans with targeted goals for recycling and/or reducing dependence on non-renewable natural resources, and specific timelines to meet those goals. Progressive business leaders are leveraging their resources to help solve for some of the biggest environmental and social issues of our era.

As economic volatility took hold of global markets, many of us were empowered to build our own businesses or start new careers. The "great resignation" forced employers to reach out to potential workers, offer higher levels of training and compensation, and take their flexibility needs into consideration to attract and retain talent. The silver lining for entrepreneurs as well as workers was a new sense that they can chart their own futures.

Corporate leaders who remain uneducated about the importance of environmental, social, and governance (ESG) considerations will not be leading for long. They not only risk losing customers, but they also risk losing the interest of investors, both institutional and retail. Here are a few reasons why:

- Leaders who are unaware of social and environmental policies risk fines, reputational damage, and loss of customers and investors.

- Businesses that aren't prepared to compete for employees and investors in this new Green Economy—those that can't adjust their operations toward climate and clean energy awareness—may be incapable of attracting the best talent, customers, and investment dollars.

- ESG investments are set to hit $53 billion by 2025[1] and will likely account for one-third of all global assets under management by that time. Investors must move in the direction of ESG—and ensure the companies they invest in do, too—if they expect to support portfolio growth.

- Companies are encountering more investors who use proxy voting to hold boards accountable for lack of progress on ESG. These investors have the power to restructure company governance, and vote in new board members who can help these companies pivot toward ESG.

The purpose of this book is to investigate how companies are advancing the ESG agenda, to discuss the role that investors, governments, and NGOs can play in these efforts, and to develop an understanding about how this ESG focus can benefit society, especially those who have been most acutely affected by these negative impacts.

Corporate commitment to solving social and environmental problems through ESG policies and actions requires that the C-suite in particular reckon with their company's own environment, climate, and societal footprint. Just as attaching a unit of value is how a company understands whether a new strategy or product is impacting their goal or target, attaching a unit of value to business efforts on climate, environmental, and societal impact supports a company in identifying if they are meeting their goals toward ESG.

Climate and environmental issues, social issues, and business governance may seem like separate concerns, but they are actually not; they need to be tackled in tandem. Businesses, investors, and other organizations have enormous resources, especially when they partner together. By thinking through ESG considerations, we can approach sustainable business planning in the same methodical way we approach product and revenue planning: hand-in-hand. We've seen that a best practice for sustainable business is not to silo these concerns off in a separate ESG department, but rather to include ESG concerns in all business operations, product planning, and overall risk and opportunity evaluations.

Business leaders are accustomed to managing several issues at once, such as mitigating risk while monitoring costs and simultaneously driving revenue. But for some reason, some corporate participants feel they don't have the resources and/or knowledge to improve their enterprises' environmental and social standings simultaneously. But you can. It's all about shifting how you see things. Changing the lens of how you view the world means changing your mindset; learn to see not just problems, but also see solutions—particularly how you can create solutions from your unique perspective as a business leader. In practice, this means considering climate, innovation, or worker health benefits of a business proposal simultaneously with revenue generation of the proposal. Considering ESG impacts alongside profitability helps us identify risks and opportunities to our businesses, as well as risks and opportunities to our employees, customers, and shareholders who support our businesses. We can walk and chew gum at the same time. The chapters in this book explain how businesses can work with investors, governments, and NGOs to achieve ESG goals, while also achieving revenue goals.

This book is for several groups of people. For corporate leaders, this is a book for those who are seeking to improve existing operational processes and business investments, promoting a greater consideration of ESG within their business model. They recognize that thinking through environmental, social, and governance impacts on operations and investment decisions is a key method for differentiating themselves from their competition. Some of these readers may already be familiar with these concepts but are ready to grow and improve in how they implement ESG considerations.

For other readers, whether their work entails managing an investment portfolio or leading a business, this book may serve as an introduction to the topic, to help them understand what ESG and sustainability mean on a business level—how they affect customers, supply chains, investors, and other market participants. They need clarity on how ESG and sustainability manifests in markets and regions where they do business and where their businesses invest. There is a need for foundational knowledge on how

ESG and impact their firm holistically, financially, reputationally, operationally, and from a regulatory perspective.

For all readers, regardless of their level of knowledge, this book is a framework for creating value for customers, society, suppliers, shareholders, communities, and other stakeholders, while keeping up with market demands and growing the business.

Before launching into how an ESG focus can create change in social, climate, and business environments, let's first take a look at how we've arrived at this point. We'll start with origins of impact investing and a history of ESG concepts, how these considerations have grown from relative obscurity in the corporate world, and how they have come to dominate today's business headlines.

Note

1. https://www.bloomberg.com/professional/blog/esg-assets-may-hit-53-trillion-by-2025-a-third-of-global-aum/.

Chapter 1

History of Environmental and Corporate Entanglement

In spring 2021, a small hedge fund called Engine No. 1 successfully infiltrated and changed the board of the oil behemoth Exxon. In a series of maneuvers that will surely go down in the history of game-changing investments, an activist investor used stealth and strategy to take over the board. Chris James, Engine No. 1's founder, began his initiative in December 2020 with a focus on reducing and eliminating greenhouse gases from the company's operations, which would in turn help boost long-term profits, especially considering the brutal year that oil companies were experiencing at the time.[1] That strategy ultimately led to seating three candidates on the board who agreed with James about shifting Exxon's fossil fuels focus: a refining executive, a renewable products expert, and a former US Assistant Secretary of Energy.[2] This was a major coup, considering Exxon was heavily invested in oil and natural gas at the time, with relatively little investment in renewables.[3] Since then, there has been a gradual increase in major investments in renewable technologies, but there is still much work to be done.[4]

It's not often that an investor is so determined to shift the very business model of a company with such an unyielding culture as Exxon. As you'd expect, nothing about Exxon's May 26, 2021, shareholder vote on board members was normal. For starters, Exxon's leaders reportedly called for a recess only 40 minutes into the meeting.[5] Perhaps, this was done to allow time for engaging investors who might be swayed by Chris James et al.'s determination to bring in environmentally focused board members. Typically, a hedge fund with less than $275 million assets under management wouldn't have stood a chance against a Goliath such as Exxon, which was worth around $260 billion at the time of the meeting. However, Engine No. 1 was not alone: additional investors were also advocating for change. As the Engine No. 1 bloc steadily gathered support, it also appealed to investing giants such as BlackRock, Vanguard, and State Street, who held larger stakes in the company. It was the support and votes of these firms that cemented Engine No. 1's success in winning three Exxon board seats (out of four total nominations).[6]

Two key factors were at play during Engine No. 1's historic infiltration—factors that we are increasingly seeing across the investor and corporate landscape.

First, consumers, not-for-profits, employees, and retail investors are demanding that corporations participate in climate- and environment-focused activities, ranging from a reduction of fossil fuel usage, to improved water and waste management. Over the long haul, companies will either change to meet these expectations or suffer the consequences of losing their "social license" to operate.

Second, institutional investors are responding to these demands that are put forward by staff, clients, and activists outside the company. Investors are using a variety of methods to push companies toward a greener economy, such as insisting on transparency about environmental, social, and governance (ESG) issues, and using their votes to change corporate boards.[7] Perhaps even more surprising is just how visible the social-change component is becoming; how investors are harnessing resources in the *S* space as well as the *E*.

Just like Engine No. 1's ascension to the Exxon board, effective change begins with clear goals. To fully understand how conceptions of ESG have become increasingly integrated with corporate strategy and how this will change the way we do business, this chapter will consider the complex socio-political context that brought us to where we are now with ESG.

Impact Investing: What Is It?

Impact investing seeks to generate financial returns while also creating positive social or environmental change.[8] It is a nontraditional way of thinking about investing in the sense that impact investors consider a company's commitment to corporate social responsibility as a factor in their investment decisions. In 2016 Sir Ronald Cohen, chairman of Global Steering Group, stated,

> Impact investment is a response to the needs of impact entrepreneurs that want to improve lives and the planet in a similar way that venture capital and NASDAQ were for tech entrepreneurs. It is very difficult to separate a market into its components. We need change at the investor level. We need change at the investment manager level, and we need change at the entrepreneurial level. I am glad to say that this change is beginning to be visible to scale.[9]

The umbrella term *impact investing* is usually understood to encompass ESG and socially responsible investing (SRI). SRI takes the approach of harm avoidance: these investors typically choose companies with similar, or industry leading beliefs around human rights and environmental responsibility.[10] Companies that implement ESG initiatives attempt to reduce their negative impacts on society and create positive ones. The *E* includes such factors as emissions reduction, embracing renewables, and tackling water scarcity. The *S* incorporates human rights, health and safety issues, and corporate responsibility. The *G* encompasses shareholder rights and board structures, among other factors. Largely ignored until recent years, the number of companies publishing ESG reports has increased from 50 in 1993 to over 7,000 in 2015. Change is coming quickly: 37% of S&P 500 companies published ESG data by the end of 2019, but that had increased to 54% by year-end 2020.[11]

ESG is no longer a surface-level ethical discussion. It has now evolved into a discussion about metrics and relative evaluations of individual companies. The traditional tension between profitability versus responsible investing is falling away as they merge under the umbrella of ESG.

Contrary to widespread belief, the interests of ESG investors are not limited to climate change—as investors are diverse, so, too, are their socio-political priorities. Instead, ESG takes in a wider conversation about corporate change across a variety of disciplines. As the discussion has evolved from mere rhetoric to an urgency for real change, investments are evolving to meet a larger need. Today, more than a third of all the investment assets in the United States fall under this broad category of sustainable and responsible investing. Make no mistake: ESG investing is a key force keeping pressure on companies to prioritize their environmental and social commitments.

Another term that often arises during conversations about impact investment is *sustainable business*, which describes organizations that employ "green" practices to ensure that products and manufacturing processes address sustainability concerns while still maintaining profitability.[12] They examine financial *and* nonfinancial components when strategizing overall performance metrics and improvements. Leaders of businesses that focus on sustainability attempt to consider the effect of their practices on both the environment and society, seeking to positively impact on both. They consistently monitor the widespread effects of their business operations to ensure that their short-term decisions about revenues, costs, and other factors do not result in long-term negative environmental and social consequences.

Impact investors often look for sustainable businesses when making investment decisions. Climate and environment tend to be top of mind when we think about sustainable business, but some investors are asking for more. Sarah Bratton Hughes, head of ESG and sustainable investing at American Century Investments points out that human resource practices can make or break a business just as climate practices can.

> Human capital is the ultimate scarce resource. Yes, climate change is going to impact every company you're invested in. However, you can isolate your portfolio from a lot of that risk based on the sectors and industries that you allocate to. You cannot do the same with human capital. Employees are a material stakeholder, in every single company you're invested in. From an investment perspective, the hardest thing to do is to get your hands around a corporation's culture.

> Juliette Menga, director of investments, chair of ESG/ Sustainable Investing Committee at Aetos Alternatives Management echos the thought that climate and employee issues should be equally as important to a company.

> Just about every sector will be impacted by climate change, one way or the other. Depending on which part of a sector a company is in, it may have a lower carbon footprint than another company, but all companies will be impacted. Same thing with social and human capital. Every company needs to have employees that are stable, happy, and safe.

Examining both the *E* and the *S* through a lens of equal importance is a new approach for some. After all, most of the sustainability narrative discussions center around corporate climate and net

5

zero commitments. From a wider perspective, conversations about impact investment overall are relatively new, but their foundations can be found in spiritual and religious doctrine, as well as the environmental and social justice movements.

Religious Doctrine and Impact Investment

An example of how socially responsible investing has its origins in culture and religion can be seen with Islamic finance. Islamic finance is an over $2 trillion industry that is expected to grow 10 to 12% between 2021 and 2022.[13] Although Islamic finance took a hit during the pandemic, that level of growth is still positive.

Business leaders globally care about Islamic finance for two main reasons. First is scale: Islamic banking accounts for a 6% market share of global banking assets, including a variety of commercial, wholesale, and other types of banks. Second is asset focus: Islamic banking's primary edge is its reliance on tangible assets such as real estate as opposed to less straightforward investments such as derivatives.[14] The current scale and growth of Islamic finance along with the types of assets Islamic banking's earnings come from make for an interesting proposition for businesses and investors.

Islamic finance's alignment with ethical finance practices demonstrates how spiritual practice can integrate a philosophical framework with investing.[15] Their customs are Sharia-compliant and rooted in the rich history of Islamic faith and culture. With assets forecast to reach about $3.5 trillion within the decade, investors and financial services firms across the globe are seeking to learn more about serving the growing sector of Islamic finance.

Umer Suleman is the head of advisory board for for Wahed, UK, the world's largest Islamic fintech. He also sits on the board of the UKIFC and serves as business and economics advisor to the Islamic Council of Europe. In a 2021 interview, Suleman shed some light on the philosophy of Islamic finance:

As a whole, it comes under the science of general social contracts as opposed to worship. That's important because, within the general principle, everything is permissible unless it's been specified that it is not. The multitude of different ways in which you can interact with each other financially are generally allowed other than those transactions which contain interest, which is strictly prohibited in Islam and other faith traditions that came before us.[16]

These principles function as a screen to weed out transactions and investments such as pornography, arms, and alcohol. "On top of this, we have certain principles which bring about good stewardship of investing," said Suleman.[17]

The question of social impact is deeply embedded in Islamic finance. According to Suleman, unbridled capitalism can eventually break the underlying organization. He pointed to the last financial crisis as an example, explaining that profits were privatized and losses were socialized. This inequity drove people toward safer investments and more social consciousness about the real cost of their return.

I think people are genuinely waking up to the question of "what is value" and creating value itself. Is it enough that a company has pure profit growth versus an increase in the number of employees? If a company has made slightly less profit than it made the year before, but increased its staffing 5% to 10%, for me that company has a massive take because through its business operations, it has enabled more people to be employed and more families to be supported. This is value and something that should be celebrated. It has given us social profit, and not just pure profit. As people become more educated and get used to ESG-based

7

investments, they will become the norm and more embedded in our general investments. Then, you'll see creativity and profits start to rise in a sustainable manner.[18]

The foundations of impact investing are not unique to the Islamic world. Similar philosophies can be found in many major religions. Whether we are buying stocks, mutual funds, or exchange-traded funds, we support and profit from the activities and decisions of that business. If viewed through a religious or spiritual lens, a responsibility exists to avoid investments in companies that intentionally cause harm for the sake of profit.

Social Justice and Impact Investing

The foundations of modern responsible investment culture can also be seen in the Civil Rights Movement. One example is the corporate response to George Floyd and Breonna Taylor protests. Through committing to increase diversity, equity, and inclusion, professing support for colleagues of color internally, or addressing the issue via social media, company leaders agreed change was needed in private corporate spaces and public places. Critics complained these efforts were largely "performative" (meaning, superficial gestures intended for public consumption, rather than systemic change) but some firms did commit to quantifiable strategies. For instance, Goldman Sachs announced it would "only underwrite IPOs in the US and Europe of private companies that have at least one diverse board member."[19] In 2021, they increased this to two diverse candidates.

Still, the charge that many corporate responses to the Floyd protests were "performative" was not without merit. Unfortunately, one result of these "performances" is loss of public trust, which leads to loss of reputation. When businesses lose the trust of their consumers and others, consequences may include long-term revenue loss.

Customers cutting ties with businesses that run afoul of social issues isn't a new thing: the relationship between social justice and the business sector has a long history. The Dryades Street boycotts in 1960 provide an example.[20] At the start of the Civil Rights Movement, New Orleans's main shopping avenue was Canal Street, where all stores were white-owned, with segregated facilities that did not serve Black Americans at their lunch counters, even though Blacks made up almost 40% of the city's population at the time. The second-busiest shopping avenue was Dryades Street. These stores were also white-owned, but their customer base was overwhelmingly Black. Though Black customers were allowed to use the facilities, they were kept from employment within the stores, with the exception of an occasional janitorial position. It's interesting to note that many of the storeowners on Dryades Street were Jewish; they were themselves segregated from owning stores on the more profitable Canal Street, which was owned by the city's Christian majority.

In late 1959, members of the Southern Christian Leadership Conference and the National Association for the Advancement of Colored People organized the Consumers' League of Greater New Orleans to fight employment discrimination by the Dryades Street merchants. There was already precedent for action like this. For example, Harlem had its own campaign in 1934 where Blacks refused to shop where they weren't allowed to work.[21] After months of negotiation with no progress, the league launched a boycott of the businesses. During the week before Easter—typically a time of increased business revenue—shoppers were replaced by citizens picketing the stores.

Although a few stores began hiring some Blacks, most persisted in their refusals, which drove the continuation of the boycott. As many stores closed permanently or moved into white areas of the city, the once-lucrative Dryades Street dried up. By late 1961, the economic leaders of New Orleans were feeling the impact of the boycott, so they formed a coalition to negotiate with the protestors.

These negotiations resulted in some modest changes as stores began to desegregate and slowly increase Black employment. The Dryades and Canal Street boycotts and pickets promoted solidarity among Blacks within the city and used economics as a tool for influencing business actions. As part of the Civil Rights Movement, these boycotts occurred within a collective effort to use impact as a tool for driving social change.

Sometimes customers are also investors and owners. Other times they are not. Either way, the important thing to remember is that businesses build good reputations mostly because of customers. When that reputation, or social license to operate, is challenged by customers and communities, businesses suffer—and so do the businesses' investors and owners. When businesses are economically influenced toward positive social impact—with fair employment practices, as has been the case in many civil rights movements in general—we see the other side of the coin: how societal pressures on a business can force a business's hand. It is important that leaders ensure proper values are integrated into their business culture to encourage principled approaches to worker issues, such as equitable hiring, compensation, and even workplace safety. Savvy business leaders and investors know that once a business loses customers, it's costly to get them back.

Another origin of impact investing can be found in global social movements such as the pressures imposed on South African businesses during apartheid. In response to the system of oppression, numerous countries and foreign investors divested from South Africa, marking a dramatic change from the wealth of investment that previously flowed into the country thanks to its abundance of sought-after natural resources.[22] The two largest sectors for South African investment were mining and manufacturing at that time. Although these sectors grew steadily throughout the 1960s, they declined sharply in the 1970s as companies and people began pulling out of the country. Direct investment fell to less than 30% of the country's revenue, with the remainder coming from foreign loans. Divestment efforts spread throughout the 1980s as college-aged citizens became more vocal with their demands for divestment. It became a widespread movement throughout the United States, which put greater pressure on private and public agencies to completely divest any stocks of companies still doing business within the country.

The strategies increasingly affected South Africa as corporate heavyweights such as IBM and General Motors withdrew from the country and it became too expensive to continue operations there. In 1986, the University of California sold $3.1 billion in stock to divest itself from investments in South Africa. Various faith organizations, unions, and states followed suit, and Congress passed the Comprehensive Anti-Apartheid Act, banning new investment in the country. By 1988, 155 universities had divested. Investment in the country had become minimal and the country was in full economic decline, which forced South Africa to abolish apartheid and change its oppressive policies. Since then, foreign investment returned to the country with South Africa establishing itself as a viable country for investment.

A debate raged—and continues to this day—about the value of divesting versus engagement. In the 1980s US President Ronald Regan supported "constructive engagement" of the white South African minority; this included limited economic sanctions. Many saw this as a failed foreign policy effort, and supported divestment.[23] There is still active debate about whether investors should wholly divest from companies who are considered "bad actors" or whether to engage with them to influence change.

Recent social justice movements have evolved, and they now address contemporary concerns in somewhat different ways, like *buycotting* or actively purchasing from brands that align with consumer values.[24] For example, the "Buy Black" movement gained momentum over summer 2020. The initiative highlighted the plight of Black-owned businesses hit particularly hard by the pandemic, while

11

also championing the support of Black-owned business in general, as a method of addressing racial injustices.

The Foundations of Environmental Sustainability

As mentioned earlier, the *E* in ESG is a huge part of this discussion, with green investing and the like. Indeed we're only recently seeing significant talk, followed by unfortunately much more limited action, about social investing the way we have seen around environmental issues over the past few decades.

In a speech before the Stanford Graduate School of Business, Sir Ronald Cohen stated,

> The majority of us today feel that the world cannot go on in the way that it is doing. Something has got to change . . . [but] what is it that has to change? Capitalism has served us well for 250 years, but we are at the stage where the consequences of a capitalist system are so great that governments can't cope with them. Governments across the world are looking at social and environment issues without having the tools or resources to bring credible responses to them.
>
> Philanthropists . . . can't bring the answer either. So, the conclusion has to be that the private sector has to get involved in finding solutions to social and environmental issues at scale.[25]

Many of the "consequences" that Cohen speaks of can be traced back to harm caused during the Industrial Revolution. Although this era brought about extensive innovation and incredible profits, it also resulted in massive environmental and social problems, such as child labor (as much a driver of anger at the time as we see with pollution today), exploitation, slum-living and land theft. From railroads and oil fields to factories and steel foundries, the foundation was laid for companies to conduct business in ways that didn't consider long-term societal or environmental best interests.

Driven by the abundance of available resources, Europe's Industrial Revolution started in Britain in the 1700s before quickly advancing across the continent.[26] For Europeans, industrial growth encouraged mass movement to cities in search of jobs, but the negative results included overly crowded cities and unhealthy living conditions. As industrialization spread, national economies thrived, but many of the people saw a decline in living standards due to lengthy work days, cholera outbreaks, and rising inequality as well as environmental damage in the form of air pollution, water pollution, and deforestation. Centuries of industrialization and environmentally harmful activities have contributed to the current problems of global warming, but rapid acceleration of this during the 20th and 21st centuries are also to blame.

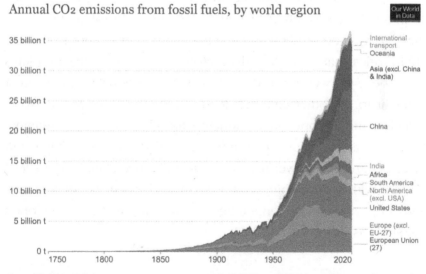

Annual CO_2 emissions from fossil fuels, by world region

Source: Global Carbon Project
Note: This measures CO_2 emissions from fossil fuels and cement production only – land use change is not included. 'Statistical differences' (included in the GCP dataset) are not included here.

CO_2 emissions from fossil fuels over the centuries.
Source: Hannah Ritchie, Max Roser and Pablo Rosado (2020) / OurWorldInData.org. / Licensed by CC BY 4.0

History of Environmental and Corporate Entanglement

Countries in Asia, Africa, and Latin America did not experience vast industrial expansion until far more recently, but they are being forced to do so in a world that has been shaped by the poor practices that began during the Industrial Revolutions in Europe and America. So-called developed countries had the "privilege" of growing and expanding their industries with no regard to the lasting effects of their business decisions and operations. Government regulation was minimal at best, and there were no widespread demands for more responsible business practices until the environmental movement really took off in the 1960s. Essentially, countries in Europe and North America had the freedom to act in a vacuum with no regard for the consequences that future generations would face.

These days, as African, Asian, and Latin American countries experience their own forms of industrial expansion, these countries are doing so under the watchful eye of international government oversight and and the global community. Critics point out developed countries have severely damaged the environment for centuries, yet they are now demanding that emerging countries adhere to sustainability rules that may slow their growth to alleviate the problems many believed were caused by Western expansionism. Critics say it is unfair to ask other countries to slow their growth because North America and Europe have suddenly found sustainability religion. Whether this is fair or unfair, most agree that business leaders and investors are in a powerful position to influence climate and social change within developing countries in a way that is collaborative and supportive, while continuing to move the needle in developed countries as well.

Trains and Steel: Learning from History

Investors and businesses are recognizing the effects of industrial production, such as steelmaking, which is one of the largest CO_2

emitters. The main ingredient in the production of steel is iron ore, which is mined from the earth.[27] Of the more than 2,000 million tons of iron ore mined annually, about 95% is used by the steel industry. It is the world's most produced commodity by volume, only following crude oil and coal. It is also the second most-traded commodity behind crude oil. Mining iron ore is extremely energy intensive. The steel industry also creates water pollution from the heavy metals and acid draining from the mines. This acid drainage can continue for thousands of years, even after mining activities have ceased.

Businesses are attempting to course correct by using recycled ferrous scrap, burning coal to cut down on emissions, and other methods.[28] This is an example for other sectors to follow, and it is also an example of how businesses and investors can learn from historical workplace social injustices so as to not repeat them, especially in today's age, when a business's reputation affects customer loyalty, which may affect investment dollars received.

The railroad industry, which was deeply involved with the steel business—both because steel was a vital component of trains and railroads and also because trains were the primary way steel was transported—provides an additional example of how the lack of safety, low pay, and irresponsible practices resulted in long-term negative impacts.[29] Today's manager or business strategist would be hard-pressed to prove that the benefits outweighed the immediate social consequences. Most notably the forced relocation of Native Americans, resulting in the widespread destruction of Native American cultures and ways of life. The Chinese workers who helped construct the railroad also suffered harm.[30] They endured dangerous work conditions while being compensated significantly less than US workers and were forced to live in tents instead of the train cars provided for white workers. Frigid weather and incidents, such as accidental explosions and avalanches, killed hundreds of workers. The construction of the transcontinental railroad provides an example of how negative environmental impacts often go hand-in-hand with negative social impacts. Also, it's critical to note that the future of sustainability does not include solving an environmental problem in a way that causes a worker health or customer safety problem. Looking to the future, it's important to ensure that all aspects of ESG are given an equally high priority.[31]

Short-Term versus Long-Term Thinking

Valuable lessons emerge from the examination of actions and reactions when it comes to balancing the financial profitability of a business with important nonfinancial factors. During these seemingly impossible, no-way-out situations, successful leaders create solutions that may have short-term business impacts but also longer-term benefits—benefits that bring greater commitment from employees and publicly demonstrate how the company can serve its workers. Though it has increasingly become a topic of discussion over the past few decades, corporate short-termism has always existed within the global economy, as executives push to meet short-term performance metrics at the expense of sustainability and long-term value. They either fail to recognize or simply do not care that this type of short-sighted decision-making can ultimately prevent long-term growth and create roadblocks to financial success.

Sheila C. Bair, former chair of the FDIC, opined that efforts to prevent the 2008 financial crisis "were impeded by the culture of short-termism" in both the financial and political arenas.[32] In an attempt to quantify the impact of short-term thinking, McKinsey Global Institute designed a systematic measurement of short- and long-termism at the level of individual companies, placing them on what we call the Corporate Horizon Index.[33] Its researchers found that companies falling on the long-termism end of the spectrum significantly outperformed those on the short-term end. Business leaders can feel intense pressure to meet earnings projections immediately, or risk losing their jobs. But this can do significant damage to a brand's future: customers lose confidence in a business or industry without holistic, long-term views; investors lose confidence in a lack of accuracy in pricing of an asset, due to the fact that long-term views are not factored into management's strategy.

The short-termism that has driven business growth in the past has largely been allowed to exist because of the lack of persistent demands from investors and the public. Though small groups have occasionally focused on the idea of sustainable business, there were never as many influential voices as there are now, and these voices are now changing the way we operate.

Chapter 2 explores how today's successful companies find new, innovative ways to produce environmentally and socially friendly products. An advantage these companies have over their predecessors is the openness to shifting their view of nonfinancial considerations to align them with financial considerations.

Chapter 1 Takeaways

- Impact investing is a new way of thinking about the investors' role in the corporate world. It can take the more passive form of harm avoidance (do no wrong) or the active form of investing in companies that consciously do good.
- Social justice movements, environmentalism, and even religious beliefs are causing an evolution in our understanding of what investing is for.

- History has shown how short-term thinking on the part of corporations can lead to sustained social and environmental damage.
- The entire world is now living with the consequences of short-term thinking, where short-term business impacts and revenues have trumped longer-term views about what is most beneficial to the future of our environment and society.

Notes

1. https://www.nytimes.com/2021/05/26/business/exxon-mobil-climate-change.html; and https://www.nytimes.com/2021/06/23/magazine/exxon-mobil-engine-no-1-board.html.
2. https://www.naturalgasintel.com/engine-no-1-takes-another-seat-on-exxonmobil-board/.
3. https://www.nytimes.com/2020/09/21/business/energy-environment/oil-climate-change-us-europe.html.
4. https://www.nytimes.com/2020/09/21/business/energy-environment/oil-climate-change-us-europe.html.
5. https://www.nytimes.com/2021/06/23/magazine/exxon-mobil-engine-no-1-board.html.
6. https://www.nytimes.com/2021/05/26/business/exxon-mobil-climate-change.html.
7. Refinitiv. "What on Earth is ESG?" Youtube. (February 18, 2020). https://www.youtube.com/watch?v=cvDftLOPy4Y.
8. https://www.investopedia.com/terms/v/venture-philanthropy.asp.
9. Sir Ronald Cohen. "Impact Investing Is the Future." Stanford Graduate School of Business. (February 25, 2016). https://www.youtube.com/watch?v=VgWJZiRL7BQ.
10.
11. https://www.thecaq.org/sp-500-and-esg-reporting.
12. https://online.hbs.edu/blog/post/business-sustainability-strategies?tempview=logoconvert.
13. https://www.reuters.com/business/finance/global-islamic-finance-forecast-grow-main-markets-recover-sp-2021-05-03/.

14. https://www.businesswire.com/news/home/20211101005812/en/Islamic-Finance-Market-Outlook-2021—2026-Global-Assets-Increase-by-Double-Digits-Year-on-Year—ResearchAndMarkets.com.
15. Quotes from Refinitiv Sustainability Perspectives Podcast interview (5 May 2021).
16. Ibid.
17. Ibid.
18. Ibid.
19. https://www.goldmansachs.com/our-commitments/diversity-and-inclusion/launch-with-gs/pages/commitment-to-diversity.html.
20. https://nvdatabase.swarthmore.edu/content/new-orleans-citizens-boycott-us-civil-rights-1960-61.
21. http://www.louisianaweekly.com/new-orleans-desegregation-was-rooted-in-the-1960-dryades-st-boycott.
22. https://economyofapartheid.weebly.com/foreign-investment.html.
23. https://www.foreignaffairs.com/articles/south-africa/1985-12-01/south-africa-why-constructive-engagement-failed.
24. https://www.washingtonpost.com/news/on-leadership/wp/2018/02/28/why-buycotts-could-overtake-boycotts-among-consumer-activists.
25. Sir Ronald Cohen, "Impact Investing Is the Future."
26. https://ecsforum3.wordpress.com/2013/01/31/effects-of-industrialization-on-europes-environment.
27. https://www.theworldcounts.com/challenges/planet-earth/mining/environmental-impact-of-steel-production/story.
28. https://www.esgtoday.com/steel-dynamics-targets-carbon-neutral-steel-production/.
29. https://worldwiderails.com/how-did-railroads-help-the-steel-industry/.
30. https://www.theguardian.com/artanddesign/2019/jul/18/forgotten-by-society-how-chinese-migrants-built-the-transcontinental-railroad.
31. For instance, a 2018 incident in Ohio discharged more methane over a three-week period than the oil and gas industries of France, Norway, and the Netherlands combined over an entire year. Immediately following the incident, the responsible company claimed to be unsure about the size of the leak. It took more than a year for an accurate representation of incident to become available.
32. https://clsbluesky.law.columbia.edu/2017/10/18/is-corporate-short-termism-on-the-rise-in-the-u-s/.
33. https://www.milkenreview.org/articles/the-case-against-corporate-short-termism.

New Businesses and New Business Models

In this chapter, we'll look at two vastly different approaches that corporations have taken with regard to ESG. First, we'll look at a pair of corporations that mismanaged and misled consumers, regulators, and shareholders on ESG initiatives, and we'll investigate the reputational and financial damage that resulted when they failed to take responsibility for their company's actions. Then, we'll explore companies that experienced success in their ESG performance: what they did well, where there is still room for improvement, and what benefits were achieved both inside and outside the firm. But first, let's define exactly what companies *should be* responsible for as it relates to the environment and society.

The stakes are changing in terms of what companies were held "responsible for" in the past versus what consumers hold them responsible for now. Fifty years ago, Nobel prize–winning economist Milton Friedman championed a theory that has persisted for decades: he opined that a corporation's sole legal responsibility is the generation of profits for shareholders, without regard for other considerations such as communities, environment, and other stakeholders.[1] Business leaders around the world embraced the notion as a reason to relentlessly pursue profits at virtually any cost.

Contrast this with the growth and popularity of B Corps whose unique quality centers around ensuring groups other than corporate shareholders, like employees, communities, and even the environment receive benefit and value from the corporation. Researchers found two primary reasons firms want to be B-Corp certified: 1) as a way to stand out from competitors and be seen as genuine change agents and 2) because they believe changing the way we do business is the way to change the trajectory of the environment and social issues we grapple with today. This challenge to the traditional way of doing business not only supports people and the planet, but also aligns with values of consumers who are seeking alternatives to a profit-only business culture.[2]

Case Studies: Empty Promises

Unfortunately, some companies choose to adopt ESG promises as mere marketing ploys (similar to the performative acts discussed in Chapter 1), instead of actually working to create social value. But, as we'll see in the following examples, when those promises are revealed as fundamentally empty, those decisions can prove extremely costly.

Volkswagen

One of the most serious corporate scandals of this type was the Volkswagen (VW) emissions scandal, ultimately costing the company more than $30 billion.[3] In 2015, the Environmental Protection Agency (EPA) announced findings that Volkswagen cars sold in the United States had been equipped with a "defeat device": software placed inside of diesel engines that could detect when emissions testing was taking place and temporarily modify performance to improve results.[4] When testing was detected, the software reportedly put the vehicle into a mode in which the engine ran at a rate that, although significantly lower than normal power and performance, tested better in terms of emissions. When the testing was completed and the car was returned to regular roadway use, the engine would resume its usual level of power. The result was VW engines that emitted nitrogen oxide pollutants up to forty times greater than those allowed in the United States. Dubbed *Dieselgate* and *diesel dupe* in the press, VW eventually admitted that about 11 million cars worldwide, including 8 million in Europe, had been fitted with software designed specifically to cheat emissions tests.

Making matters worse, Volkswagen had simultaneously undertaken a widespread marketing campaign aimed at highlighting and even *celebrating* its cars' low emissions. The company marketed the diesel-powered cars as better for the environment than the competition, implying that VW possessed some type of miracle technology that enabled the creation of more affordable, "greener" diesel vehicles.[5] VW publicly asserted that its diesel engines operated at or above US national and California state requirements, while still providing owners with the good fuel economy and performance they expected. What's more, the deceptive emissions testing enabled the company to receive millions of dollars' worth of "green car" subsidies and tax exemptions in the United States.[6]

Although automobile recalls are certainly nothing new in today's environment, the VW scandal included an ESG twist. The scandal went far beyond a breach of public safety expectations: it was a breach of public trust in the company's brand. The company's image was tarnished by the scandal, which will likely have even longer-lasting consequences than a mere safety recall. Indeed, safety recalls can actually strengthen customer trust in a product or company because they are viewed as a show of transparency and goodwill. VW's actions, however, showed an intentional effort to mislead the public. Not only were consumers who purchased these vehicles duped, but so were taxpayers, whose money contributed to the more than $50 million in subsidies granted to the company.[7]

After initial denials, VW eventually admitted the truth: Martin Winterkorn, the Volkswagen Group's chief executive at the time said that the company had "broken the trust of our customers and the public."[8] Winterkorn resigned as a result of the scandal and was later ordered to pay the company about $13.7 million for "breaches of due diligence." But Winterkorn's punishment did not prevent the financial backlash that followed. On the first day of trading after the EPA's notice of violation to VW was made public, the share price of Volkswagen AG fell 20% on the Frankfurt Stock Exchange.[9] The next day, the price fell another 12%, and an additional 10.5% on the following day, dropping to a record four-year low.[10] The nation of Qatar, which was one of the company's largest shareholders with a 17% stake in the company at the time, reportedly lost nearly $5 billion as a result of stock value decreases.[11]

VW was not the only automaker affected by the scandal: share prices of German automakers BMW and Daimler also fell by 4.9% and 5.8%, respectively, demonstrating the ripple effect of breached public trust.[12] A year after the scandal, VW remained down by about 30%, and it took until 2021 for the company's stock to reach pre-scandal levels.[13]

A comparison of VW sales in the United States showed a 24.7% decline in November 2015 when compared to November 2014.[14] In addition, the respected *Consumer Reports* suspended its "recommended" rating of two VW vehicles until further testing was completed.[15] In a 2015 interview with the *Chicago Tribune*, Ellen Bloom, senior director of federal policy for Consumers Union, the policy and advocacy arm of *Consumer Reports,* stated, "Volkswagen was ripping off the consumer and hurting the environment at the same time."[14] A survey conducted by AutoPacific found that 64% of US vehicle owners lacked trust in VW and only 25% of those surveyed maintained a positive view of the company despite the scandal.[16] This widespread and highly publicized backlash meant that Volkswagen would have to invest in substantial damage control and work to improve its image in the eyes of consumers. In 2015, VW launched an ad campaign in the German media stating that the company "would do everything to win back the confidence of its customers."[17] In mid-2016, VW announced plans for substantial investments in the production of electric vehicles and promised to introduce 30 all-electric models within the decade, with electric vehicles expected to comprise a quarter of VW's annual sales by 2025. Then chief executive officer of Volkswagen AG, Matthias Müller, stated that the initiative would "require us—following the serious setback as a result of the diesel issue—to learn from mistakes made, rectify shortcomings and establish a corporate culture that is open, value-driven and rooted in integrity."[18] VW's employees also felt the effects of the scandal, with the company and labor unions agreeing to reduce the workforce by 30,000 people in November 2016, resulting from the costs of the violations.[19] In total, VW estimates that the scandal cost the company more than $30 billion.[20]

Purdue Pharma

The Purdue Pharma scandal provides a second example of what can result when corporations make false claims about their commitment to societal values. Purdue Pharma makes pain medicines, including the opioid drug OxyContin.[21] Due to the drug's high potential for addiction, many patients got hooked on a drug that was originally prescribed to them for medical reasons; some increasingly began using ingestion methods that created an elevated risk, resulting in overdose or even death. In their efforts to obtain the drugs, users began "doctor shopping" by visiting a variety of different physicians to obtain OxyContin prescriptions. These combined consequences created a situation in which addiction continuously spread as sales continuously soared.[22]

The aggressive OxyContin marketing campaign encouraged physicians to prescribe the drug, marketing the medication as "smooth and sustained pain control all day and all night." In 2001 alone, the company invested more than $200 million in its efforts to promote OxyContin.[23] The campaign consistently included data and messaging that was designed to create doubt about the risk of addiction. Promotional campaign materials, including literature for physicians and brochures for patients, claimed that the risk of addiction from OxyContin was extremely low. Meanwhile, Purdue Pharma sales representatives were trained to repeat the inaccurate assessment that the risk of addiction was "less than 1%."

We now know that Purdue Pharma executives were aware that "the pills were being crushed and snorted; stolen from pharmacies; and that some doctors were being charged with selling prescriptions." As reported by the *New York Times*, more than a hundred internal company memos included the words *street value*, *crush*, or *snort* between the years of 1997 and 1999.[24] Nevertheless, during the late 1990s, OxyContin sales brought in $2.8 billion in revenue for Purdue Pharma."[25]

In 2003, the US Drug Enforcement Administration (DEA) reported that Purdue Pharma's "aggressive methods" had "very much exacerbated OxyContin's widespread abuse."[26] In 2012 the *New England Journal of Medicine* published a study that found that "76% of those seeking help for heroin addiction began by abusing pharmaceutical narcotics, primarily OxyContin."[27] Much like the DEA, the publication suggested a connection between Purdue's marketing of OxyContin and the US heroin epidemic. By 2016, Purdue Pharma's cumulative revenue had increased to $31 billion and $35 billion by 2017.[28]

As complaints about Purdue's actions escalated, consumers made their dissatisfaction known with public protests and boycotts.

Particular ire centered on the opioid crisis in Native American communities, where overdose rates are sharply higher than in other communities.[29] The protests were largely driven by people who had lost a family member or friend to an opioid overdose. Global attention focused on the opioid crisis as lawsuits against Purdue Pharma began to pile up, spreading the controversy from the streets to the courtrooms.

In an effort to clean up their public image, Purdue officials advertised a variety of company initiatives supposedly intended to address the opioid crisis. They advertised their education and oversight initiatives in full-page ads that ran across print and digital platforms in publications including the *New York Times*, *USA Today*, *Wall Street Journal*, *Washington Post*, and Hearst Connecticut Media's daily newspapers. Critics argued that the money put into the ads should've been contributed to solutions, such as health facilities, to help end the opioid crisis.[30]

Despite their PR efforts, by October 2020 Purdue had not only lost its social license to conduct business but also its actual *ability* to conduct business: as part of a guilty plea to multiple federal charges relating to its role in the opioid crisis, Purdue Pharma agreed to pay more than $8 billion in civil and criminal fines.[31] Because the company doesn't have $8 billion in cash available, the Justice Department announced that Purdue would be dissolved as part of the settlement, and its assets used to create a new "public benefit company" controlled by a trust or similar entity designed for the benefit of the public. The Justice Department also stated that the new company will function entirely in the public interest rather than to maximize profits. Future earnings will go to paying the fines and penalties, which in turn will be used to combat the opioid crisis.

The examples of Purdue and Volkswagen are obviously quite extreme, but they demonstrate the very serious repercussions that can come to companies, their investors and owners, and society in general when environmental and social concerns are ignored. Regulatory fines, lawsuits, expensive marketing, and loss of reputation are all potential long-term costs of doing business according to the old, profit-above-all-else model. This model is expensive, irresponsible, and unsustainable for businesses that plan to participate in today's marketplace and also in the future marketplace. The old ways are being replaced with more innovative models that create long-term value for society while also generating revenue. Firms that are gaining ground are mindful of net-zero commitments, for example, and the importance of setting science-based targets while also focusing on social progress.

Important Definitions

Net zero. The goal of negating the amount of greenhouse gas produced by human activity through the reduction of emissions and the absorption of carbon dioxide from the atmosphere

Carbon neutrality. The state of net zero, defined by the balance of carbon emissions with carbon absorption

Paris Agreement. International climate change treaty that established a framework for reducing global warming

COP26. The 2021 UN Climate Change Conference, which created the objectives of committing to more ambitious targets for the reduction of greenhouse gas emissions by 2030, discussing measures to adapt to the inevitable impacts of climate change, increasing funding for climate action, particularly for developing countries

Case Studies: Goals and Plans

Having taken a look at how *not* to engage with ESG, let's turn to companies in a variety of sectors that have successfully incorporated ESG concerns into their operating strategies. It is important to remember that in these examples, as in real life, sustainability can be complex. Despite a company making positive strides in one area, they could be struggling in another aspect of ESG such as supporting the fossil fuel industry or opposing progressive governance.

Microsoft

In 2020, Microsoft announced a goal to become carbon negative by 2030.[32] In addition, the company pledged that by year 2050, it will remove all the carbon that it has emitted into the environment directly or by electrical consumption since its founding in 1975. "While the world will need to reach net-zero, those of us who can afford to move faster and go further should do so. That's why today we are announcing an ambitious goal and a new plan to reduce and ultimately remove Microsoft's carbon footprint," announced Microsoft president Brad Smith. "We will fund this in part by expanding our internal carbon fee, in place since 2012 and increased last year, to start charging not only our direct emissions, but those from our supply and value chains."[33]

Although goals are good, concrete plans are better. Microsoft's plans to meet these substantial goals include the following actions:

- Decreasing direct emissions and emissions related to the energy that the company uses to near zero by the middle of the decade
- Using Microsoft technology to help its suppliers and customers worldwide reduce their own carbon footprints
- Using a newly created $1 billion climate innovation fund to accelerate the global development of carbon reduction, capture, and removal technologies

- Making carbon reduction a major component of the company's procurement processes for the supply chain
- Creating an annual environmental sustainability report that provides updated details about Microsoft's carbon impact and its progress in the reduction plan
- Using the company's influence and voice to advocate for and support public policy that promotes carbon reduction and removal initiatives[34]

Microsoft had previously focused its efforts on avoidance offsets; their new plan changed the focus. "While it is imperative that we continue to avoid emissions, and these investments remain important, we see an acute need to begin removing carbon from the atmosphere, which we believe we can help catalyze through our investments," wrote Smith.[35]

Microsoft also published a white paper detailing its vetting criteria for choosing which initiatives and projects to support in furtherance of its carbon removal goals. This is an act not before seen in the space of corporate governance. According to Joeri Rogelj, director of research at the Grantham Institute and a reader in climate science and policy at Imperial College London, Microsoft's actions are "generating a market for that kind of service, which in itself is hugely important . . . Microsoft is not saying 'we are not doing anything today, because we want to remove a lot in the future.' They actually have a plan that combines reductions with removal."[36]

In the first year of its reduction plan, the company forecast a reduction of its carbon emissions by 6%, equating to about 730,000 metric tons.[37] Microsoft's stock prices have consistently risen between July 2020 and December 2021, corresponding with the time frame since the announcement of its carbon removal program.[38] As one of the world's largest software companies, Microsoft's impact derives not only from their own reduction of emissions but also as an industry leader.

However, critics call out Microsoft's software use in fossil fuel extractions as a contradiction to their climate progress. Additionally, they point out that their membership with trade organizations opposing key climate legislation as an example that even Microsoft has room for growth in this area.[39]

Axcelis and Kimble Electronics

Smaller tech companies such as Axcelis and Kimble Electronics are also building their own sustainability plans, showing how smaller firms can emulate the ESG success of their larger peers.

Axcelis, which focuses on design and manufacturing for the semiconductor manufacturing industry, has been certified to the International Organization for Standardization (ISO) 14001, Environmental Management System standard since 2000.[40] Much like Microsoft, Axcelis maintains a comprehensive environmental management system that specifically defines and tracks their performance related to environmental goals. The company also publishes an annual report on environmental and safety concerns to promote transparency and ensure that customers, investors, and employees fully understand the company's stance and actions toward sustainability.

The electronics and contract manufacturing firm Kimble Electronics includes electrical energy efficiency in its daily operations in an effort to reduce greenhouse gas emissions.[41] Since 2011, the company has also participated in the CDP, formerly known as Carbon Disclosure Project. CDP is a global disclosure system for investors, companies, cities, and states to help them manage their environmental impacts.[42] We'll discuss standards and frameworks such as CDP later in the book, particularly how they support companies of all sizes in the information they disclose externally, which can be used by investors, governments and society at large.

Lenovo

An increasing number of Asian companies have likewise announced their intentions to reach carbon neutrality. The Science-Based Targets initiative assists companies with cutting their emissions in line with the Paris Agreement.[43] Of the approximately 1,200 firms that have signed on, 250 are based in Asia, representing a 57% increase between 2019 and 2020. Chinese computer giant Lenovo Group Limited (Lenovo), is among the participating companies. The world's largest PC manufacturer publicly outlined its plans in May 2021. "Extreme weather has no borders," said Lenovo CEO Yuanqing Yang. "If we are truly committed to sustainable growth, we must all do our share of duty to reduce carbon footprint. If done right, we can turn the post-pandemic economic reconstruction into an opportunity to improve global ecology."[44] The company reportedly plans to use a variety of strategies, including the disclosure of emissions data, greenhouse gas reduction, and using renewable energy. Yang has also voiced a great interest in the application of intelligent technology–based solutions to reduce Lenovo's environmental impact.

> High-tech manufacturers have the power to enhance their manufacturing and supply chain systems to be not only green but also digital and intelligent, driving green transformation of the entire value chain. Across the entire lifecycle of products and services, companies can implement green purchasing, launch eco-friendly designs, build green products, accelerate green manufacturing and guide green consumption.[45]

One example is Lenovo's liquid-cooling technology, which decreases energy consumption by up to 40% while sustaining computing performance; this intelligent computing model is helping to make green high-performance computing possible. Lenovo's commitment is also evident within its manufacturing processes. Its East China manufacturing base, which produces one out of every eight PCs sold around the world, uses the Lenovo Advanced Production Scheduling System, which improves production efficiency and minimizes idle time, saving more than 2,696 MWh of electricity annually. That translates to an emission reduction of 2,000 tons of carbon dioxide, a solution comparable to planting 110,000 trees per year. Lenovo's environmental accomplishments also include its use of over 110 million pounds of recycled plastic across its product portfolio since 2005, the elimination of over 3,100 tons of packaging waste since 2008, reduced packaging consumption by 560 tons in fiscal year (FY) 2019/2020, and joining the UN's CEO Water Mandate to advance water stewardship and decrease water stress by 2050. The company also announced new climate change mitigation goals as part of its 2021 annual ESG report.[46]

Lenovo has committed to removing 1 million tons of greenhouse gas emissions from its supply chain by FY 2025/2026, integrating postconsumer recycled materials into 100% of PC products by 2025, and to reframing its social impact goals so that women will account for 27% of global executive roles by 2025, up from 21% in 2020.[47]

In November 2021 Lenovo posted record quarterly results that included historic highs for profit and revenue.[48] Its revenue experienced continuous growth of 23% year-on-year to reach $17.9 billion while the net income grew 65% year-on-year to $512 million. The company's work in the area of climate change mitigation has enhanced more than just its bottom line: Lenovo was included on

Fortune's list of the world's most admired companies for two consecutive years in 2019 and 2020.[49]

Ikea

Sweden-based Ikea has likewise publicly committed to positive climate change through its sustainability pledge, although it continues to be plagued by a negative reputation due to numerous ESG missteps. In 2012, it launched a sustainability strategy for 2020.[50] The "People and Planet Positive" strategy was established to take the company's sustainability to a new level for the purpose of driving innovation, transforming the business, and establishing new investment opportunities. In 2016, Ikea set out an updated series of goals:

- The reduction of greenhouse gas emissions from Ikea Group stores and other operations by 80%
- The reduction of greenhouse gas emissions from travel and customer deliveries by 50%
- The reduction of greenhouse gas emissions from the Ikea value chain by at least 15% in absolute terms by 2030[51]

The company also updated its 2012 strategy to include the reduction of the total Ikea climate footprint by an average of 70% per product. "Change will only be possible if we collaborate with others and nurture entrepreneurship," Inter IKEA Group CEO Torbjörn Lööf said at the time. "We are committed to taking the lead working together with everyone—from raw material suppliers all the way to our customers and partners."[52]

Though Ikea is often the butt of furniture-industry jokes, the company maintains a strong reputation among consumers, and *Forbes* has listed it as one of the world's most valuable brands.[53] In addition, The Reputation Institute ranks Ikea at number 58 among its 2017 Global RepTrak 100 listing of the world's most reputable brands. Ikea's reputation is strongest among millennials, a generation of consumers that strongly values and expects ESG initiatives from the companies they patronize.

Over time Ikea has demonstrated a commitment to ESG that goes beyond lip service. The company actively invests in environmentally sound and responsibly sourced materials as part of its commitment to operating as a responsible company for all its stakeholders.

It's important to note that even with these initiatives in place, Ikea has not escaped controversy, facing international criticism about its use of wood and association with questionable foresting practices. Most recently, a 2021 review of the company's supply chain reportedly revealed that pine wood used to make some of its most popular children's furniture likely originated from logging companies in Siberia that repeatedly violated Russian environmental laws.[54] On being presented with the findings, Ikea acknowledged use of the wood in its products, but it reportedly asserted that it was "legally harvested" and denied any wrongdoing. However, the company ended its supplier relationship with the logging company citing "practices of concern."[55] In the days immediately following news of the scandal, Ikea's stock prices fell before rebounding in a time frame corresponding to the company's public statement on the controversy. The company maintained a relatively steady stock price between late July 2021 and early September 2021, but product shortages due to global supply chain issues resulted in a troubling period at the end of 2021.

The question is, do questionable forestry practices, and accusations of greenwashing make IKEA an unsustainable company? Are they, and others like them, poor examples of ESG-focused businesses?

As noted at the beginning of this chapter, life is not always so simple. Rather than looking at companies from a lens of "totally sustainable" versus "totally unsustainable," we should look at what the company is doing to make improvements, including quantifiable metrics and ongoing monitoring. Similar to other companies that have experienced reputational issues, setting goals—as Ikea has done—and creating plans to meet or exceed them is one way to regain and maintain the trust of wary customers and investors.

National Grid

Utility companies around the world are setting net-zero emissions targets to be met by or before 2050.[56] In fact, the trend is so widespread that utility companies without net-zero targets are seen as defiant of the new normal.

National Grid is an electricity, natural gas, and clean energy delivery company operating in the United States and United Kingdom. The company announced its Net Zero by 2050 Plan. It builds on National Grid's Responsible Business Charter, which lays out the company's ESG commitments. Their plan identifies 10 key areas of focus, including the reduction of energy demand through increased efficiency and demand response. The company's demand-response program offers financial incentives to qualified participating businesses for the reduction of electricity consumption during those times when demand for electricity is generally the highest.[57] These companies are asked to reduce their electric use for at least 20 hours during the summer, typically occurring in increments of one to four hours.

National Grid's other areas of focus include decarbonization of the gas network through the use of renewable natural gas and hydrogen, the integration of innovative technologies to decarbonize heat, the investment in large-scale carbon management, and the interconnection of large-scale renewables via a 21st-century grid.[58] In October 2020, National Grid launched National Grid Renewables as the new brand name for their US renewable energy business.[59] This initiative focuses on the acceleration of clean energy transition through the development and operation of large-scale renewable energy assets, which includes solar, onshore wind, and battery storage nationwide. The program also touts a farmer-friendly and community-focused model by developing projects for corporations and utilities that reconfigure the country's electricity grid through investments in local economies and clean energy future.

However, there are other actions that undermine National Grid's community-minded efforts. In 2018, the company took away health insurance from around 1,200 of their workers after contract talks failed to produce a mutual agreement, resulting in those workers not "working on our property or for our customers, the locals are ineligible for compensation and benefits from the company" according to a company spokesperson.[60]

Further, activists' protests against National Grid's planned development of a natural gas pipeline in Brooklyn also flags a need to increase consideration of communities and neighborhoods—combining a need to improve social impact as well as environmental efforts.[61]

As we can see, when business planning, public policy support, and community engagement are combined they empower a business to achieve ESG goals. However, there is another piece to this combination; a business partner that can play a tremendous role in a company's success or failure around their business goals. That partner is the business's supplier.

Supply Chains and Sustainability

Aveda

One key to simplifying a company's sustainability efforts is to manage as much as possible internally, and when working with suppliers to know as much about your suppliers' businesses as possible. Former global president of Aveda, Dominique Conseil, did just that to develop plans for sustainability in the use of natural raw materials. In an interview, he explained his thought process:

It is better for a company that engages in sustainability to control all key processes in its operating model, to have its hands on as many things as possible. So outsourcing is an enemy here. And, of course, it also depends on who you outsource to, because you can outsource to a champion of sustainability, but it's a factor to consider.

When I left Aveda or shortly before I left, we were producing 89% of the units that we sold. So we were very much in house. We centralized manufacturing, but we were, all over the globe from a standpoint of output to consumers, and also input from supply chain, because we were using raw materials—particularly, agricultural raw materials to make essential oils, and other botanical ingredients. They were coming from the intertropical zone, mainly, but also from temperate zones all over the world. So we had complexity in some areas, and we were trying to minimize complexity and centralize in some other areas. Depending on your business model, and depending on your operating model, you need to make these calls and choose where you have complexity and where you don't. Otherwise, you end up with something that's simply not manageable.[62]

Conseil went on to point out the importance of knowing when to end business relationships when you and your supplier don't align. "If you find out that you have a supplier who disconnects when you talk about sustainability, you need to change suppliers really soon."[63]

Today, their sustainability focus continues as it relates to using postconsumer recycled material as much as possible and challenging their vendors to adhere to a rigorous recycling discipline as well.[64] In 2022, Aveda rolled out paper-based packaging material used for product samples. This material had 36 to 68% reduction in water consumption and 37 to 64% emissions reduction compared to water and emissions used in similar packaging. They did this in conjunction with environmentally conscious sample packaging firm Xela Pack.[65] This shows a consistency in their work with suppliers who share a sustainability focus.

General Mills

Many suppliers and vendors are willing to work with outside firms to create sustainable outcomes. For example, General Mills relies on farmers to deliver high-quality oats and grains to create high-quality products; to that end, the company supports their suppliers' use of regenerative farming practices.[66] This involves farmers taking a restorative approach to how they work with the soil, making it healthier while improving biodiversity and promoting carbon sequestration (helping remove carbon from the air and into the ground).[67] General Mills projects that its support for regenerative farming will help reduce greenhouse gas emissions 28% by 2025.

General Mills chief sustainability officer Mary Jane Melendez spoke to the relationship between General Mills and farmers in how the company supports the farmers' agricultural innovation and how that in turn supports General Mills overall sustainability:

> This needs to work for farmers. It has to be profitable for them. It can't just be about I'm gonna change my operations and have it be more conservative in nature in terms of conserving natural resources. They need to be able to be profitable and be able to run their business in a way that's going to be sustainable over time. And we think regenerative agriculture is a really promising one of many promising solutions that can help make changes in that area. And we've been working to bring regenerative agri-

culture practices to some of those commodities, oats and wheat, which can be greenhouse gas intensive in the way that they're grown and actually help the farmers to start thinking about soil health, water quality, and quantity, reducing the application of synthetic fertilizers, pesticides, and really start thinking about getting in tune with the natural nutrient cycle, where we allow the soil to return to health and act as the carbon sink that it's meant to be.[68]

Whereas some are already pointing to the long-term profitability of regenerative agriculture, once the method becomes more well-known and trusted, it could be a tool for consumer goods companies such as General Mills to support their supply chain, while reducing greenhouse gas emissions and costs.[69]

Final Thoughts

In this chapter we sought to discuss cautionary tales of what happens when companies do not rise to the occasion of meeting their ESG responsibilities. We also presented the alternate side, exploring how global corporations are delivering high ESG performance and the specific strategic areas behind their success.

One of the common issues we'll continue to explore (and question) is the lack of transparency and consistency about issues such as worker engagement, workplace safety, community involvement, and other concerns that fall under social, even amid continued improvements in environmental and governance. One point of consistency and agreement throughout the cases is that companies operate best when they are supported by other organizational influencers to plan and execute ESG strategies. In Chapter 3, we'll look at a specific influencer group and the impact that group has on corporations: large, institutional investors.

Regardless of sector, investors are increasingly recognizing that they have exposure to climate risks in their portfolios, and they also have a fiduciary duty to respond to that risk. These realizations typically manifest as investment decisions redirected toward companies and projects that promote clean technology, which provides investors with the power to promote change within the most carbon-intensive companies and sectors. We also see an increasing number of investors challenging corporations to use social engagement levers to empower workers with more positive workplace experiences. Corporate executives, their boards, and investors have a common stake in moving toward ESG, despite obstacles that may make the relationship challenging.

Chapter 2 Takeaways

- Companies that compromise their ESG responsibilities may experience long-term reputational damage as well as heavy fines.
- Financial damage can extend beyond fines; it can include costly marketing campaigns to improve firm's image and win back customers.
- Large corporations that achieve outstanding ESG performance have baked sustainability into their business operations in various ways:
  - Retooling how they do what they do (Microsoft, Ikea)
  - Shifting precisely what they do (National Grid)
  - Engaging firms in their supply chain (Aveda and General Mills).
- The same companies that have achieved outstanding ESG performance can still underperform in other important areas, demonstrating that there is still much work to do.

Notes

1. https://qz.com/work/1975970/company-scandals-in-the-age-of-corporate-responsibility/.
2. https://hbr.org/2016/06/why-companies-are-becoming-b-corporations.
3. https://www.youtube.com/watch?v=OQ1cliM0b0Q&t=22s.
4. https://www.bbc.com/news/business-34324772.
5. https://www.economist.com/science-and-technology/2016/01/12/the-dieselgate-dilemma.
6. https://www.motortrend.com/news/taxpayers-paid-51m-in-green-car-subsidies-linked-to-vw-diesels/.
7. https://www.motortrend.com/news/taxpayers-paid-51m-in-green-car-subsidies-linked-to-vw-diesels/.
8. https://www.theguardian.com/business/2015/sep/20/vw-software-scandal-chief-apologises-for-breaking-public-trust.
9. Cremer, Andreas. "Volkswagen AG Shares Plummet after Admitting It Cheated on Emission Tests." *Financial Post*. Reuters. (21 September 2015).
10. "Volkswagen Shares Slump for Third Consecutive Day as Emissions Scandal Escalates." *The Daily Telegraph*. (23 September 2015).
11. Kottasova, Ivana. "Volkswagen Emission Cheating Costs Qatar $5 Billion." CNNMoney. (September 22, 2015).
12. "Volkswagen Shares Slump for Third Consecutive Day as Emissions Scandal Escalates." *The Daily Telegraph*. (September 23, 2015).
13. "Volkswagen Diesel Emissions Scandal: The Toxic Legacy." *The Independent*. (September 17, 2016).
14. Welch, David, and Dana Hull. "Volkswagen of America November Vehicle Sales Down 24.7%." Bloomberg US. (December 2, 2015).
15. https://www.chicagotribune.com/business/ct-volkswagen-owners-0921-biz-20150921-story.html.
16. "Volkswagen's Reputation Takes Big Hit with Vehicle Owners; AutoPacific Predicts Tough Road Ahead." AutoPacific. (October 6, 2015).
17. Meier, Christian. "VW entschuldigt sich mit riesiger Werbekampagne." (October 4, 2015).
18. "VW Plans Huge Investment to Become Electric Cars Leader." *BBC New*. (June 16, 2016).
19. "Volkswagen Is Said to Be Cutting 30,000 Jobs." *Fortune*. (November 18, 2016).
20. https://www.reuters.com/article/us-volkswagen-results-diesel-idUSKBN2141JB.
21. "About Purdue Pharma L.P." (September 6, 2015).
22. Roberts, Sam. "Opinion: Raymond Sackler, Psychopharmacology Pioneer and Philanthropist, Dies at 97." *New York Times*. (19 July 2017).
23. https://www.ncbi.nlm.nih.gov/pmc/articles/PMC2622774/.

24. Meier, Barry. "Origins of an Epidemic: Purdue Pharma Knew Its Opioids Were Widely Abused." *New York Times*. (29 May 2018).
25. Meier, Barry. "In Guilty Plea, OxyContin Maker to Pay $600 Million." *New York Times*. (May 10, 2007).
26. Keefe, Patrick Radden. "The Family That Built an Empire of Pain." *The New Yorker*. (October 23, 2017).
27. Smith, Jason. "Kingpins: OxyContin, Heroin, and the Sackler-Sinaloa Connection." *New England Journal of Medicine*. (March 7, 2016).
28. Keefe, Patrick Radden. "The Family That Built an Empire of Pain: The Sackler Dynasty's Ruthless Marketing of Painkillers Has Generated Billions of Dollars—and Millions of Addicts." *The New Yorker*. (October 2017).
29. https://www.industryweek.com/leadership/companies-executives/article/21215749/pharma-giants-to-pay-590-million-to-us-native-americans-over-opioids.
30. https://www.legalreader.com/purdue-issues-campaigns-aimed-battling-opioid-crisis/.
31. https://finance.yahoo.com/news/ap-exclusive-oxycontin-maker-plead-134849205.html.
32. https://news.microsoft.com/2020/01/16/microsoft-announces-it-will-be-carbon-negative-by-2030.
33. https://blogs.microsoft.com/blog/2020/01/16/microsoft-will-be-carbon-negative-by-2030/.
34. Ibid.
35. Ibid.
36. https://www.bbc.com/future/article/20211028-why-not-all-net-zero-emissions-targets-are-equal.
37. https://blogs.microsoft.com/blog/2021/01/28/one-year-later-the-path-to-carbon-negative-a-progress-report-on-our-climate-moonshot/.
38. https://finance.yahoo.com/news/microsoft-plans-become-carbon-neutral-045238074.html.
39. https://www.theguardian.com/environment/2021/nov/27/its-critical-can-microsoft-make-good-on-its-climate-ambitions.
40. https://www.axcelis.com/about/corporate-responsibility/focus-on-sustainability. ISO 14001 is a type of quality-management standardization for organizations.
41. https://www.kimballelectronics.com/esg.
42. https://www.cdp.net/en.
43. https://www.eco-business.com/news/asian-companies-claim-they-are-going-net-zero-but-are-their-targets-realistic-ambitious-or-greenwash/.
44. https://news.lenovo.com/pressroom/press-releases/lenovo-ceo-outlines-commitments-to-a-greener-future/.

45. https://news.lenovo.com/pressroom/press-releases/lenovo-ceo-outlines-commitments-to-a-greener-future/.
46. Ibid.
47. https://news.lenovo.com/pressroom/press-releases/iwd-time-to-break-the-bias/.
48. https://news.lenovo.com/q2-2021-22-key-achievements-and-milestones-infographic/.
49. https://news.lenovo.com/pressroom/press-releases/lenovo-recognized-fortunes-2019-worlds-most-admired-companies.
50. https://www.designorate.com/ikea-sustainable-design-strategy-part2.
51. https://www.environmentalleader.com/2018/12/ikea-greenhouse-gas-emissions/.
52. Ibid.
53. https://www.forbes.com/sites/pamdanziger/2018/01/17/ikea-gets-no-respect-but-it-should/?sh=2c0848a284d1.
54. https://www.nbcnews.com/science/environment/ikea-likely-sold-furniture-linked-illegal-logging-forests-crucial-earth-n1273745.
55. https://www.nbcnews.com/science/environment/ikea-likely-sold-furniture-linked-illegal-logging-forests-crucial-earth-n1273745.
56. https://www.forbes.com/sites/scottcarpenter/2020/10/15/us-utility-companies-rush-to-declare-net-zero-targets/?sh=25110568693b.
57. https://www9.nationalgridus.com/aboutus/a3-1_news2.asp?document=10793.
58. https://www.nationalgridus.com/News/2020/10/National-Grid-Releases-Net-Zero-by-2050-Plan/.
59. https://www.nationalgrid.com/national-grid-ventures/what-we-do/renewable-energy.
60. https://www.masslive.com/news/boston/2018/07/national_grid_union_workers_lo.html.
61. https://web.archive.org/web/20200219135830/https://gothamist.com/news/national-grid-fracked-gas-pipeline-brooklyn-protest.
62. Dominique Conseil interview with the author (February 11, 2022).
63. Ibid.
64. https://www.aveda.com/living-aveda/responsible-packaging.
65. https://www.americansalon.com/business/aveda-reaches-new-sustainable-packaging-milestone.
66. https://www.greenbiz.com/article/general-mills-danone-dig-deeper-regenerative-agriculture-incentives-funding.
67. https://www.forbes.com/sites/forbesbusinesscouncil/2021/08/19/regenerative-agriculture-the-next-trend-in-food-retailing.
68. Mary Jane Melendez interview with the author (March 10, 2022).
69. https://www.no-tillfarmer.com/articles/10526-farm-study-regenerative-ag-practices-increase-profits-improve-soil-health.

The Partnership between Investors and Corporations

The evolution of ESG as an investment focus has increased engagement between many investors and the firms in their portfolios. Investors increasingly view themselves as partners working with firms—sometimes voluntarily and sometimes under duress—to incorporate sustainable practices into business models, meet industry innovation challenges, and generate revenue. These corporations and investors work together in pursuit of five main objectives:

1. **Opportunities gained** from meeting and even surpassing evolving consumer expectations, rather than seeing these trends as merely onerous requirements (and only meeting the bare minimum)

2. **Mitigation of risks** through compliance with established regulations (such as environmental, human rights, and ethics), as well as addressing ESG issues *without* forced regulation

3. Lowering "cost of capital" by **managing reputational damage** that may result from scandals such as environmental contamination, worker injuries, corruption, or litigation; managing these elements may lead to lower interest rates for borrowed funds as there is a perception of reduced risk for lenders

4. **Increasing revenues** by producing climate-friendly and socially beneficial products that increase market share; consumers reward responsible companies with loyalty and increased consumption

5. **Reducing operational costs** through increased efficiencies, such as more renewable forms of energy and materials, resulting in long-term reduction in costs because renewables and recycled materials lead to incremental cost reductions year after year

Financially Material ESG Factors

ESG factors, ranging from worker health to supply chain management to water use, may not have been called out as "material"—or necessary information to make investment decisions—in the past. Today, it's imperative to know that ESG factors can have negative or positive impacts on a company's revenues and operational model. Thus, that ESG-related information is material in making investment decisions. When CFOs report on how their company is progressing, it is wise to engage the sustainability officer to ensure investors, the public, and other stakeholders are aware of the firm's financial performance, as well as steps they are taking to improve any current or past damage to the climate or the welfare of those involved in their business.

Investors and other providers of capital are increasingly interested in how a company identifies which ESG topics are most financially impactful to their firm and how they build policies and plans to decrease risks and seize opportunities associated with those material topics.

Juliette Menga of Aetos Alternatives Management—where she serves as director of investments, chair of ESG/Sustainable Investing

Committee—shares her view on how corporate leaders can take a favorable approach to reporting on issues and topics that are most important to their specific business.

> I think the most successful CEOs, in terms of integrating ESG, are those that really embrace the concept, and integrate it as part of their strategic planning, and really take the time to understand what is material for their business.
>
> ESG does not mean the same thing for every company. It depends on your sector, your industry, your company's specific geography and what your company does [what it produces]. Take the time to understand material factors for your company and integrate it into your strategic planning. Take the time to understand how to hire the right people or consultants to help the company do that. Bring in decision makers. Really integrate ESG in the process.[1]

Awareness of a company's internal sustainability efforts and how they might benefit a company's operations (or not) is just as important as understanding how the company could be damaging to the environment, both directly and indirectly. In March 2022, the SEC announced their first proposal to call on companies to include climate-related risks that may come directly from goods they produce or even indirectly—such as from corporate vehicles or electricity they use—in their annual reports. Opponents have argued that the environmental impact of even basic daily activities such as business-office maintenance and the delivery of products, are not material and thus should not count. Supporters of this proposal have responded that "full disclosure" should be true full disclosure, and that includes details that are considered potentially minor, marginal or tangential.[2]

47

Regardless of your personal take on that debate, you need to recognize that what is considered material to your business is rapidly changing. Be prepared to communicate with stakeholders about your current performance and, if necessary, also be prepared to explain how you plan to improve. The following case studies demonstrate how companies can successfully partner with their own investors to make positive change in the ESG arena.

Engine No. 1 and Exxon: A David and Goliath Story

Following its gain of three seats on the Exxon board (as discussed in Chapter 1), Engine No. 1, a small hedge fund with less than $275 million assets under management, faced considerable criticism over its choice to invest in a fossil fuel giant and substantial doubt as to its capacity to craft a new framework within the corporation; transforming the culture of such a large company is not an easy task. Though the hedge fund's actions were inspired by specific goals—enhancing shareholder value, reducing carbon emissions, and transforming Exxon into a global leader in profitable clean energy—Engine No. 1 did not immediately provide specific recommendations for how to accomplish these objectives. As stated in one *MarketWatch* article, "a lack of specificity indicated that it was not truly informed about the operations of Exxon Mobil or how to manage its long-term future." The article noted that the fund's activism had yet to result in increases in Exxon's stock prices. "Whatever increase in the stock since Engine No. 1's activism became public can be attributed to a rise in oil prices that have benefited all oil and gas companies."[3]

Engine No. 1 executives have a different take on their progress, asserting that Exxon has reduced oil and gas production in a "meaningful" way in the months since its successful proxy campaign. Noting that genuine change takes time, Engine No. 1's website states, "Since we launched our campaign, ExxonMobil's share price has increased, although not nearly enough to make up for the billions in value that have been destroyed. However, we believe that preserving these gains and creating long-term value creation will require real change."[4] The fund has shared some valuable insights into the framework that it used in its unprecedented Exxon board challenge by publishing an investment framework that advocates for a connection between value and corporate activities affecting climate and society.

Wharton School management professor Witold Henisz, who also serves as an advisor to the firm, argues that the distance between ESG goals and traditional metrics of success is a matter of perception. "Engine No. 1 attaches a value to a company's impact on climate change, water consumption, workforce diversity or human rights. In the absence of company data that allows this, it uses models that draw on sources such as the United Nations and the International Labor Organization."[5] He explained that, from Engine No. 1's perspective, the disconnect between ESG scores, or how firms are rated on their ESG footprint, and the material financial value actually seen from ESG improvement, makes it more difficult for investors that want to focus their capital on decreased emissions.[6] To exemplify its model in action, Engine No.1 CEO Jennifer Grancio highlighted how Exxon included only about 10% of its total carbon emissions in its reduction targets, because the data excluded the emissions that resulted when customers burned its fuel. She said there is substantial potential for increased value if companies are fully transparent about emissions and take affirmative steps to reduce them.

The Partnership between Investors and Corporations

In 2019 the Trump Administration's Department of Labor sought to reduce ESG investing through policy. The policy was designed to argue that institutional investors were going against their fiduciary duty, or duty to put clients' interest first, by selecting socially responsible investments. It didn't allow ESG investments to be a "default" option—a win for the fossil fuel industry. The Biden Administration's focus changed so that now investors are encouraged to take ESG into consideration during their portfolio analysis.

Source: https://www.santafenewmexican.com/news/business/federal-assault-on-sustainable-investing-will-hurt-investors/article_01f3126e-e621-11ea-9bc7-932498c45535.html.

DSM Venturing: Investing in Sustainable Food Systems

DSM Venturing is finding success in the sustainable food industry by putting health and nutrition at the forefront of their investing focus. They empower small businesses with funding to support innovative, adaptive programs for producing foods more sustainably.

The production and consumption of food accounts for well over 20% of global greenhouse gas emissions and more than 90% of the world's freshwater consumption.[7] Global population growth will likely increase these emissions by an additional 49% by 2050, even as many other sectors such as energy and transport are set to see a decrease over the same time frame. A sustainable global food system would have dual ESG benefits—meaning, it would benefit both the environment and human society—especially given that hundreds of millions of people suffer from undernourishment and the erosion of fertile topsoil (which can take centuries to replenish) at an alarming rate. The world needs to produce and consume sustainable, affordable, and healthy food to promote the health of people and the planet.[8]

DSM Venturing describes itself as a "global purpose-led, science-based company specializing in nutrition, health & sustainable living."[9] It is one of the investors behind Meatable, a Dutch food startup that has raised more than $170 million in funding from 15 investors.[10] Founded in 2018, the company produces lab-grown, cultivated meat with the goal of preventing the slaughter of animals, while also reducing land and water use and greenhouse gas emissions.[11] In addition to the environmental benefits, the company's process also targets consumer health by eliminating the use of antibiotics in livestock farming.

In September 2021, Meatable announced an agreement with DSM to "make cultured meat affordable and accessible on a large scale."[12] Meatable is waiting for regulatory approval before selling a ground meat product on the market; company executives expect this to occur as of 2025. The DSM-Meatable partnership shows how small businesses can attract investments on a scale far larger than they could normally expect, especially when sustainability is baked into their business model. Alternative meat is an industry that seeks to meet ESG standards while also attracting lucrative investments. Reports show that the industry raised more than $3 billion in investments in 2020.[13] That equates to more than the investments of any

51

single year in the industry's history. This level of investment exemplifies the attractiveness of sustainable protein production solutions as viable investment opportunities. But startups and alternative food production companies are not the only ones acting on these investment changes.

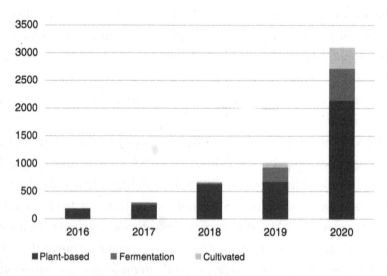

Investment in alternative meat companies has increased considerably since 2016.
Source: https://www.credit-suisse.com/media/assets/corporate/docs/about-us/research/publications/the-global-food-system-identifying-sustainable-solutions.pdf.

Tyson Ventures: Sustainable Investing amid Scandal

When a brand is caught up in environmental scandals, it is challenging for that brand's investment arm to profess a dedication to supporting sustainability and be taken seriously. Further, investors rightfully aim to reward *tangible* operational, product, and behavioral changes in the area of sustainability—not just talk. Tyson Foods and their investment arm Tyson Ventures present an example of this dynamic, as well as the improvements needed to ensure a company plans for and meets sustainability goals.

"Large strategic food and beverage players also increasingly are interested in scaling businesses that can demonstrably help them achieve ambitious, publicly declared sustainability or social governance goals," stated Erin VanLanduit, managing director, Tyson Ventures, the venture capital arm of Tyson Foods.[14] "Sustainability is a consideration in all of the investments that we make on behalf of Tyson. We have some very large and public goals related to sustainability that Tyson has put out there in the past few years. So we do think very carefully about where we're putting our money because we do want to drive towards those sustainability goals." She said that Tyson Venture's interests lie in water management, land stewardship, soil health, greenhouse gas reduction, and animal welfare.

But it must be pointed out that, even with these ESG investment interests, Tyson is not above its own environmental missteps. The company produces one of every five pounds of all the meat consumed in the United States, processing more than 35 million chickens, 424,000 pigs, and 130,000 cattle per week.[15] Though the company has made moves in recent years to increase its use of renewable energy and announced plans to stop using antibiotics in its chicken and pork, one *Huffington Post* article referred to the company's efforts as "lipstick on an antibiotic-juiced pig."[16]

In 2016, the organization Environment America named Tyson as the top water polluter among agribusinesses.[17] In 2020, the state of Alabama sued Tyson for damages caused by wastewater pollution from one of its facilities, which killed an estimated 175,000 fish. Tyson has also faced criticism within the social aspect of ESG for its irresponsible treatment of workers throughout the pandemic. Its governance was also called into question with allegations of price fixing in order to cheat smaller farmers and consumers.

Realistically, Tyson's mishandling of key environmental and social challenges can force their investors to demand immediate change—such as action aimed at removing waste and increasing transparency in paying their farmers—as a requirement for their investment dollars. However, the Tyson Limited partnership has maintained its position as the company's largest shareholder, and in 2019, John R. Tyson took reigns as chief sustainability officer, exemplifying that the family is still very much in the driver's seat.[18]

Long-term reputational risk and costs from litigation make it difficult for Tyson's investment arm to have credibility in the marketplace as an investor who puts dollars into projects concerning animal welfare and water management. Sustainability starts at home, and this situation points to the need for investment groups to manage the reputation of the brand with which they are most closely affiliated.

Jana Partners: Increasing Revenues and Improving Products

Neuberger Berman is an institutional investor that, until recently, has always taken a traditional buy-and-hold approach to money management. But in 2017, with threats to its roughly $200 million investment in Whole Foods looming (this was pre-Amazon takeover of Whole Foods), Neuberger Berman decided to take action by pressuring hedge funds to become activist investors.[19] (Activist investors are shareholders who use their stake in a corporation to place pressure on the company's management to take some type of action.) Jana Partners, an $8.5 billion hedge fund responsible for some very high-profile corporate shake-ups, became involved. Although neither Neuberger nor Jana discussed their relationship publicly, the two firms seemed to agree on concerns and to be collaborating on addressing them.[20] For example, Jana voiced concerns about Whole Foods' customer service, as well as the quality of the produce offered, these can be considered as community engagement and product quality issues falling squarely under the *S* in ESG. Jana cited additional issues for Whole Foods to work out about workers' schedules and executive behavior. Investors gave the company clear directives on areas of improvement and, faced with these mandates, Whole Foods complied. The company's stock jumped 10%, resulting in millions of dollars in increased value for Neuberger's stake in the company.

Jana Partners also had a lot to do with changes that occurred within ConAgra Brand, resulting from criticisms of the company's failure to meet consumer demand for more organic and environmentally friendly foods and packaging.[21] The result was a shift toward greater sustainability, as well as an increase in ConAgra's share price once the news broke that Jana was an investor.

Investors Balance ESG and Revenue

Although activist investors can further ESG initiatives of a company, the opposite result is also possible, as demonstrated by the ouster of Danone's CEO and chairman Emmanuel Faber, who was appointed chair of the International Sustainability Standards Board (ISSB) in 2022.[21] After taking a substantial hit during the pandemic, the global food company experienced less-than-stellar market performance. In response, activist shareholders made numerous demands, which business experts have referred to as a small coup that forced Faber out.

A highlight of Faber's four-year leadership had been a strategy he called "One Planet, One Health," which involved a strategy to include Danone's environmental performance as a primary indicator of the company's overall achievement. This showed that sustainability wasn't just a nice to have but rather meeting certain environmental targets was a critical strategic input baked into the company plans and approach. This, along with his many other environmental policies, brought him significant recognition from environmentalists and climate activists. As *Forbes* stated in March 2021, "Emmanuel Faber will enter history as one of the leading executives promoting stakeholder capitalism and centering core business units around ESG objectives."[22] But many investors were more focused on the drop in sales that Danone experienced at the time, especially in comparison to competitors Nestlé and Unilever.[23]

Faber's controversial ousting highlights the gap that still exists between promoters of sustainable business objectives and traditional corporate advocates. Faber's environmental practices were seen as an impediment to a strong market share and stock price increases by activist investors. Consider the numbers from a February 2021 *Barron's* article: "Since the month Faber took over, Danone's stock price has risen by 8% to about 55 euros ($66). Compare that with the performance of rival Nestle (NESN.Switzerland), whose shares are up 50% over the same period, or Unilever (UL), which is up 73%. Danone is also trailing the competition on other financial metrics, such as price/earnings ratio." But balance this in context of the "gender-balanced" board of directors and sustainable product focus during his tenure, and we see both sides of the coin when looking at ESG in context of stock price.[24]

This Danone case offers some extremely important observations about the realistic ability of executives to promote ESG at their firms. First, companies must seek out investors whose goals are in line with their own. If ESG ranks as a high priority within the corporate culture, the company needs investors who are willing to accept some short-term losses for the long-term benefits to society and the world. Second, pioneering investors are needed to craft innovative business models that combine sustainability with desirable shareholder returns, which is a serious challenge particularly if we're only looking at short-term returns. This highlights the importance of communication about ESG initiatives between companies and investors. Valerie S. Grant, managing director and portfolio manager at Nuveen, a TIAA Company, said that, as companies review their overall corporate and ESG strategies, they should communicate their long-term goals and aspirations along with an outline of the steps that should be taken to reach those goals.

It helps to frame that for investors so that we actually know what to expect. Then, when we see some variability in earnings or some volatility, we don't overreact. At least for the strategy that I manage, we tend to be longer term holders that look at the long-term performance of a company, the communication is very critical. Some companies are still not doing that very well. They have their ESG targets and then, in another part of the company, they have their investor relations function, but they don't necessarily integrate the two which will become increasingly important.[25]

Short-term costs are an inevitable part of the sustainability equation, and businesses typically pass them on to shareholders, suppliers, or customers. But a happy medium is possible. Arturo Bris, professor of finance, International Institute for Management Development, offered Swiss-based Vestergaard as an example of a company that mastered the fine balance between sustainability and desirable returns.[26] Vestergaard sells products that help rural African populations access clean water; the company was financed by selling carbon credits. It was a business model that simultaneously benefited customers, users, suppliers, and owners. "A chief executive running a business like that should be safe from being removed for caring too much about sustainability," asserted Bris.[27]

Columbia University Business School professor Angela Lee, who also founded the investment group 37 Angels, describes the perceived struggle between impact and returns as a spectrum. "Some people believe that you can have impact or you can have financial gain. Some people think you have to take a concession on one or the other. I am somebody who does truly believe that it can be a win-win and our portfolio proves that." She said the portfolio includes 50% impact—meaning half is dedicated to improving society—while maintaining a

57

top performance. "So we have not had to take any sort of concession on financial returns in order to invest in companies that have impact."[28]

In order to see those financial returns, investors and corporate leaders have to factor the roles consumers, regulators, societal trends, and other market forces play.

Nikita Singhal, managing director, co-head of Sustainable Investment & ESG at Lazard Asset Management, points out that investors examine sustainability issues as well as a company's handling of those issues and how that plays out in its market position.

> I am really focused on understanding sustainability trends, and in this context—whether it's social inequalities or climate change—how are those trends likely to get priced into capital markets? I encourage research analysts to think about what are the likely catalysts that are going to drive the 'pricing-in' of these issues? And what we have found is that can be very contextual—driven by sector, region or something entirely idiosyncratic. Typical catalysts can include things like changes in regulations, so, there might be auto emissions regulations, or building emissions regulations, regulations around diversity requirements. There may also be changes in consumer behavior around specific sustainability issues, such as the expectation to reduce plastics in consumer packaging that impacts the plastic packaging industry and its supply chain. And lastly, there may also be disruptive technologies like EVs, renewable energy or LED lighting, whose pace of accelerated adoption can act as a market catalyst. [This] can really impact the reputation of companies, their ability to maintain or garner new market share, their cost of capital, or a specific line item that impacts their long-term financial productivity.[29]

Activist Investors and Governance

As highlighted in these food and beverage industry examples, activist investors can exhibit substantial influence over the operations and executive decisions of a business. These individuals and businesses leverage their capital to gain voting rights on a board of directors through the purchase of large numbers of company's shares. The overarching goal is to affect the strategic directions of executives, particularly in relation to the management of resources, as well as risk and return.[30] Activist investors typically look for companies that suffer from some type of managerial flaw. They then seek to affect through their influence or by replacing the existing management, thus their focus on the governance aspect of ESG.

There are generally a few types of activist investors. First, extremely affluent individuals may function independently as activist investors. Two examples are Bill Ackman, founder and CEO of Pershing Capital, and David Einhorn, founder and president of Greenlight Capital. Second, private equity firms can also assume an activist role by taking control of a public company for the purpose of taking it private. The third type of activist investors are hedge funds, which can act like individual activist investors or private equity firms in the ways they take control of public companies. The main goal of a hedge fund is usually the generation of return for investors, but in a way that may be more aggressive and riskier than with other funds.

It's worth noting that whether we're talking about individual activist investors or large-scale hedge funds, the field is currently dominated by white men—quite ironic when you consider the broad goals of ESG. But as with the investment world in general, the activist-investor space also has a need for greater diversity.

Sometimes individual activist investors transform into hedge funds to better leverage their capital. For example, Jana Partners was founded as a hedge fund in 2001 by Barry Rosenstein for the purpose of engaging in shareholder activism and socially responsible investing.[31] In addition to Whole Foods and ConAgra, Jana has also made activist investments in such major corporations as Apple Inc., Tiffany's, PetSmart, Marathon Petroleum, and McGraw Hill.[32]

Churchill Capital Corporation: SPACs and ESG

Firms are now creating new, innovative techniques to drive business objectives, and the special purpose acquisition company is a good example. Churchill Capital Corp operates as a special purpose acquisition company (SPAC), also known as a blank-check company. According to its Bloomberg company profile, this publicly traded company "aims to acquire one and more businesses and assets, via a merger, capital stock exchange, asset acquisition, stock purchase, and reorganization."[33] In 2021, Churchill Capital announced plans to enter the electric vehicle game through a merger with Lucid Motors, which is led by a former Tesla engineer.[34] The merged company is listed on NASDAQ, trading under the name Lucid Group.

In early 2021, Bloomberg reported that Churchill Capital had sought to raise between $1 billion and $1.5 billion from institutional investors in support of the merger, which demonstrates the influence that institutional investors had in the creation of the Lucid Group. This merger did not happen without challenges, though: Churchill reportedly struggled to secure the backing of all shareholders. Prior to the vote, the company felt the need to send shareholders a reminder about voting their shares. According to a report by *The Street*, this has become a pretty common tactic among SPAC mergers because retail investors are typically shorter-term holders than institutional buyers and they "may not even realize that they should be voting as of the record date."[35] This is an example of a company whose leader had a competitive background (e.g., former Tesla) to be a player in an emerging market (electric vehicles) and was able to leverage the SPAC as a means to enter into what may be considered a high-growth market. The lesson here is there may be diverse ways—such as SPACs—to garner necessary investment support to enter a space where ESG considerations are clear to the market.

PGIM Real Estate and Invesco: Improving Efficiency, Mitigating Risk

The real estate industry is benefiting from a focus on energy and water efficiency. Green buildings are more than a trend, and investors are looking to capitalize on the shift toward operational and cost efficiencies, as well as more consumer demand for commercial and residential real estate with a foundation of sustainability.

Real estate development is a key contributor to carbon emissions through the use of concrete and steel, in terms of energy mix and efficiency (or lack thereof). From a social perspective, the lack of affordable housing built for families has very real consequences around health and well-being. A growing need to innovate in the industry in both environmental and social fields has led to an increased appetite for ESG investing within real estate. According to the Environmental and Energy Study Institute due to the use of fossil fuels and propane in heaters and furnaces in real estate, buildings nationwide account for 40% of the country's carbon emissions.[36]

Michele Jean Le Goff is a senior analyst, ESG at PGIM Real Estate, and she appeared on Refinitiv's Sustainability Perspectives podcast in March 2021.[37] PGIM, formerly known as Prudential Asset Management, has about $1.5 trillion assets under management. Le Goff explained that, as real estate has played an increasing role in advancing sustainability, investors have become extremely interested in assets that are more productive and less damaging to the environment while also providing greater value. "Investors expect baseline energy efficiency in their real estate throughout the asset, from the ground up. So, we are deploying technology to protect the asset as well as to uncover opportunities for improvement in building performance." She said that expectations also exist for benchmarking energy throughout the building in real time so that all investments can be green rated. "This is very valuable data for investors to know in terms of capital placement as well as how their investments are performing year over year."[38]

Another major component of ESG within the real estate industry is risk mitigation. As Le Goff explained, "It's important to remember that, before the climate discussion was mainstreamed, it was the underwriters of the property's insurance that really underwrote any type of risk to the properties, including those that are weather related." She said that it took a while for climate risk to become a widespread conversation with an industry-wide understanding about mitigation strategies that can be taken in addition to underwriting on specific investment. "For example, we can leverage climates analytics to seize opportunities," stated Le Goff. "We can use capital projects on properties to enhance climate resiliency for high-risk properties to make lease payments more durable." She described water conservation, the mitigation of water loss, waste reduction, and indoor air quality as additional environmental concerns within the real estate industry. Getting a handle on water loss and waste reduction can support greater operational efficiency and reduced operational costs.[39]

Greater attention paid to environmental concerns contributes to the growth and "mainstreaming" of investing conversations on topics such as climate risk.
Source: Nuthawut / Adobe Stock

In 2020, global investment manager Invesco launched the world's first green exchange traded fund (ETF).[40] According to the company's website, the Invesco MSCI Green Building ETF will generally invest 90% of its total net assets in securities in the index, which are companies that provide exposure to the environment impact theme of "green building" by including the design, construction, redevelopment, retrofitting, or acquisition of green-certified properties to promote mechanisms for raising capacity for effective climate change mitigation and adaptation. The ETF reportedly prefers companies with proven commitments to energy efficiency, healthier indoor air quality, and environmentally aware construction practices. Ali Ingram, director and sustainability lead in JLL's European office investment team, said, "It's great that vehicles such as Invesco's ETF will not only concentrate on real estate companies but also on companies focused on retrofitting existing buildings and those who are innovating. To meet climate objectives, the rate of building renovations will need to at least double.

It's the biggest challenge faced by the sector today as it looks to maintain its attraction to investors and chase down net-zero goals."[41]

Nuveen: Opportunities That Go beyond Expectations

Nuveen is the investment manager of the Teacher's Insurance and Annuity Association (TIAA), which is the top financial services provider for employees in the academic, research, medical, cultural, and governmental fields.[42] In 1970, TIAA began strategizing its voting proxies to vote for or against specific initiatives instead of blanket voting in support of or opposition to company management. During this decade, TIAA also helped form the Investor Responsibility Research Center to create fact-finding surveys to report on social issues within investments. Throughout the 1980s and 1990s, TIAA expanded its responsible investment efforts through various small business and community investment programs. In 1998, TIAA was one of eight insurance companies to create and fund Impact Community Capital (ICC) to generate purpose-driven investments. The company reportedly became one of the first to "deliver capital in scale for affordable housing."[43] Since its formation, ICC has originated more than $1.9 billion of investments for affordable housing, health care, childcare, and economic development. TIAA's CEO Thasunda Brown Duckett, one of the few Black women heading up a Fortune 500 firm, shows TIAA's focus on C-suite-level diversity, which is another way it can be a model for their competitors.

As TIAA's investment manager, Nuveen puts forth the following statement about responsible real estate investing:

Responsible investing drives better outcomes for investors, our communities and the planet and is an integral part of our process. By embedding environmental, social, and governance (ESG) factors into investment research, due diligence, portfolio construction and ongoing monitoring, we seek to improve clients' long-term performance and reduce risk.[44]

Allison Spector, director of sustainability in the real assets and private markets team at Nuveen, the US asset manager, told the *Financial Times* that she has seen a greater awareness surrounding risks and opportunities, revealing that Nuveen is fielding an increasing number of client questions about ESG portfolio details.[45]

Michele Le Goff, from PGIM Real Estate, spoke about the connection that exists within the real estate sector between health equity and social equity, explaining that about 70% of green certifications have to do with underlying health metrics.[46] She said that the industry is starting to take affordable housing as a serious aspect of impact investing. "We are finally able to combine impact, which is social equity in housing as well, and implementing social equity in development projects." She gave the real-life example of an impact value fund spinoff that transformed a former military base near Washington, DC, redeveloping and repositioning it into a mixed-used development with development techniques such as green certifications. "One component of that was affordable housing, which resulted in capital placement from investors with interests in impact funds," she explained.[47]

Here we can see the interconnectedness of environmental, as well as social and health concerns, that drive today's environmental justice movement. A community's health, or lack thereof, can be traced directly to living conditions. We are aware of the abysmal living conditions that too many people have to endure: lead in pipes, asbestos in floor tiles, or mold from a leaky roof. Investors who finance this sector would do well to advise their real estate business partners to ensure materials and construction practices create living

65

and working quarters that do no harm to the environment or to those who inhabit those spaces.

Final Thoughts

Institutional investors play various roles in their engagement with companies, depending on their size, scale, and capabilities.

Large money managers are increasingly partnering with smaller activist investors to meet common goals. The benefit of these relationships is shown when the investors come together to influence companies to increase their level of climate awareness, improve products for consumers, or ramp up other areas that serve to improve the company's ESG footprint while also increasing financial value.

Certain investors have a primary interest in certain industries, and thus they focus on sustainable investment in those industries. These investors have capabilities and knowledge for those markets and can move the needle in innovative ways, while disrupting and creating competition among the more staid, larger industry leaders.

The marketplace continues to debate whether investors should use their influence to help firms recalibrate when they are perceived to misuse natural or human capital, or whether they should label such companies as "bad actors" and totally divest from them. But total divestiture does not seem to be where the future is headed. Many investors see the future as one in which they convert companies that are performing poorly into better stewards by giving guidance on how they can better plan and execute on sustainability goals. Increasingly, we cannot dispute the fact that investors and the companies in their portfolios are partners; they have an interdependent relationship to meet objectives on mitigating risk that can result in ongoing costs or large fines, exploiting opportunities to meet societal demands, and improving returns.

In Chapter 4, we will look at corporate ESG initiatives through the lens of another important partner: governments. Similar to asset managers, governments can be investors as well as lenders in a company's sustainability and social responsibility initiatives. But governments as stakeholders present different types of engagement and opportunity for businesses. For one thing, they have the power to regulate and fine business that do harm to environment and society. Today's global focus on infrastructure improvements as well as the prevalence of a variety of sustainability and social bonds means that government-corporate ESG partnerships will deepen, as will the challenges and opportunities that accompany them.

Chapter 3 Takeaways

- Corporations and investors work together in pursuit of five main objectives: opportunities gained, mitigation of risks, managing reputational damage, increasing revenues, and reducing operational costs.
- Large asset managers are partnering with activist investors who have the access and know-how to ensure companies in their portfolios understand sustainability threats and to recalibrate to improve their corporate ESG standing.
- Investors are enabling startups to develop new business models that disrupt older, staid corporate models and challenge their market share. These new models range from arenas such as renewable energy to electric vehicles to sustainable food and beverages.
- One of the biggest debates in the ESG space is whether corporate sustainability can coexist with the desire to increase revenue.

Notes

1. Juliette Menga interview with the author (December 10, 2021).
2. https://www.nytimes.com/2022/03/21/business/sec-climate-disclosure-rule.html.
3. https://www.marketwatch.com/story/engine-no-1-is-all-talk-no-strategy-with-exxon-mobil-11629127035.
4. https://reenergizexom.com/the-case-for-change.
5. https://www.reuters.com/business/sustainable-business/exclusive-engine-no-1-investment-framework-aims-tie-company-valuations-climate-2021-09-13/.
6. https://www.reuters.com/business/sustainable-business/exclusive-engine-no-1-investment-framework-aims-tie-company-valuations-climate-2021-09-13/.
7. https://www.credit-suisse.com/about-us-news/en/articles/news-and-expertise/sustainable-food-as-an-investment-opportunity-202106.html.
8. Ibid.
9. https://www.dsm.com/corporate/about.html.
10. https://www.crunchbase.com/organization/meatable/company_financials.
11. https://www.globenewswire.com/news-release/2018/09/30/1587407/0/en/Meatable-to-Feed-the-World-with-Breakthrough-Single-Cell-based-Meat-Technology.html.
12. https://myprivacy.dpgmedia.nl/consent?siteKey=PUBX2BuuZfEPJ6vF&callbackUrl=https%3a%2f%2fwww.volkskrant.nl%2fprivacy-wall%2faccept%3fredirectUri%3d%252fnieuws-achtergrond%252fdsm-stapt-in-kweekvlees-met-start-up-meatable-groen-diervriendelijk-en-hopelijk-rendabel%257ebf7d8bdf%252f (Translated).
13. https://gfi.org/blog/2020-state-of-the-industry-highlights.
14. https://www.foodnavigator-usa.com/Article/2020/09/29/Environmental-social-governance-goals-emerge-as-top-priority-for-investors-in-food-beverage.
15. https://www.huffpost.com/entry/tyson-foods-environmentalism-regulation-sustainability_n_5a9562d6e4b0699553cc7656.
16. Ibid.
17. https://www.ecowatch.com/tyson-foods-2020-public-health-2649618702.html.
18. https://talkbusiness.net/2011/01/tyson-partnership-succession-plans-revealed/ andhttps://www.tysonfoods.com/news/news-releases/2019/9/tyson-foods-names-john-r-tyson-chief-sustainability-officer.
19. https://www.nytimes.com/2017/04/25/business/dealbook/money-managers-take-off-the-gloves-in-dealing-with-companies.html.
20. https://www.forbes.com/sites/frankvangansbeke/2021/03/20/sustainability-and-the-downfall-of-danone-ceo-faber-12/.
21. https://omaha.com/business/its-not-just-conagra-and-cabelas-businesses-everywhere-targeted-by-investors-pressing-for-change/article_868b2440-8004-11e5-b359-fbcce03e9ed1.html.

22. Ibid.
23. https://time.com/6121684/emmanuel-faber-danone-interview/.
24. https://www.barrons.com/articles/
activist-investor-takes-aim-at-danone-what-that-could-mean-for-the-
stock-51612431006.
25. Valerie Grant interview with the author (December 16, 2021).
26. https://theconversation.com/danones-ceo-has-been-ousted-for-being-progressive-
blame-society-not-activist-shareholders-157383.
27. https://theconversation.com/
danones-ceo-has-been-ousted-for-being-progressive-blame-society-not-activist-
shareholders-157383.
28. Angela Lee interview with the author (December 3, 2021).
29. Author Interview. Nikita Singhal. January 18, 2022.
30. https://corporatefinanceinstitute.com/resources/knowledge/trading-investing/
activist-investor/.
31. https://www.reuters.com/article/us-hedgefunds-jana/activist-investor-jana-
hired-staff-for-new-socially-responsible-fund-idUSKBN1HO200.
32. https://www.brown.edu/about/administration/corporation/members/
barry-rosenstein.
33. https://www.bloomberg.com/profile/company/9990401D:US.
34. https://www.thestreet.com/investing/churchill-shareholders-lucid-motors-spac-
acquisition.
35. https://www.thestreet.com/boardroomalpha/spac/cciv-lucid-vote-thursday-
spacs.
36. https://angeles.sierraclub.org/climate_action_team.
37. https://shows.acast.com/refinitiv-sustainability-perspectives-podcast/episodes/
esg-in-real-estate.
38. Ibid.
39. Ibid.
40. https://www.us.jll.com/en/trends-and-insights/investor/real-estate-has-its-first-green-
building-etf-what-next.
41. Ibid.
42. https://www.nuveen.com/en-us/institutional/investment-capabilities/real-
estate/responsible-property-investment.
43. Ibid.
44. https://www.nuveen.com/en-us/institutional/investment-capabilities/
real-estate/responsible-property-investment.
45. https://www.ft.com/content/c4daafa4-5de4-4391-9bba-e2a1733d9bba.
46. https://shows.acast.com/refinitiv-sustainability-perspectives-podcast/episodes/
esg-in-real-estate.
47. Ibid.

The Partnership between Investors and Corporations

The New World of Bonds

The global ESG bond market is set to reach $1.5–1.8 trillion in 2022, up from $520 billion in 2020.[1] Given both the size and expected future growth of this market, corporate leaders should consider educating themselves about it. Why? Because ESG bonds are here to stay. The market is growing. They are increasingly important to your stakeholders, including investors and customers.

I want to start this chapter with a brief explanation of bonds, the mechanics behind them, and a comparison between corporate and government bonds. Understanding how government and corporate bonds work gives business leaders insight into why investors are attracted to government bonds as well as corporate bonds. After some brief comments on bonds in general, this chapter discusses a variety of ESG bond types, such as green, blue, and social. Just as important, this section describes why issues such as water conservation and climate change, as well as improvements in health care and job creation, are important to stakeholders, and how businesses and governments may be in a position to help solve these issues.

The Basics of Bonds

Bonds are, as defined by the US Securities and Exchange Commission:

> a debt obligation, like an IOU. Investors who buy bonds are lending money to the company (or government entity)

issuing the bond. In return, the company (or government entity) makes a legal commitment to pay interest on the principal and, in most cases, to return the principal when the bond comes due, or matures.[2]

Buying bonds differs from the purchase of common stock, where the purchaser obtains equity in the company and may also receive regular dividends. Corporate bonds do not provide equity in the company, only interest and principal on the bond, which stays the same regardless of the company's profitability or stock price. Although corporate bonds make up the largest section of the US bond market, treasury bonds and other government bonds also comprise a significant portion.

Corporate bonds are a tool that companies use to quickly access cash without the dilution of ownership that can result from issuing additional stock.[3] The money brought in by corporate bonds can be used in a variety of ways, including the purchase of new assets, research and development, mergers and acquisitions, or to fund stock buybacks. Bond holders are paid interest at regular intervals throughout the life of the bond, and when the bond "matures," they are repaid the initial investment, or principal.

Naturally, bond purchasers want some assurance that their money is safe. Often they turn to one or more of bond-rating agencies for counsel; the big three are Standard & Poor's (S&P), Moody's, and Fitch. Taking into consideration factors such as financial stability, potential for growth, and current debt, these agencies issue letter grades that help investors understand the level of risk involved in a particular bond. Bonds that are rated from AAA or Aaa to BBB or Baa are classified as "investment grade."[4] Based on their growth potential and small likelihood of default, they are typically issued at lower yields when compared to less creditworthy bonds. Conversely, bonds with a BB or Ba rating or below, as well as bonds that are not rated, are classified as junk bonds.[5] Junk bonds are not literally "junk," but they are determined to have a greater risk of default, so they are issued at a higher yield, due to the perception that they represent a higher risk to investors; junk bonds are sometimes called high-yield bonds for that reason. Investment experts generally agree that a diversified investment portfolio should include highly rated bonds of various maturities as a resource for a steady income stream over the life of the bond.[6]

When governments need to borrow funds, they can also issue debt obligations in the form of bonds. These bonds can be sold to individuals, other government agencies, and businesses, as well as to state and local governments. Government bonds may also be sold to foreign individuals, businesses, and governments. The purchaser essentially lends money to the government for the necessary purpose, and over the course of time, that government pays the money back to the purchaser with interest. Government bonds from developed countries are generally regarded as low-risk investments due to the government's backing (we discuss how a country's risks are evaluated in Chapter 5); US Treasury bonds are considered some of the safest investments across the globe.[7] That is why treasury bonds are often used by investment funds to satisfy fiduciary requirements, as well as by individual investors who appreciate the guarantee of receiving their principal and interest according to an established schedule. Government of Canada Bonds (GoCs), UK Gilts, German Bunds, Japanese Government Bonds (JGBs), and Brazilian Government Bonds are other examples of sovereign government bonds.[8] Historically, the United States, Japan, and Europe have been the biggest issuers of government bonds.

For the purposes of this chapter, another important type is the emerging market bond. These are sovereign and corporate bonds issued by developing countries.[9] This market has significantly developed since the 1990s, expanding to include a wide variety of bonds

73

issued in major external currencies, such as the US dollar and the euro, as well as local currencies. Emerging market bonds carry varying growth prospects, and some investors view them as useful for diversification of investment portfolios.

The most significant difference between government and corporate bonds is the risk of default for each type. Government bonds are typically viewed as less risky, though bonds issued by countries do carry various degrees of risk, depending on the stability of a particular country's finances.[10] Corporate bond risk comes in a few different flavors, such as default risk (meaning, if the issuing company goes out of business, the bond holder may not get their money back) and event risk (when an unforeseen event renders a company unable to generate income).

Bonds for Environmental and Social Progress

The growth of sustainable investing often depends on using debt capital as a tool for funding projects that address environmental or social concerns. For example, so-called green bonds raise capital for projects that advance specific sustainability initiatives.[11]

The first green bond was issued in 2007 by the European Investment Bank and World Bank. It was titled Climate Awareness Bond, and its proceeds were used to further projects dedicated to renewable energy and energy efficiency. The World Bank issued its first green bond in 2008 for a group of Scandinavian investors. In 2013, the first corporate green bonds were issued by Vasakronan, a Swedish property company.[12] Other large corporations soon followed, including SNCF, Apple, Engie, ICBC, and Credit Agricole. The state of Massachusetts issued the first municipal green bond in June 2013 for sustainability purposes such as supporting energy efficiency and habitat restoration. Gothenburg, Sweden, issued the first green city bond a few months later to finance projects that mitigate climate change through low-carbon, clean tech investments and adaptive measures to climate change through sustainable and climate-change resilient projects.[13] Since that time, US states have become common issuers of green bonds; municipalities in other regions have also become green bond issuers, including the Province of Ontario, the City of Johannesburg, and the Province of la Rioja (Argentina).

No uniform standards exist for green bonds at this time. There is no legal definition or standards governing what constitutes a green bond and what does not. Instead, issuers have self-identified their bonds as "green"—a practice that may result in greenwashing accusations if investments aren't vetted adequately.[14] A consortium of investment banks established the "Green Bond Principles" in 2014 to offer some guidance.[15] These voluntary best-practice guidelines promote transparency, accuracy, and integrity of all data disclosed and reported by issuers to stakeholders. The GBP includes four core components:[16]

1. **Use of proceeds**, which recognizes the various categories for potential green bonds

2. **Process for project evaluation and selection**, which addresses the process for identifying projects appropriate for funding

3. **Management of proceeds**, which addresses the handling of funds pending investment

4. **Reporting**, which focuses on the frequency of reports by issuers

The GBP also provides broad suggestions for types of green projects that are worthy of bonds, including energy, buildings, transportation, water management, nature-based assets, and information technology.

Recent efforts to regulate green bonds underscore the growth of these sustainable investments. Credit-rating agencies such as S&P Global and Moody's have instituted green evaluation services to grade bonds on a scale of their "greenness." This represents a major upgrade from the generic classifications that have been widely relied on by investors, with social bonds also becoming a key area of investment that will be discussed later on in this chapter.

Governments abhor a regulation vacuum, and it's safe to assume that the current lack of standards will not last much longer. A voluntary green-bond standard is set to be adopted by European legislators; European Green Bond Standard also referred to as EUGBS, the standard is expected to provide a model for regulation and standards worldwide, and in all likelihood will become mandatory at some point. In addition, China and India have created issuance guidelines for the green bond market.[17]

Many countries are investing in developing sustainable finance taxonomies to define with greater granularity whether investments can be considered green or sustainable. For example, the EU taxonomy will form the basis for labeling green investment funds, the classification of companies' economic activities as sustainable, and the certification of green bonds issued under the European Green Bond Standard. Business leaders will need to be aware of these developments to integrate them successfully in their businesses.

Blue Bonds: Protecting Water Sources

Another type of environmental bond has evolved out of the green bond—the blue bond—which was designed to help protect the world's oceans.[18] Though they are relatively new, blue bonds operate much like any other: investors provide capital to issuers that repay the debt with interest over time. However, the proceeds are dedicated to oceanic conservation projects, such as the reduction of marine plastic waste. In his March 2021 appearance on the Refinitiv Sustainability Perspectives podcast, Thomas Schumann of Thomas Schumann Capital explained that water and climate are interlinked and interdependent; 9 of the 10 worst global risks relate to water, such as flooding, droughts, and fresh water availability.[19] Because investors increasingly use water risk as a proxy for climate change risk, Schumann Capital sponsored the creation of the world's first benchmark water risk index, which tracks water risk inequities and provides global capital markets with the first-ever "water footprint."

In April 2019, Morgan Stanley became the first financial services firm to commit to the development of systemic solutions to the problem of plastic waste. The Morgan Stanley Plastic Waste Resolution is designed to "prevent, reduce and remove 50 million metric tons of plastic waste from entering rivers, oceans, landscapes and landfills by 2030."[20] In early 2021, the company served as sole underwriter of a blue bond for the World Bank, with $10 million going toward plastic waste reduction efforts in oceans and the sustainable use of marine resources. In May 2021, the Asian Development Bank (ADB) committed $5 billion over five years to the Action Plan for Healthy Oceans and Sustainable Blue Economies. This commitment seeks to accelerate blue bond investments by partnering technical assistance funding with private capital.[21]

Blue Bond Success Stories

In October 2018, the World Bank facilitated the world's first blue bond: an agreement to divest a percentage of the Republic of Seychelles's debt in exchange for the country increasing its protection of marine resources.[22] Proceeds from the $15 million bond issuance targeted expansion of marine-protected areas, improved governance of priority fisheries, and the development of the Seychelles's ocean-dependent economy.[23] The success of the Seychelles bond served multiple purposes. It helped stabilize the country's credit rating—which is valuable from the perspective of foreign investment and business opportunities—and it provided an injection of capital into its economy, while also advancing ocean sustainability. The country also benefitted from the creation of high-value jobs and an increase in food security. This is a common occurrence with green, blue, and social bonds: they often provide overlapping benefits.

Another example of a successful blue bond came from the Asian Development Bank (ADB), which launched the Action Plan for Healthy Oceans and Sustainable Blue Economies in 2019.[24] This bond looks toward United Nations Sustainable Development Goals to identify support areas. The UN has framed its 17 development goals—which range from "Good Jobs and Economic Growth" to "Reduced Inequalities" and "Clean Water and Sanitation"—as an opportunity for world leaders and others to be involved in creating a healthy, sustainable world economy. The Action Plan supports ADB's developing member countries in their movement toward those goals. ADB will expand financing and technical assistance for ocean health and marine economy projects to $5 billion between 2019 and 2024; blue bonds will play a vital role in that expansion.

ADB also recognizes that marine plastic pollution presents a major crisis for Asia and the Pacific, damaging the region's marine economies. This damage to the marine economy means reduced fish stocks and increased ecosystem degradation, which will lead to reduced biodiversity alongside a decline in tourism and business opportunities. The convergence of these problems could lead to poverty and even food scarcity. Just as there are overlapping benefits to marine health, there are overlapping problems with unhealthy oceans and water sources. It's important to be aware of these factors, as businesses play an important role in impacting them directly, or indirectly through their value chain activities.

Social Bonds: Private and Government Issuance

The environment is not the only target of sustainable bonds. Social bonds are issued to fund projects that promote beneficial outcomes such as improved education, health care, clean drinking water, and good-paying jobs.[25] The Spanish Instituto de Credito issued the first formal social bond in January 2015, which sought to spark employment—which was experiencing a double-digit downward trajectory for youth between 2013 and 2018—by offering affordable loans to small and mid-sized enterprises in Spain.[26]

The following are additional examples of social bond project categories:

- Basic infrastructure
- Access to essential health and educational services
- Affordable housing
- Employment
- Microfinancing
- Food security

These programs generally target vulnerable populations such as those living below the poverty line, individuals with disabilities, displaced individuals, and those in need of training and education.

Similar to the GBP, the International Capital Markets Association (ICMA) created a Social Bond Guidance to define the structure, reporting, monitoring, and documentation of social bonds. The Guidance states, "Social Projects are projects, activities and investments that directly aim to help address or mitigate a specific social issue and/or seek to achieve positive social outcomes especially, but not exclusively, for target population(s)."[27]

In May 2020, Bank of America issued a $1 billion corporate social bond to support pandemic relief; it was the first such offering by a US commercial bank.[28] The four-year bond pays interest semi-annually at a fixed rate of 1.486% for the first three years and will pay interest quarterly at a floating rate thereafter. "The world is in a fight against COVID-19 and we are committed to doing our part by supporting the companies and professionals who are on the front lines," said Bank of America vice chairman Anne Finucane at the time. "The proceeds from this offering will help deliver critical resources for the companies involved in the testing, diagnosis, treatment and prevention of this insidious virus, while providing investors an opportunity to join us in this all-important effort."[29] Bank of America has offered numerous ESG bonds over recent years, including green bonds focused on clean energy and a social bond supporting affordable housing and community development financial institutions.

Bank of America was the first US-based commercial bank to issue a COVID-19 related social bond, but not the last. The African Development Bank launched a $3 billion "Fight COVID-19" social bond—the world's largest dollar-denominated social bond at the time.[30] Later in 2020, the US-based Ford Foundation issued $1 billion in social bonds to support nonprofit organizations affected by COVID-19, making it the first nonprofit foundation to offer a social bond within the US corporate bond market.

The social bond market is set to reach $300 billion in 2022; much of this surge can be attributed to health and research efforts due to the pandemic during the prior two years.[31] Investors, banks, governments, and even not-for-profits continue to partner to address critical issues. With the rise of public interest in climate justice, social inequity, and global pandemics, the social bond market is poised to reach new peaks. Business managers should understand what's important to their stakeholders, including investors, customers, and society. The better they do this, the better they will (1) understand stakeholders' concerns about the future and (2) align their corporate goals and resources to solving those problems in communities where they do business and where their employees live.

Social Impact Bonds

Social impact bonds (SIBs) are not really traditional bonds as much as they are agreements between governments or other entities and investors to share savings that were achieved as the result of a successful social program. For example, in 2010, the London-based not-for-profit firm Social Finance, along with other charities, entered a contract agreement with investors to reduce the recidivism rates of inmates in Peterborough jail by 7.5% over one year. The program—which included recognizing inmates' behavior patterns and counseling—exceeded expectations, reducing recidivism by 9%. Investors were paid their initial investment plus an annualized 3% return because of the outstanding, quantifiable success.

Unfortunately many SIBs have floundered, and investors neither received their initial investment nor any extra return. SIB program successes have yet to garner the same popularity and the same numbers as actual ESG bonds. The concept of SIBs is quite new and there are innovations yet to be seen in this area. Critics point to the fact that the model is complicated and it takes several years to measure success and that programs are usually pretty tailored to very specific circumstances, so they are unable to scale.[32]

Sustainability Linked Bonds: Measuring Performance

A fairly new tool in the ESG landscape is the sustainability-linked bond (SLB). These bonds aren't tied to specific projects; instead, the issuer commits to strengthening performance in a specific sustainability target, and that commitment is linked to the bondholder's coupon payment.[33] The consequence of missing the specific sustainability target is having to pay out a higher interest on the bond. As a result, it is in the issuer's best interest to meet the target they committed to. For example, Enel, an Italian power company, issued a bond where interest rates would be determined by their success in transitioning a large amount of their energy generation to renewables by the end of 2021.[34] Failure to meet the stated increase in renewables would result in them paying out a one-time 25 basis point (0.25 per cent) extra interest on the bond. In January 2022, Enel SpA announced that they believed they had achieved their target.[35]

SLBs offer a number of attractive features for borrowers and lenders. Because sustainability-linked financing is geared toward performance and outcomes rather than activity, bond issuers have flexibility to use the proceeds as they see fit. Many lenders and investors like that SLBs add a defined sustainability component to their loan portfolios. They also appreciate them as a tool for keeping borrowers accountable for the commitments to sustainability.

As interest in SLBs has expanded, the ICMA released the Sustainability Linked Bond Principles.[36] They included guidance for the selection of key performance indicators, creation of sustainability performance targets, bond characteristics, reporting, and verification of performance targets. Business managers might recognize that SLBs operate a lot like most business targets: if a performance target isn't met, there is a consequence, but when expectations are met, it is a success. This is how success is measured in corporate environments and, some argue, how we should attempt to measure our ESG efforts: with solid numbers as well as other qualifying measurements including how we'll continue to act on opportunities and mitigate risk.

ESG Bonds

Bonds with a special purpose issued to raise the funds for socially responsible investment, such as improving the environment, society, and governance.

Social Bond

Special-purpose bonds issued
for solving social problems

ESG Bonds

Green Bond

Special-purpose bonds issued
for eco-friendly projects

Sustainability Bond

Special-purpose bonds where green
bonds and social bonds are combined,
for the use of the raised
funds for a wider variety of purposes

A breakdown of the different bond types.
Source: https://news.skhynix.com/sk-hynix-issues-usd-1-billion-green-bond-how-will-the-investment-be-used/.

Municipal Bonds and ESG

In general, ESG integration into the municipal bond market remains underdeveloped. As noted in an October 2021 article by investment manager Nuveen, there are a couple of reasons for this disparity.[37] For one, the municipal market lacks third-party ESG ratings. A relatively low number of municipal bond investors are embracing ESG considerations in their analysis. As such, too few municipal strategies explicitly incorporate ESG factors or ratings. What's more, those that do typically place their focus on direct social and green bonds as opposed to municipal bonds, which can arguably contribute the same effect. Also contributing to the disparity is an inaccurate belief that municipal bond investments are inherently ESG driven, due to their focus on public services.

Increased demand for ESG factors in municipal bonds is being driven in large part by investors. Also, in the United States, a greater focus on building climate-resilient infrastructure may result in an uptick in municipal bonds that include environmental and social elements. For businesses with close ties to their local communities, understanding these types of infrastructure changes—and the role ESG will continue to play in those changes—may help increase understanding of their customer base. This could range from variations in how employees and customers commute (e.g., from car to rail), to upticks in business development or tourism that might drive sales.

Why Green Bonds Are Good for Business

In 2021 the total value of sustainable bonds rose to $1 trillion. The green bonds category (which includes blue bonds) leads the pack, with more than $489B in sales; social bonds reached $193B despite seeing substantial drops in the last two quarters, sustainable company bonds followed with $186B; and sustainability bonds round out the list with about $37 billion in sales. Sustainability-linked loans surged by 300% to more than $700 billion in 2022. The focus of much of the investing has evolved over time. Global concerns about COVID-19 financial strain, racial injustice, and health disparities drove investor interest in particular products, as did the resulting recessionary environment for vulnerable communities. As a result, social-bond issuance hit $147.7 billion in 2020, representing an incredible 720% increase from the previous year.[38] This rise was not repeated in 2021, and there has been a notable drop in the last two financial quarters of 2021.

Nevertheless, experts believe that this trend will continue into the foreseeable future, with global green bond sales expected to hit $1 trillion in 2022, according to Refinitiv data.[39] The explosion of interest in ESG bonds should send a clear signal to corporations that investors are paying attention to their social and environmental impacts.

Danske Bank and Luxembourg Stock Exchange, along with supporting analysis from the University of Reading Henley Business School conducted the 2020 Green Bond Treasurer Survey.[40] More than 85 treasurers from 34 countries participated in the survey, collectively representing 686 green bonds. The survey highlighted some interesting findings:

- Of respondents 98% responded that their green bond attracted a new, more diverse pool of investors through greater visibility.

- Of respondents 91% asserted that green bonds resulted in improved engagement with investors compared to conventional bonds. Dialogue concerning the use of proceeds, frameworks, and reporting gave investors a greater understanding of the business.

- Of respondents 88% communicated plans to issue more green bonds, along with 15% who reported a willingness to reopen current bonds. Among the reasons cited for repeat bond issuance, an established investor base and greater visibility were mentioned the most.

- Of respondents 70% reported a higher demand for green bonds than conventional equivalents.

These responses demonstrate the many benefits that companies can experience from green bond issuance. Even more striking is the fact that 48% of survey respondents described green bond costs as being similar to those of conventional bonds, and an impressive 42% labeled green bond costs as lower than conventional. This is strong evidence that the "greenium," or paying a premium for green bonds over standard ones, is quickly becoming a myth as new risks arise for companies which fail to innovate. The benefits of green bonds more than account for any increased costs in establishing new infrastructure.

Along with the financial benefits, ESG bonds also help companies address new sustainability objectives. The bonds can spur new lines of business and open companies up to new opportunities. The enhanced visibility and reputation that comes from an ESG bond also leads to a larger scope of investors, including those with green mandates.

Infrastructure and Sustainability: Global Initiatives

Various governments worldwide have implemented partnerships with businesses on large-scale infrastructure plans that include bonds that are meant to yield sustainable results. But creating a balance between infrastructure and sustainability can be a difficult challenge, because large-scale infrastructure plans are often at odds with environmental interests.

The China Belt and Road Initiative (BRI) is an ambitious global infrastructure development program adopted by the Chinese government in 2013 with the goal of developing trade routes and infrastructure connecting China with the rest of the world. When introducing the BRI, Chinese President Xi Jinping asserted that the strategy must be "green and sustainable."[41] As such, the Chinese government has endorsed several "Green Investment Principles" for the incorporation of low-carbon and sustainable practices into BRI.[42] In BRI countries, $57.4 billion in green bonds were issued in 2019.[43]

From a social and environmental perspective, some experts say that China's investments in infrastructure projects in developing countries are filling a foreign capital gap widened by Western countries.[44] In an effort to build their supply chains, China recognized the critical need for capital that existed in many of these countries and stepped in to fill that need. But although some point to several examples of Chinese debt being successfully managed and resulting in green energy advancements in developing countries, many analysts assert that these investments have been predatory in nature. The Council on Foreign Relations noted that "skeptics worry that China is laying a debt trap for borrowing governments."[45]

The following are some examples of controversies that have plagued BRI:

- Former Malaysian prime minister Najib Razak signed the East Coast Rail Link infrastructure deal with China as part of BRI.[46] The deal was associated with a broader corruption scandal involving Razak and was eventually canceled.

- BRI in Kenya, specifically the standard-gauge railway (SGR), has fallen short of its initial promise. Kenya already experienced pandemic-related economic challenges. Critics see the deferred debt of SGR as worsening Kenya's already difficult fiscal problems. Additionally, in 2019 Kenya's Ethics and Anti-Corruption Commission "suspended compensation for SGR land acquisitions in light of widespread accusations that National Lands Commission officials were demanding kickbacks to facilitate legitimate compensation payouts to landowners."[47]

- A 2021 report by International Forum for Rights and Security described BRI as a "threat to climate change" because almost 90% of its projects use fossil fuels in a carbon-intensive manner.[48]

Pointing to BRI's reputation for harmful environmental and social impacts, lack of transparency, predatory lending, and corruption, some observers express the hope that Western democracies will present viable alternatives. For example, South Africa, a major producer of coal, entered into an $8.5 billion deal with the United States, the European Union, and other European nations for improved clean energy alternatives and assistance for workers negatively affected by advancements away from coal.

In 2021, US President Joe Biden introduced the Build Back Better World (B3W) plan during the June G7 summit.[49] The stated goal of B3W is the creation of "a values-driven, high-standard, and transparent infrastructure partnership" to help finance projects in developing countries. "There's an urgent need for infrastructure development in countries—infrastructure that prioritizes . . . the fight against climate change from the moment the spade goes in the ground, and jumpstarts the green economic growth," Biden said in November 2021.[50] But the ultimate fate of B3W is in doubt as negotiations continue within the US Congress. Observers question whether B3W will be able to meet a level with the quantity of investment promised by BRI.

Other regions have also implemented their own green development efforts. In 2016, the European Union announced a multibillion-euro infrastructure program to counter China.[51] In 2021, Saudi Arabia introduced the Saudi Green Initiative as a regional and cooperative approach to climate action.[52]

As these examples show, businesses need to be mindful of not only the opportunities but also the risks that are inherent in development partnerships. Ensuring sound governance, overseeing of third-party suppliers' practices, following regulations, and reaching consensus are ways to avoid even the perception of corruption or lack of commitment when it comes to building sustainable infrastructure.

Final Thoughts

Corporate and government bonds that include ESG factors are help-ing to fund a wide variety of projects, from sustainable buildings to climate-resilient infrastructure, to programs aimed at reducing health inequities. From a governmental perspective, a variety of ESG-focused tools—whether green or blue bonds, sustainability-linked bonds, or social bonds—can support a region's workforce and environmental development. In turn, improved development makes investing and doing business in the region mutually profitable to a business, its investors, and the community itself.

In Chapter 5, we'll explore more about how regions are rated according to their level of sustainability. We'll also look at how to use information from those rankings to make decisions about how to engage from a vendor or partnership perspective.

Chapter 4 Takeaways

- When bonds are created to advance environmental protec-tion or societal equity, they can support healthy regions and countries where we can build thriving businesses, reducing risks that come with lack of job growth, fiscal uncertainty, and governmental instability.
- Most green bond proceeds are used for green projects and backed by the issuer's entire balance sheet.
- There are several types of sustainability bonds, and they are all gaining popularity in the marketplace: green bonds and their subset, blue bonds, social bonds, and sustainability-linked bonds.

- These bonds are being used to fund programs that address pandemic-related health inequity, job growth, climate, and infrastructure and other environmental and social challenges.
- Although these bonds are popular, some are plagued with questions about corruption. Businesses must be mindful of governance, supplier oversight, and regulations to have successful partnerships with governments and other entities.

Notes

1. https://www.spglobal.com/ratings/en/research/articles/220207-global-sustainable-bond-issuance-to-surpass-1-5-trillion-in-2022-12262243; and https://www.bloomberg.com/news/articles/2022-02-01/esg-bond-boom-takes-over-the-world-with-1-8-trillion-in-sight.
2. https://www.sec.gov/files/ib_corporatebonds.pdf.
3. https://www.investopedia.com/financial-edge/0612/how-to-invest-in-corporate-bonds.aspx.
4. https://www.investor.gov/introduction-investing/investing-basics/glossary/investment-grade-bond-or-high-grade-bond.
5. https://www.investor.gov/introduction-investing/investing-basics/glossary/high-yield-bond-or-junk-bond.
6. https://www.investopedia.com/financial-edge/0612/how-to-invest-in-corporate-bonds.aspx#citation-2.
7. https://www.investopedia.com/articles/investing/073113/introduction-treasury-securities.asp#citation-24.
8. https://www.pimco.com/en-us/resources/education/everything-you-need-to-know-about-bonds.
9. Ibid.
10. https://www.marketreview.com/corporate-vs-govt-bonds/.
11. https://www.climatebonds.net/market/best-practice-guidelines.
12. https://www.climatebonds.net/market/explaining-green-bonds.
13. https://unfccc.int/climate-action/momentum-for-change/financing-for-climate-friendly/gothenburg-green-bonds#.
14. https://www.climatebonds.net/market/best-practice-guidelines.
15. https://www.cambridgemarketinsights.com/post/cmi-explains-the-rise-of-green-bonds.
16. https://www.climatebonds.net/market/best-practice-guidelines.

17. https://www.climatebonds.net/market/best-practice-guidelines.
18. https://www.morganstanley.com/content/dam/msdotcom/ideas/blue-bonds/2583076-FINAL-MS_GSF_Blue_Bonds.pdf.
19. https://shows.acast.com/refinitiv-sustainability-perspectives-podcast/episodes/world-water-day-special-episode.
20. https://www.morganstanley.com/content/dam/msdotcom/ideas/blue-bonds/2583076-FINAL-MS_GSF_Blue_Bonds.pdf.
21. https://www.adb.org/news/adb-launches-5-billion-healthy-oceans-action-plan.
22. https://www.morganstanley.com/content/dam/msdotcom/ideas/blue-bonds/2583076-FINAL-MS_GSF_Blue_Bonds.pdf.
23. https://calvertimpactcapital.org/investing/partner/seychelles-blue-bond.
24. https://www.adb.org/news/adb-launches-5-billion-healthy-oceans-action-plan.
25. https://www.icmagroup.org/sustainable-finance/the-principles-guidelines-and-handbooks/social-bond-principles-sbp/.
26. https://social-bonds.net/History-of-Social-Bonds/ and https://www.statista.com/statistics/813014/youth-unemployment-rate-in-spain/.
27. https://www.icmagroup.org/assets/documents/Regulatory/Green-Bonds/June-2020/Social-Bond-PrinciplesJune-2020-090620.pdf.
28. https://newsroom.bankofamerica.com/press-releases/corporate-and-financial-news/bank-america-issues-1-billion-corporate-social-bond.
29. Ibid.
30. https://www.cnbc.com/2020/06/23/social-bonds-are-surging-as-conscious-investing-turns-mainstream.html.
31. https://www.bnymellonim.com/uk/en/intermediary/news-and-insights/insight-social-bonds-and-sure/ and https://www.ifc.org/wps/wcm/connect/c7b96f2a-bce0-4d5a-9ca1-feb8baa0466e/FY21+IFC+Social+Bond+Impact+Report.pdf?MOD=AJPERES&CVID=nZWSf4p#.
32. https://www.ft.com/content/ddf55a2e-7472-11e8-bab2-43bd4ae655dd.
33. https://idbinvest.org/en/blog/development-impact/esg-investors-look-returns-sustainability-linked-bonds-are-hot-new-thing.
34. https://www.businesstimes.com.sg/opinion/unresolved-dilemmas-from-sustainability-linked-finance.
35. https://www.bloomberg.com/news/articles/2022-01-05/enel-set-to-hit-goal-with-first-batch-of-climate-linked-bonds.
36. https://www.sustainalytics.com/esg-research/resource/corporate-esg-blog/sustainability-linked-bonds.
37. https://www.nuveen.com/en-us/insights/municipal-bond-investing/Innovation-in-ESG-municipal-bond-investing.
38. https://www.bloomberg.com/professional/blog/sustainable-debt-issuance-exceeds-730-billion-in-2020/.
39. https://www.etftrends.com/fixed-income-channe/esg-bond-market-looking-forward-to-another-strong-year/.

40. https://www.climatebonds.net/resources/press-releases/2020/04/green-bond-treasurer-survey-issuers-identify-multiple-benefits.
41. https://www.reuters.com/article/us-china-silkroad-idUSKCN1S104I.
42. https://www.refinitiv.com/perspectives/future-of-investing-trading/green-leadership-belt-road-initiative/.
43. http://green-bri.com/green-finance.
44. https://www.fpri.org/article/2022/01/u-s-china-sustainable-infrastructure-collaborative-opportunities-green-partnerships-must-begin-in-africa/.
45. https://www.cfr.org/backgrounder/chinas-massive-belt-and-road-initiative.
46. https://www.chathamhouse.org/2021/09/what-chinas-belt-and-road-initiative-bri.
47. https://www.fdd.org/analysis/2020/05/04/below-the-belt-and-road/.
48. https://www.republicworld.com/world-news/china/chinas-bri-project-poses-significant-threat-to-climate-change-environment-iffras-report.html.
49. https://www.voanews.com/a/build-back-better-world-biden-s-counter-to-china-s-belt-and-road/6299568.html.
50. https://www.whitehouse.gov/briefing-room/speeches-remarks/2021/11/02/remarks-by-president-biden-in-meeting-on-the-build-back-better-world-initiative/.
51. https://foreignpolicy.com/2021/10/04/belt-and-road-initiative-bri-build-back-better-us-china-competition-west/.
52. https://news.un.org/en/story/2021/10/1103992.

Rating Regional ESG Progress

One important but easily overlooked aspect of managing ESG risks and opportunities centers on the countries where companies and their suppliers are located. Corporate leaders should care about environmental, social, and governance risks and opportunities in various regions because their companies—and the suppliers that service their companies—have a responsibility to enhance the regions and communities where they do business.

Thinking about how your company and suppliers impact communities can offer a holistic approach to assessing your sustainability efforts, sustainable products, practices, and policies. Your long-term planning should consider the sustainability of the goods you produce, how they are produced, and how your direct or indirect operations might impact the areas where you do business. For example, your products may be produced in a country that has loose or no human rights regulations. In those cases, your planning should include supplier screening for human rights issues.

Consideration of regional risks has become integral to ESG investing in recent years. The phrase *regional risks* is shorthand for the challenges à company faces in a specific location due to the economic environment, regulatory environment, and even the likelihood of physical climate catastrophes. Rating organizations assess the financial ability of regions to withstand environmental, social, or external interruptions.[1] These ratings offer information that benefits corporate leaders and investors. Corporate leaders benefit from these ratings by gaining a greater level of clarity about which global regions are best positioned to handle the shocks that can negatively affect the corporations based within them. The location of a company may have a significant impact on its investment performance and may also dictate its exposure to challenging environmental, economic, and sociopolitical variables. Understanding how these location-related variables may affect (1) your firm, (2) the content of your corporate disclosure to the public, and (3) investors' views of the suitability of your company for their portfolio should all play a role in how you approach potential risks to doing business in certain locations.

Country-risk ratings, viewed through an ESG lens, look at a nation's wealth in context of the growth and health of its natural and environmental resources as well as its workforce and economic activity.[2] Investors gain a holistic assessment of a country's current risks, as well as some emerging ones that may not be immediately present. This forward-looking approach helps business leaders and investors anticipate potential challenges or events when making investment decisions. ESG-risk exposure, along with the management of that risk, affects the long-term sustainability and competitiveness of a nation's economy, which can make a country more or less appealing to investors.[3]

This chapter will help you understand how to identify regional investment opportunities and risk as well as helping you better assess the impacts of your operations in foreign regions. Arming yourself with the right information is the first step in making these investment decisions.

Russia, Sanctions, Reputational Damage

Russia's invasion of Ukraine provides an instructive example of the kinds of risks investors need to consider.

When the war began in February 2022, some were perplexed to see the western world responded primarily with sanctions rather than direct military aid. However, as more and more companies pulled their enterprises out of Russia, we saw just how punishing sanctions could be and their increasing potency as a weapon of proxy-war in a globalized economy—from crashing the vodka market to impacting world-wide oil supply. We also saw how tightly wound a country's reputation is with (1) foreign investors' appetite for opportunities in that region and (2) the livelihood of workers in the region.

From restaurants to retailers, there was a mass exodus of businesses from Russia by early March 2022. Indeed, companies that had not shuttered or at least paused business in Russia found themselves having to defend that decision to an angry public. The departure of luxury brand Dior supported the understanding that hitting the purses and wallets of the wealthy might increase their disillusionment with Putin's regime in general and the invasion in particular.

In time we saw consequences go much deeper than that. In an interview with *The Guardian*, Maria Shagina, an international sanctions specialist at the Finnish Institute of International Affairs and the Geneva International Sanctions Network, spoke directly about the reputational issues at play with Russia.

> Of course, the Kremlin expected that the west would impose sanctions, but I am not sure they expected just how toxic Russia would become. These companies are not just leaving because of sanctions, but primarily because they believe that Russia is uninvestable right now. That it is not right to do business there.[4]

Let's unpack what it means for a country to be "uninvestable." For one, there is the impact on the Russian markets. Sanctions included freezing $630 billion of Russian Central Bank assets. Then, there is the fall of Russia's currency, the ruble, which traded less than one cent on the dollar by March 2022—a decrease of 35% year to date at that point.[5] Meanwhile, the shutdown of Moscow's stock exchange marks the longest shutdown in the country's history.[6]

On its own, the situation suggests a bleak outlook for Russia's economy; one suspects the country will remain "uninvestable" for the foreseeable future. But what further exacerbates this issue of reputation and investability is the impact these financial shocks are currently having on citizens and workers. This is especially the case for workers employed by foreign-owned companies. For these workers, the short- to medium-term future looks bleak. Foreign businesses are leaving the region and taking their jobs with them. There is an expectation of growing unemployment, which further stifles the economy. In February 2022, inflation in Russia rose to its highest in seven years: up to 9.15% from 8.73% just a month earlier. "[Russian investment is] certainly not something for anyone who is unwilling to take an extreme amount of risk because the reality is that many international investors simply want out and price doesn't really matter," said Yung-Yu Ma, chief investment strategist at BMO Wealth Management.[7]

Many foreign countries that suspended Russian operations promised to continue to pay local workers. In stepping up to pay employees, management teams showed they valued human capital, even though they disagreed politically with the decisions made by their government. Of course, no one was sure how long operations would be down and how long these paychecks were to keep coming. When Russian leaders began floating the idea of bringing in local management and seizing ownership of—that is, nationalizing—companies that exited Russia, critics saw this as further isolating the nation. White House press secretary Jen Psaki even alluded to legal action that may result from "any lawless decision by Russia to seize the assets of these companies."[8]

The confluence of an already exhausted supply chain, foreign ire, domestic protests, and investor exits can affect national reputations in ways that may have consequences for years to come. This is a consideration a business leader needs to have top of mind when deciding where they want to operate and who they want to include in their supply chains. Regimes with well-documented human rights abuses and expansionist foreign policy have in the past been treated as reasonable places to invest as long as they appear to be relatively stable. But as investors learned after Russia's invasion of Ukraine, turning the other way to such abuses may have very serious real-world costs—both human and economic. In choosing a new region to work in, to some extent you take on the burden of its potential future political decisions as well.

The Role of Country-Risk Ranking Providers

Now that we understand why regional risks are important, let's take a detailed look at country-risk ranking providers and how they develop their extensive reviews, including which elements and variables are most important to their processes. Here are some of the most significant players in country-risk ranking.

MSCI

MSCI provides decision support tools and services for the global investment community and has also created an ESG government ratings database to "identify a country's exposure to and management of environmental, social, and governance (ESG) risk factors and explain how these factors might impact the long-term sustainability of its economy."[9] Taking a long-term view of sustainability, MSCI seeks to complement the traditional government debt analysis of a country's credit worthiness. They provide country profiles and screening factors related to a variety of values- and mission-based issues, such as child or forced labor, armed conflict, and participation in international conventions. Using a seven-point scale, in which AAA is the highest score and CCC is the lowest, MSCI ESG Government Ratings scores are derived from the three pillars of ESG. The company says that it seeks to answer the following questions with its ratings:

- What ESG risks are countries exposed to, based on their natural, financial, and social resource availability and their political governance structures?
- How does the country being rated actually manage and enable its resources?
- Is that country's management and performance commensurate with its ESG risk exposure?[10]

MSCI ESG Government Ratings: ESG Risk Factors

Pillar	Risk factor	Sub-factors (Exposure)	Sub-factors (Management)
Environmental Risk	Natural resource	• Energy security risk • Water resources • Productive land and mineral resources	• Energy resource management • Resource conservation • Water resource management
	Environmental externalities and vulnerability	• Vulnerability to environmental events • Environmental externalities	• Environmental performance • Impact of environmental externalities
Social Risk	Human capital	• Basic human capital • Higher education and technological readiness • Knowledge capital	• Basic needs • Human capital performance • Human capital infrastructure • Knowledge capital management
	Economic environment	• Economic environment	• Employment • Wellness
Governance Risk	Financial governance	• Financial capital	• Financial management
	Political governance	• Institutions • Judicial and penal system • Governance effectiveness	• Political rights and civil liberties • Corruption control • Stability and peace

Source: https://www.msci.com/documents/10199/5c0d3545-f303-4397-bdb2-8ddd3b81ca1b.

Refinitiv

In 2020, Refinitiv announced its adoption of country sustainable development goals scores (SDGs) as metrics for comparisons at the country level.[11] The scores are used as a transparent and objective measure of a nation's performance across each of the SDGs, as well as submetrics. The comparisons, which are calculated annually with the current data, cover more than 240 countries. Countries are separated into risk bandings that range from very high to very low, with companies located within high- and very high-risk countries warranting increased investment scrutiny.[12] In developing the methodology, Refinitiv references more than 300 independent sources from respected organizations such as the World Bank, the UN, World Economic Forum, and the World Factbook to assess levels of political, economic, and criminal risk to evaluate countries.[13] Political risk looks at factors such as civil liberties, political stability, rule of law, and political terror. The economic risk considers poverty, GDP, tax concerns, and credit sovereign ratings among other factors. Criminal risk is determined based on factors such as crime rates, corruption, exploitative labor, and threat financing.

High-level scores structure

There are three levels of detail applied to each of the 210 countries included in the benchmark group:

1. An overall SDG score
2. A score for each of the 17 United Nations Sustainable Development Goals
3. A score for each of the 148 metrics

SDG number	SDG description	Number of indicators	Current coverage score[1]	Coverage percentage
1	No Poverty	12	4	33%
2	Zero Hunger	14	4.5	32%
3	Good Health and Well-Being	26	8.5	33%
4	Quality Education	11	2.5	23%
5	Gender Equality	14	3	21%
6	Clean Water and Sanitation	11	3	27%
7	Affordable and Clean Energy	6	3	50%
8	Decent Work and Economic Growth	17	6	35%
9	Industry, Innovation and Infrastructure	12	6	50%
10	Reduced Inequalities	11	2.5	23%
11	Sustainable Cities and Communities	15	1	7%
12	Responsible Consumption	13	1.5	12%
13	Climate Action	8	0.5	6%
14	Life below Water	10	0	0%
15	Life on Land	14	5	36%
16	Peace, Justice and Strong Institutions	23	7	30%
17	Partnership for the Goals	25	3.5	14%
	Totals	242	61.5	25%

[1] Coverage assessment based on the following criteria - full match = 1 point; partial match = 0.5 points; and no match = 0 points

Source: https://www.refinitiv.com/content/dam/marketing/en_us/documents/
methodology/refinitiv-country-sdg-scores-methodology.pdf

Sustainalytics

Sustainalytics also provides country ESG ratings, using an assessment of a nation's prosperity in consideration of "its access to, and management of, natural, human and institutional wealth."[14] With data compiled by the World Bank, Sustainalytics groups country assets into three categories.

1. **Natural and produced capital** includes infrastructure, energy independence, and natural resources.

2. **Human capital** involves access to water and sanitation, as well as life expectancy and mean years of schooling.

3. **Institutional capital** assesses rule of law, corruption, and political liberties.[15]

ESG performance, trends, and events can have a significant impact on a nation's ability to manage its wealth with an eye toward sustainability. Investors can supplement traditional bond analyses with data provided by Sustainalytics to make more informed decisions and streamline reporting requirements within a fixed income portfolio.

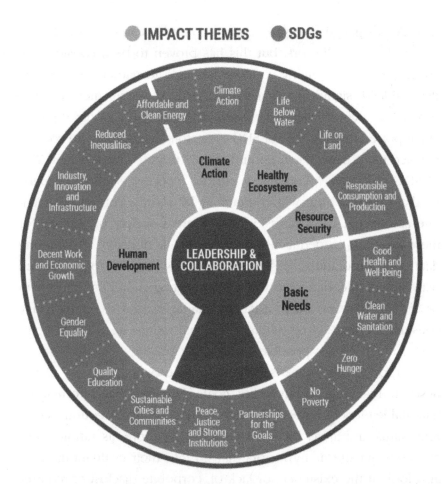

Metrics are aligned to Sustainalytics' proprietary ESG Impact Framework and the UN Sustainable Development Goals (SDGs). These metrics enable investors to analyze and report on the environmental and social impact of their portfolio investments.

Source: https://www.sustainalytics.com/impact-metrics

Corporate Disclosures and National Sustainability

As evident in the approaches used by rating providers, analysis for prospective investors may consider details about a country's progression toward United Nations Sustainable Development Goals (UN SDG).

In order to gauge that progression, countries can be scored on a range of SDG indicators, but this has proven to be a considerable challenge, because many countries struggle to gather the requisite data. Indeed, significant data gaps exist in the assessment of SDG progress at a country level. Between 2015 and 2019, countries generally reported on only 55% of SDG indicators. In addition, no country reached more than 90% reporting and 22 reported on less than 25% of SDG indicators.[16] Looking at current reporting statistics, experts predict that reporting will continue to be insufficient for the accurate assessment of progression. There are a variety of reasons for these reporting inadequacies; the main one is difficulty of gathering data from corporations. Business leaders may continue to be plagued with lack of adequate data when investigating countries to invest in or expand into. In these instances, managers and executives may consider looking across different regional ratings agencies to compile as much data as possible to make decisions.

Corporate disclosure is essential to the overall success of nations in reaching sustainability goals. Without that information, national leaders lack necessary information about the country's current status and areas for improvement. Therefore, as rating agencies consider the many factors that go into their evaluations, they also look at the existence, or lack of, corporate disclosure requirements for large corporations. It is critical for company leaders to provide transparent information for their sustainability practices to support analysis of the environmental, social, and economic health of the regions where they're doing business. This information is key to supporting the health of the communities where the business is located.

This section provides insight into regulations that are being adopted in various regions. It's critical to realize that just because the region you work in doesn't have particular regulations *yet*, that doesn't mean you shouldn't work toward understanding regulations in general. Even if you are not directly operating in the regions where these regulations exist, you may have some indirect responsibility due to activities in your value chain (e.g. every link in the chain of the process to produce your goods or services). Additionally, stakeholders form specific expectations based on the best practices from these regulations that they apply to any company. Therefore, companies should have the knowledge about these regulations to grow and be competitive in the future.

Governments from 38 of the world's largest 50 economies have either implemented, or are in the process of crafting, ESG disclosure requirements for corporations.[17] These initiatives can take a number of different forms. Some, such as Saudi Arabia's disclosure of management remuneration requirement, focuses on the single issue of corporate salaries. Others focus on numerous issues. The European Union is largely regarded as ahead of the curve in this arena due to its taxonomy, the Sustainable Finance Disclosure Regulation and the Non-Financial Reporting Directive. EU taxonomy is a classification system that establishes a list of environmentally sustainable economic activities to assist in scaling up sustainable investment. It offers EU companies, investors, and policymakers detailed definitions of which economic activities can be considered environmentally sustainable.[18] Published in the *Official Journal of the European Union* in June 2020, the Taxonomy Regulation establishes the following six environmental objectives:

1. Climate change mitigation

2. Climate change adaptation

3. Sustainable use and protection of water and marine resources

4. Transition to a circular economy

5. Pollution prevention and control

6. Protection and restoration of biodiversity and ecosystems[19]

The climate-focused Sustainable Finance Disclosure Regulation (SFDR) applies to all EU-based financial market participants.[20] Some of the required disclosures include a description of governance arrangements for assessing and managing climate-related risks and a detailed listing of principal climate-related risks related to company operations.[21] Aiming to minimize greenwashing and provide a more transparent view of sustainability investments, the SFDR came into effect in 2021 for the European Union and was phased in for the United Kingdom in 2022.

The European Union Non-Financial Reporting Directive establishes regulations for companies to include nonfinancial statements either in their annual reports or in a separate filing.[22] Established in 2018, it requires that companies disclose data on environmental protection, social responsibility and treatment of employees, respect for human rights, anti-corruption and bribery, and diversity on company boards. The directive applies to public interest companies in the European Union with more than 500 employers. Corporate leaders need to understand these regulations because they—or similar iterations—will likely become global and need to be adopted in the near term.

In February 2021, the European Supervisory Authorities published the details for disclosure under SFDR.[23] It required reporting from "European listed and large public-interest companies with more than 500 employees and that have either a balance sheet total of more than 20 million euros or a net turnover of more than 40 million euros."[24] These companies must publish reporting on policies related to environmental protection, social responsibility and treatment of employees, respect for human rights, and anti-corruption and bribery. They must also report on the diversity in company boards in relation to the ages, genders, and educational and professional backgrounds of board members.

Several Asian Pacific countries have also demonstrated an interest in ESG corporate disclosures as a way of promoting investor transparency and driving ESG efforts. Both the Singapore Exchange and the Stock Exchange of Hong Kong demand some level of ESG reporting from listed companies.[25] Meanwhile, South Korea's green posting system includes a requirement that listed companies post the state of their green technology certification and greenhouse gas data within their annual reports.[26] In furtherance of the country's goal to achieve carbon neutrality by 2060, China Securities Regulatory Commission announced plans to enforce environmental reporting requirements for publicly listed companies.[27] As mentioned earlier in the chapter, the relevance to you as a business leader is the fact that this type of regulation is likely to become more global in nature. The better insight you have today, the more it can support your regional growth opportunities in the future.

The Reporting Exchange, an online platform to help businesses navigate their corporate reporting responsibilities, characterizes Australia as a leader in the Asian Pacific region for the area's sustainable finance efforts.[28] More than 80% of a country's reporting relate in some manner to environmental issues such as climate change, emissions, and corporate accountability.

Australia was an early adopter of ESG reporting. In 2007, the National Greenhouse and Energy Reporting Act introduced a mandatory reporting framework for the country's largest 500 corporate entities, as determined by greenhouse gas emissions and energy production/consumption. Following the repeal of the act in 2014, Australia dropped to a "very low-performing" ranking in Germanwatch's analysis of country's responses to climate change.[29] However, the reporting requirements established within the act still exist in Australia; it is the world's longest-running national greenhouse gas reporting system.

Closer to home, ESG disclosure requirements in the United States remain a work-in-progress. Recent statements from the Security Exchange Commission (SEC) suggest the appearance of formal regulations in the near future, likely resembling the UK model. In a March

2021 statement, John Coates, acting director of the SEC Division of Corporation Finance, stated:

> Going forward, I believe SEC policy on ESG disclosures will need to be both adaptive and innovative. We can and should continue to adapt existing rules and standards to the realities of climate risk, for example, and the fact that investors increasingly are asking for ESG information to help them make informed investment and voting decisions. We will also need to be open to and supportive of innovation—in both institutions and policies on the content, format and process for developing ESG disclosures.[30]

He went on to explain that though the SEC could lead the way in developing a comprehensive effective ESG disclosure system that provides investors with the data they seek, the following questions need to be answered:

- What corporate disclosures are most useful?
- What is the right balance between principles and metrics?
- How much standardization can be achieved across industries?
- How and when should standards evolve?
- What is the best way to verify or provide assurance about disclosures?
- Where and how should disclosures be globally comparable?
- Where and how can disclosures be aligned with information companies already use to make decisions?[31]

The discussion about these questions underscores the SEC's concern that the development of new corporate disclosure requirements should focus on data that is directly material to investment decisions.[32]

One driver of this focus may be the concerns that private companies are already burdened by the vast number of regulations placed on them by the SEC. Critics argue that new ESG regulations will prove too much for these companies to handle. However, the evolution of impact investing has created an environment where ESG is absolutely material to investment decisions, so the SEC's attempted designation should not be a difficult hurdle for most.

Critics of ESG standards-reporting often blame their resistance on the notion that the requirements will break the proverbial camel's back.
Source: https://www.pionline.com/article/20181015/PRINT/181019959/sec-must-say-no-to-esg-regulation.

According to a report by Principles for Responsible Investing, companies that are located within countries where comprehensive ESG reporting is mandated have a 33% better ESG rating score than corporations in countries without those mandates.[33] The report offered a number of possible reasons, including the positive impact that these mandates have on the behavior of corporate leaders. Forcing a company to examine its internal process can lead to improved risk management. In addition, governments that regulate ESG disclosures may lower risk exposure within the country with their proactive approach. These regulations also work to normalize corporate sustainability as a formal part of conducting business. Enhanced data also lead to better investor analysis and more effective engagement for long-term value.[34]

The number of countries mandating corporate disclosures will likely continue to grow. In 2015, the Financial Stability Board created the Task Force on Climate-related Financial Disclosures (TCFD) to develop recommendations for the promotion of climate-related disclosures "that could promote more informed investment, credit, and insurance underwriting decisions and, in turn, enable stakeholders to understand better the concentrations of carbon-related assets in the financial sector and the financial system's exposures to climate-related risks."[35] With a commitment to greater transparency and market stability, TCFD asserts that accurate and timely data will enable companies to better incorporate climate-related risks and opportunities into their strategic planning. The recommendations, released in 2017, were structured on governance, strategy, risk management, and metrics and targets. Efforts such as these are expected to stimulate increased disclosures in the years to come.

Although they are voluntary, these recommendations are viewed by many as a step in the direction of an internationally recognized set of reporting guidelines. Regulators across the globe are drafting or finalizing rules regarding the disclosure of ESG data within annual reports and regulatory filings. These changes will prove significant as they affect the way that business gets done in response to what matters to investors in today's environment. An October 2021 article by professional services firm Deloitte refers to this evolution as a "tectonic shift" setting off a chain of ESG disclosure reactions.[36] The internet has created an increasingly empowered consumer base, which includes savvy investors who expect companies to address ESG concerns with transparency. They want to invest in organizations that operate with an eye toward caring for their workers, their communities, the environment, and the world as a whole. As stated in the Deloitte article, there is a "global dialogue" occurring between companies and these more informed stakeholders. "Today, people from around the globe, including employees, suppliers, business partners, members of the community, activists, and society at large, are equal participants—stakeholders—in a direct dialogue with your company about what they expect from your business."[37]

Because there are no universal criteria, there are two primary issues with corporate reporting: (1) reporting standards vary widely and (2) not all regions require companies disclose their sustainability data. Without comparable data, investors have a difficult time accurately assessing ESG performance. Even though the number of companies that voluntarily report ESG data is increasing, their data is very difficult to compare. This can be due to different reporting standards, different levels of disclosure on the same standard, or different methodologies employed by reporting entities. This leads to a huge issue in comparability, making the data difficult to employ in informed decision-making.

In June 2021, the G7 finance ministers and central bank governors made a public commitment to addressing ESG concerns and promoting multilateral economic cooperation.[38] In addition, a report by the International Organization of Securities Commissions (IOSCO) highlighted the essential role of the financial sector in furthering a more sustainable future, asserting the importance of comparable ESG data.[39] Though countries have increasingly developed individual reporting requirements, varying regulations across multiple jurisdictions create a risk for fragmentation in the global business market, which is why global consistency must be a priority.[40] Poor-quality ESG ratings create potential barriers to sustainable investments and to clarity about businesses' responsibility in terms of how and what they communicate. Investors and corporate leaders need improved data and improved disclosure guidance. As for regions where disclosure responsibilities are evident, lack of consistency makes it challenging for companies to understand how and what to disclose from one region to the next. The shift toward greater harmony in regional disclosure will benefit companies and investors. In the meantime, looking at information from a variety of ratings providers may be the most effective way to navigate the current data landscape.

What Do International Sustainability Standards Mean for Corporations and Investors?

Sustainability standards will help you gain a clearer understanding of what to report, how to report, and what investors and other stakeholders are interested in knowing about your firm. We are swiftly moving from not having one clear approach to having a global approach that will empower efficiency in your reporting.

In November 2021, the International Financial Reporting Standards Foundation, which oversees production of international accounting standards, announced the creation of the International Sustainability Standards Board (ISSB), which would "deliver a comprehensive global baseline of sustainability-related disclosure standards that provide investors and other capital market participants with information about companies' sustainability-related risks and opportunities to help them make informed decisions."[41] The ISSB is composed of several frameworks and standards (such as, Sustainability Accounting Standards Board, International Integrated Reporting Council, and Task Force for Climate Related Financial Disclosure), which craft sustainability standards with the goal of eliminating fragmentation and streamlining the creation of a single set of international standards.[42] Once adopted by the IOSCO, implementation will be up to individual countries, and will provide a type of quality badge. Reinhard Dotzlaw, partner at KPMG, argued that "the creation of globally consistent and transparent sustainability disclosure standards focused on long-term value creation will strengthen our capital markets by helping investors make better decisions. The hope now is that jurisdictions globally get behind the new ISSB."[43]

Corporations will benefit from the ISSB's uniform guidance for corporate disclosure, including what data should be considered financially material to shareholders. Investors will have transparency and comparability when doing company analysis, comparing peer companies across an industry and making decisions.

One critique of the ISSB approach is its climate-first focus—observers point to a lack of attention to social aspects. Critics argue that if we don't tackle climate and social issues in tandem—given that they are intricately connected—then there may be a continued delay in developing social standards. However, social standards might be difficult to apply internationally, due to varying attitudes and opinions among different cultures and customers.

Global Companies and Their Suppliers: Workers, Health, Safety, and Human Rights

We have examined a variety of environmentally focused policy discussions, but let's pivot to look at countries taking a more robust approach to specific social policies and regulations. Representing the *S* pillar in ESG, these approaches stand to benefit workers, not just at a specific company, but within a company's entire supply chain. As we see greater emphasis on consistent climate and environmental regulation, I believe focus on regulations and even proactive policies centered on workers and other social policies will uptick. Companies that operate in multiple countries—or have vendors that operate in multiple countries—will need to be increasingly attentive to these policies in order to remain compliant. In this section, you'll learn how to future-proof your business to be compliant with these changes and perhaps find new opportunities as well.

Although small and mid-sized enterprises (SMEs) have not yet been regulated under some of the current policies, they will still feel the impact as countries actively work to expand the scope of these requirements to encompass smaller firms. For example, the EU has shared their plans on developing the SME-focused standards through European Financial Reporting Advisory Group (EFRAG). In addition, these smaller companies cannot escape the opinions of society—sometimes referred to as their "social license"—as consumers continuously hold businesses of all sizes to the same standards of worker safety and human rights and inclusion. Small companies that act as suppliers and vendors for large companies will also be subjected to monitoring by their customers. In fact, companies may increasingly be required to disclose the policies and practices of their own suppliers' efforts to ensure their employees' well-being in regions where they do business. Thanks to educated and demanding stakeholders, companies of every size have an external incentive to pursue sustainability—namely, gaining a competitive edge.

The push to punish large corporations for the abuses they and their suppliers commit overseas has gained popular appeal in recent years, though legislation and enforcement targeting such practices hasn't caught up to the public ire and scrutiny into workplace hazards and tragedies. In April 2013, an eight-story commercial building called Rana, located within the Savar Upazila of Dhaka District in Bangladesh, collapsed.[44] The official death toll was 1,134 with more than 2,500 people injured. In the days that followed, garment workers demanded the arrests of building owners and factory operators.[45] They argued that substandard building practices, administrative failures, and ignored warning signs all led to the deadly collapse. (More than 40 people were charged with murder for their role in the disaster.) The impact of the Dhaka building collapse was felt world-wide because the affected factories had provided garments to high-fashion brands in the United States, the United Kingdom, Spain, Italy, Germany, and Denmark.[46] The horrendous Rana collapse highlighted the lack of responsibility that large corporations take when abuses within their supply chains lead to substantial harms internationally. Proactively addressing the risks, transparently reporting them, and internally managing them can help avoid these situations.

In 2017, France passed the French Duty of Vigilance Law, which establishes a legal obligation for the country's largest companies—defined as those with more than 5,000 employees in France and/or more than 10,000 employees worldwide, including affiliates' employees—to prevent human rights violations and environmental problems that result from not only their own activities but also the activities of companies they control, their suppliers, subcontractors, and even suppliers of subcontractors.[47] It empowers parties and communities affected by harmful actions to hold companies accountable through the mandatory development of a vigilance plan and/or financial compensation. Impacted parties have the option of using civil action to argue the company's liability and request compensation for resulting damages. In combination with this compensation, the judge may also impose a fine of up to 30 million euros.[48]

Several other countries had previously adopted voluntary codes of conduct related to supplier supervision. For instance, the United Kingdom's Modern Slavery Act of 2015 was crafted to provide law enforcement with tools to fight modern slavery, including severe punishments for perpetrators and enhanced protections for victims.[49] The EU's Non-Financial Reporting Directive, established in 2018, requires organizations to publicly disclose nonfinancial information related to employee engagement, board diversity, environmental matters, anti-corruption, and respect for human rights.[50] But the Duty of Vigilance Law was the first binding legislation to cover all human rights abuses and expand corporate obligations across the entire supply chain. An article by the International Bar Association notes that the French Duty of Vigilance Law went further than the UK and the EU legislation by "establishing not only a reporting obligation but also a monitoring obligation."[51]

Though it represents a historic step forward, the Vigilance Law is far from ideal. First, not many French companies fall within the law's limited definition of a large company with 10,000 employees. "This definition is outdated because it measures companies by the number of staff they have, which reflects traditional manufacturing notions of size," said Els Reynaers Kini, senior vice-chair of the IBA's Environment, Health and Safety Law Committee. "These days there are successful companies in industries which don't have so many employees."[52] Other concerns involve the lack of possible criminal prosecution for culpable company directors and the burden of proof that victims must meet when seeking enforcement. These communities may not have the financial means to stand up against large corporations, which can further deepen the gap that exists between large offending corporations and their victims.[53] Countries must not only speak to their commitment to doing no harm but also accept responsibility and quickly put corrective actions in place when their operations or services harm employees, customers, or the general public.

Other countries have also begun moving in the direction of mandating human rights actions at the corporate level. In June 2021, the German parliament passed legislation requiring the country's largest companies to be actively diligent in the prevention of human rights and environmental abuses within their own business and supply chains.[54] Under the law, companies must complete a risk analysis on unsafe working conditions, child exploitation, forced labor, inadequate pay, and human rights–related environmental standards. Initially limited to companies with more than 3,000 global employees, including foreign companies with subsidiaries in Germany, beginning in 2024, the legislation will apply to companies with more than 1,000 employees. Compliance with the law will require transparency on the part of suppliers to large German companies, which may include regular audits, the monitoring of operations, and the implementation of similar measures for their own suppliers to meet requirements throughout the supply chain.

Ranking Countries on ESG

The RobecoSAM Country Sustainability Ranking provides a comprehensive analysis of countries' performances on various ESG metrics. As of October 2021, Finland ranked at the top, largely based on its commitment to addressing environmental and political risk, followed by Sweden, Denmark, and Norway.[55] Outperforming the European Union average across all 15 ESG criteria, Finland's high environmental scores were key in its elevation to top performer. According to Robeco:

> Finland's strong environmental protection policies have been effective at reducing pollution, promoting natural conservation and safeguarding biodiversity. And with nearly a 40% share of renewables in the energy mix, it also leads the world in transitioning its energy sector to a low-carbon future. Moreover, robust institutions have helped it contain Covid-19 caseloads and largely avoid the pandemic's economic knock-on effects.[56]

On the one hand, the prevalence of Nordic nations at the top of the list is no surprise. The region widely adopted ESG investing strategies as early as the 1980s, even before such strategies had an official name.[57] Nordic societies have long prioritized community interests: the region led the way in establishing women's voting rights, equal opportunity, environmental protections, and governments regulations to combat corruption. Laws relating to sustainable and social responsibility in business are part of that larger context. Nordic companies were early adopters of practices that promote a high-level of social responsibility and future sustainability. Their commitments are evident in the annual reporting of most Nordic companies, which helps elevate these countries in their sustainability rankings.[58]

On the other hand, Australia, which is heavily dependent on fossil fuels, has a history of undermining indigenous rights, and has failed to deal adequately with forest fires, are seeing their troubles intensify. As stated in a Robeco Insights report, "the cost of inaction is likely to increase in the coming years. A recently released report from the Climate Council finds that the cost of extreme weather has more than doubled since the 1970s and amounted to AUD 35 billion over the past decade. By 2038, these costs could increase to even AUD 100 billion every year."[59]

ESG, Emerging Markets, and Business Growth

Although the importance of recognizing which countries top the lists of sustainability ratings may be obvious, countries ranking low on the list should also be considered by the leaders of companies, for a number of reasons.[60] First, sometimes doing business in these countries is simply not avoidable. Second, it can be cruel to local people to simply starve these countries of investment, especially when citizens may have little say in the way the country is run.[61]

Zimbabwe is a great example of an emerging nation that ranks low on the list but has key mineral resources—including platinum, chrome, gold, and diamonds—that are much-needed by global industry and therefore vital to Zimbabwe's future economic growth. The country performs poorly on ESG metrics due to political and social repression; it also suffers from over-exploitation of natural resources, often by foreign actors who have historically utilized corruption to get what they want. Consequently, there are a multitude of issues to wrangle with if you are to do business ethically in Zimbabwe. One way forward is to partner with the locals where you are considering doing business. Engage with the community to understand their environmental and social challenges, and work together to devise a plan on how you might hire from within the community, build rapport with other businesses in the area, and generate value that is beneficial for *both* your company and the community at large. A commitment toward supporting the area and its people—and, importantly, sticking to the mutually agreed upon commitment—can go a long way in building trust, establishing a strong working relationship, and doing business ethically.

The overall importance of these bottom-ranking countries lies in the fact that they often provide the supply chain resources and labor to companies in other countries. The widespread use of global supply chains requires companies to consider the ethical and legal practices of their contractors and subcontractors. Merely making public declarations against improper practices is not sufficient. Companies need to take real responsibility for the sourcing and manufacturing of their products. Even the best-run multinational in the world can still suffer negative publicity if their providers are not operating in accordance with widely recognized ESG standards.

The chocolate industry is an instructive example of this problem. In 2001, Nestle—one of the largest and most recognizable consumer brands in the world—signed onto an industry agreement to eradicate child labor occurring on their cocoa farms in Ghana and the Ivory Coast. Yet, the company continues to face criticism and accusations about the use of child labor in its supply chain. A group of survivors of child labor on cocoa farms in Mali filed a class action lawsuit against "Big Chocolate," which includes not only Nestle but also Mars, Hershey, Cargill, and more. In June 2022, the US Supreme Court ruled that the case could not go forward; because the abuse did not occur on US soil, the Court found that the plaintiffs lacked standing to sue in US courts.[62] But although the corporations won out in this particular suit, legal experts cautioned firms to not assume that they will always be safe from legal repercussions of illegal activity overseas.[63] Further, child labor in the chocolate industry remains a social injustice issue that needs to be addressed, not to mention an unending PR headache. Nestle issued a statement to the effect that the "risk of child labor" in its supply chain cannot be "fully removed," but that they are "determined to tackle the problem."[64]

To best analyze this issue, it is useful to briefly explore the characteristics of emerging market (EM) countries. Typically, these nations are moving away from traditional economies, based in agriculture and raw materials, and toward industrialization and the adoption of a free market or mixed economy.[65] Investing in these economies can do great things for local talent and can bring great benefit to both a company and a region. Five defining characteristics of an emerging market include low income, rapid growth, high volatility, currency swings, and high potential returns. That high volatility can stem from a number of causes, including rapid social change, external price shocks, domestic instability, and natural disasters. Many EM economies are particularly vulnerable to natural disasters due to their reliance on agriculture. Devastating earthquakes have overwhelmed Haiti, for example, droughts plague the Sudan, and tsunamis affect Thailand. EM countries are also more susceptible to currency and commodity swings, such as those related to fuels and food. Their limited political power means that they lack the ability to influence these changes for their own protection.[66]

Investing in Emerging Countries

For all those reasons and more, investment in EM countries have historically been considered hit or miss. Political conflict, currency crises,

Gambling on Green

and social upheavals sometimes leave investors deflated about their prospects. But each region is different, and one set of circumstances may not fit all locations. The right conditions can bring substantial rewards and the possibility of robust growth and positive portfolio returns. Factors that raise risks, when properly managed and monitored, may also present rewards for companies and investors. Data is essential for making these decisions, and lack of quality data may be a culprit in lack of knowledge of certain regions' ESG standing.

Although there is much room for ESG disclosure improvement among EM countries, some governments are crafting relevant policies. China offers a useful example. Though it is classified as an emerging market based on general criteria, its position as the second-largest economy in the world sets it apart from the other EM countries. However, poor availability and quality of ESG data in China creates a major obstacle, limiting investors' ability to identify viable investment opportunities. As stated by Piotr Mazurkiewicz, lead environmental and social policy and risk officer at the International Finance Corporation, "It's time to get serious. Without the data, it's very tough to make investment decisions and emerging markets are missing out."[67]

According to research from the Emerging Markets Institute conference, EM economies are, in spite of data issues, consistently making notable progress in their ESG efforts.[68] This is partly due to increased pressure from investors to meet stated commitments and comply with any existing mandates. Investors, companies, and consumers increasingly hold EMs accountable for their ESG practices. Many of these countries operate under standards that greatly differ from those of their counterparts in developed markets. These variations may include labor and product-safety practices, environmental protections, accounting requirements, and shareholder rights. The challenges business leaders face in emerging markets may seem robust, but they are not insurmountable.

Final Thoughts

Corporate responsibility to ESG factors goes much further than the benefits to customers and employees; companies also have a responsibility to the regions where they do business. When corporations understand disclosure requirements of the regions where they and their suppliers are located, that supports the environmental and social progress of that region. Clearly, there is difficulty in understanding sustainability standards across various regions because there is not yet a global standardization, but this is improving due to the introduction of the ISSB. It is up to businesses to go above and beyond what is now deemed as adequate. This includes ensuring compliance with climate-related guidance, but also ensuring the safety and health of their workers. Companies (regardless of size) that can get ahead of the curve of providing an inclusive, safe place for workers as well as sustainable products and services for their customers will see themselves well positioned for growth in the future, while also supporting the economies of the communities where they are located. This can be the case for regions that are already models for sustainable growth as well as emerging regions.

In Chapter 7, we will discuss how companies and governments can work together to ensure they are progressing the economies of their communities and growing the companies that are investing in those regions. When these partnerships are approached with a spirit of cooperation and mutual benefits—including benefitting the greater good—the result can be a fertile business environment as well as healthy workforces and communities.

Chapter 5 Takeaways

- Sustainability is about not only your company operations but also how your company's products and manufacturing policies affect climate, employees, suppliers, and corporate actions in the communities where you do business.
- Attention to how you are benefiting or harming ESG efforts in the regions where you operate can provide you with a holistic view of how your company is performing in the context of society's broader ESG commitments.
- Regional disclosure lacks consistency; this is problematic for businesses because there is no uniform approach to what and how to disclose. It's also problematic for investors because without consistent corporate disclosure, they may not have clarity on specific regional risks and opportunities.
- As climate and environmental disclosure is inching toward a level of global standardization, disclosure requirements for worker and supplier policies (the "S" in ESG) remain inconsistent.
- Tragedies caused by poor safety standards continue to draw public ire and pose significant risk to the company reputations; this is true even if the guilty party is a supplier.
- Emerging markets historically have been seen as risky, but with the appropriate data and analytics, companies and investors may see opportunities.

Notes

1. https://www.unpri.org/fixed-income/a-practical-guide-to-esg-integration-in-sovereign-debt/4781.article.
2. https://www.sustainalytics.com/investor-solutions/esg-research/country-risk.
3. https://www.msci.com/documents/10199/5c0d3545-f303-4397-bdb2-8ddd3b81ca1b.
4. https://www.theguardian.com/world/2022/mar/09/history-can-be-funny-muscovites-get-used-to-life-without-dior-and-mcdonalds.
5. https://markets.businessinsider.com/news/stocks/russia-stock-market-shut-moex-ukraine-foreign-currency-sales-stopped-2022-3.
6. https://www.bloomberg.com/news/articles/2022-03-04/russia-keeps-stock-trading-closed-in-nation-s-longest-shutdown.
7. https://www.reuters.com/markets/deals/russian-rouble-weaker-early-moscow-trade-2022-03-09/.
8. https://apnews.com/article/russia-ukraine-putin-business-europe-economy-d205d9feeda7c4dc5a365d65375f8555.
9. Ibid.
10. Ibid.
11. https://www.refinitiv.com/en/media-center/press-releases/2020/october/refinitiv-debuts-country-sustainable-development-scores-to-measure-how-extensively-a-country-meets-un-sdgs.
12. https://www.refinitiv.com/content/dam/marketing/en_us/documents/methodology/refinitiv-country-sdg-scores-methodology.pdf.
13. https://www.refinitiv.com/content/dam/marketing/en_us/documents/brochures/country-risk-ranking-brochure.pdf.
14. https://www.sustainalytics.com/investor-solutions/esg-research/country-risk.
15. Ibid.
16. https://blogs.worldbank.org/opendata/are-we-there-yet-many-countries-dont-report-progress-all-sdgs-according-world-banks-new.
17. https://www.unpri.org/policy/how-effective-are-corporate-disclosure-regulations/211.article.
18. https://ec.europa.eu/info/business-economy-euro/banking-and-finance/sustainable-finance/eu-taxonomy-sustainable-activities_en.
19. Ibid.
20. https://www.refinitiv.com/content/dam/marketing/en_us/documents/fact-sheets/sfdr-principle-adverse-impact-indicator-coverage.pdf.
21. https://assets.publishing.service.gov.uk/government/uploads/system/uploads/attachment_data/file/1056085/mandatory-climate-related-financial-disclosures-publicly-quoted-private-cos-llps.pdf.
22. https://www.greenfinanceplatform.org/policies-and-regulations/non-financial-reporting-directive-nfrd-directive-201495eu-and-proposal.

23. https://www.bloomberg.com/professional/blog/the-relationships-between-sfdr-nfrd-and-eu-taxonomy/.
24. Ibid.
25. https://www.financeasia.com/article/esg-disclosure-rules-set-to-advance-sustainable-bond-market/473718.
26. https://www.unpri.org/policy/how-effective-are-corporate-disclosure-regulations/211.article.
27. https://esgn.asia/a-unified-standard-needed-to-take-esg-to-the-next-level/.
28. https://www.cdsb.net/sites/default/files/sustainability_aus_report_web.pdf.
29. Ibid.
30. https://www.sec.gov/news/public-statement/coates-esg-disclosure-keeping-pace-031121.
31. Ibid.
32. https://www.sec.gov/news/speech/can-the-sec-make-esg-rules-that-are-sustainable.
33. https://www.unpri.org/policy/how-effective-are-corporate-disclosure-regulations/211.article.
34. Ibid.
35. https://www.fsb-tcfd.org/about/.
36. https://www2.deloitte.com/us/en/insights/topics/strategy/esg-disclosure-regulation.html.
37. Ibid.
38. Gov. UK. "G7 Finance Ministers and Central Bank Governors Communique" (June 5, 2021).
39. IOSCO, "Report on Sustainability-Related Issuer Disclosures" (June 2021).
40. https://www2.deloitte.com/us/en/insights/topics/strategy/esg-disclosure-regulation.html.
41. https://www.ifrs.org/groups/international-sustainability-standards-board/.
42. https://boardagenda.com/2021/11/04/cop26-plans-revealed-for-new-international-sustainability-standards/.
43. https://home.kpmg/xx/en/home/insights/2021/11/sustainability-reporting-climatechange-issb.html.
44. Tansy, Hopkins. "Reliving the Rana Plaza Factory Collapse: A History of Cities in 50 Buildings, Day 22." *The London Observer*. (April 23, 2015).
45. "Garment Workers Remain Restive." *The Daily Star* (April 28, 2013).
46. https://growensemble.com/rana-plaza/.
47. https://media.business-humanrights.org/media/documents/files/documents/French_Corporate_Duty_of_Vigilance_Law_FAQ.pdf.
48. Ibid.
49. https://www.gov.uk/government/collections/modern-slavery-bill.
50. https://www.esgenterprise.com/esg-reporting/overview-eu-non-financial-reporting-directive-nfrd-reporting/.

51. https://www.ibanet.org/article/1324A0D4-268F-40D1-AD30-F863BA212D39.
52. Ibid.
53. https://www.complianceweek.com/france-adopts-multinational-duty-of-care-law/2696.article.
54. https://www.aperio-intelligence.com/2021/07/01/germanys-new-supply-chain-act-will-make-human-rights-due-diligence-mandatory.
55. https://www.robeco.com/en/key-strengths/sustainable-investing/country-ranking/.
56. https://www.robeco.com/en/insights/2022/01/a-new-northern-light-emerges.html.
57. https://www.alfredberg.com/nordic-sustainable-and-socially-responsible-investing-an-old-habit-in-a-strong-esg-environment/.
58. https://www.alfredberg.com/nordic-sustainable-and-socially-responsible-investing-an-old-habit-in-a-strong-esg-environment/.
59. Ibid.
60. https://www.robeco.com/en/insights/2022/01/a-new-northern-light-emerges.html.
61. https://www.robeco.com/en/insights/2022/01/a-new-northern-light-emerges.html.
62. https://www.bbc.com/news/world-us-canada-57522186.
63. https://www.mcginnislaw.com/news-Supreme-Court-Sides-with-Nestle-and-Cargill.
64. https://www.msn.com/en-us/money/companies/new-lawsuit-claims-nestle-mars-hershey-use-cocoa-farmed-by-trafficked-children-in-west-africa.
65. https://www.thebalance.com/what-are-emerging-markets-3305927.
66. National Center for Biotechnology Information. "Food vs. Fuel: Diversion of Crops Could Cause More Hunger" (August 5, 2021).
67. https://business.cornell.edu/hub/2021/12/02/esg-pressure-takes-center-stage-2021-emerging-markets-institute-conference/.
68. https://news.cornell.edu/stories/2021/12/esg-pressure-takes-center-stage-2021-emerging-markets-institute-conference.

Chapter 6

The Role of Ratings

hroughout this book, we have examined case studies of firms
using sustainability considerations to gain competitive advantage, as well as those that have mismanaged and misled stakeholders on sustainability initiatives, suffering reputational and financial
damage. In Chapter 5 we discussed the value of insight into regional
ESG progress for business leaders. As we discovered, country ratings, along with existing and upcoming regulations, are especially
important to understand when you are considering expanding into a
region, or when onboarding suppliers operating in another country.
Later in the book (in Chapter 9), we will identify key standards and
frameworks that executives need to consider when building their
company's own ESG reports.

For now, a pressing question a business leader needs to answer
is: how will the information about your corporation's sustainability
efforts be gathered, scored, and used by investors and other stakeholders? It's the role of ESG ratings companies to deliver objective,
transparent insights that investors, asset managers, companies, not-
for-profits, even consumers, and other stakeholders can rely on when
assessing company ESG performance or building a portfolio.

This chapter will give you details about the evolution of these
largely for-profit firms, along with the scope of factors and methodologies they use to craft ratings on your company. Importantly, this
section will also explore strategies your company can implement to

support positive scores and results, while sharing how investors can ensure full use of the scoring data to make the most shrewd investing decisions.

How Are ESG Ratings Used?

Traditionally, investors have relied on financial reports when assessing company portfolios and making investment decisions. But ESG ratings provide insight into the nonfinancial aspects of a business that are also important and material in driving the business's value.[1] Investors want access to comprehensive data all at once, instead of spending substantial time combing through lengthy reports. They also expect to see evidence regarding the inclusion of ESG into the company's growth strategy and a level of commitment at all levels of leadership. Without the innovation of ratings agencies, investment firms would be forced to review a variety of reports and frequently update news and data in order to gauge a company's ESG status.[2]

However, there is a fair amount of evidence that suggests an investor should look at more than just the rating alone. Aaron Yoon, an assistant professor of accounting and information management at the Kellogg School, and George Serafeim, professor of business administration at Harvard Business Schools, conducted a study to determine whether ratings accurately predict positive and negative future ESG-relevant company news.[3] "The general complaint in the industry and in academia is that ESG ratings can have huge discrepancies among them," Yoon said in the research paper. Yet, he argues that the inconsistencies can be used to an investor's advantage. Investors often try and create their own ratings by comparing data between ratings agencies and using their own analysts, which enables them to see which companies are effectively overstating their ESG value and heading toward scandal and who are understating it. In conclusion, he stated, "We find that ESG ratings do predict future ESG news."[4]

Let's consider how some investors have used ESG ratings. A 2020 survey by the think tank and advisory firm SustainAbility polled 25 investors about their views on ESG ratings and how they use them in their corporate ESG analysis.[5] Many of the investors interviewed, reported using ratings several times a week in their work and using a variety of ratings to fill in gaps where some ratings cover different areas or even can present a different view of a company. A number of investment firms have crafted their own key performance indicators (KPIs) regarding ESG research, building out an ESG methodology in house. Investors also may use their in-house system with external ratings as well. Rather than using ratings as straightforward determinants (i.e. "yes, we will invest" or "no, we won't") some companies surveyed by SustainAbility tend to focus more on the data *beneath* the ratings. Executives at these firms tend to view ratings as just a starting point for determining whether or not further research and engagement is appropriate. This reliance on the underlying data is also driven by the efficiency offered by ratings agencies. Investors can easily access ESG data and feed it into their internal scoring systems. Some investors stated that they use ratings as an initial screen for specific investment products or portfolios, helping them identify the best-performing companies from the worst.[6] This gives an indication of how you as a business leader might approach your scores. It might be a good investment to bring in a consultant or even a data scientist to support you in looking at key ESG data areas that map up into ratings. We'll explore those sub-categories that make up the ratings later in the chapter, but know for now there may be a benefit in being attentive to details of your sustainability efforts as well as the big picture.

Investors are not the only stakeholders who benefit from ESG ratings. Companies can also benefit from the assessments; for instance, ratings may provide clarity on where a company excels and where there is room for improvement—this acts as a benchmark against which any additional data can be compared. The various metrics reviewed by ratings agencies can provide a detailed examination of a company's operations, processes, outreach, and governance—all of which are factors that can either elevate or decrease a company's value. They provide a valuable outside perspective that many businesses would not otherwise receive. By responding to ESG questionnaires, business leaders can gain a heightened awareness about the significance of managing ESG activities throughout all functions of the company.[7] Used effectively, the outcomes can spark important internal discussions about potential opportunities, as well as looming risks. Ratings also help companies evaluate how they stack up against their competitors in ESG matters; this knowledge can be used to advance strategic decision-making while improving shareholder relations and increasing investment.

Experts advise companies to choose more than one ESG ratings provider to work with, because investors often use multiple ratings when making investment decisions. Data contributions should be transparent to promote a comprehensive review. Global management consulting firm Sustainserv advises that companies communicate with their investors to get their insights on what they want ESG policies to accomplish in the business.[8] It is also suggested that companies research the ESG data of their competitors, using that information to perform an internal analysis to identify gaps and address them. According to Sustainserv, small consistent steps are preferable to major overhauls that may not pan out. Companies should establish and action KPIs and implement procedures that demonstrate a true dedication to ESG objectives.[9]

Having said that, it's important to understand that the various ESG ratings providers have their own proprietary methodologies; this reality can lead to some variances in scores.

The next part in this chapter explains the different methods used by ratings providers; and toward the end of this chapter, we will delve into the details of the consistency challenges with the ESG ratings.

ESG Rating Providers and Their Methods

Before examining the unique qualities and methodologies of the various ESG rating providers, here is a list of some of the ratings agencies we will be discussing. The alphabetized bullet points below by no means constitute a complete list of ratings companies; rather, these are some of the most-used ratings agencies within the ESG ratings space.

- **Bloomberg ESG Data.** A service from Bloomberg Financial LP, Bloomberg ESG Data was launched after the firm's 2009 acquisition of New Energy Finance. Using a scoring system of 1 to 100, the service collects data on more than 10,000 companies, or approximately 88% of the global equity market. Bloomberg ESG Data tracks 120 different indicators, ranging from climate, waste, and pollution to executive compensation, political contributions, and community relations.[10]

- **CDP.** Unlike many of the firms on this list, the Carbon Disclosure Project (now known simply as CDP) is a nonprofit. Beginning in 2002 with just 35 investors who were seeking climate-related disclosures, CDP now has offices in 50 countries and collects data on thousands of mid- and large-cap companies. CDP's data are more circumscribed than most: they focus on climate change, water security, forests, and biodiversity. Their view is that good stewardship in these areas is representative of good management overall. Firms are given annual letter grades that range from A to F, and CDP makes those grades easily accessible online.[11]

The Role of Ratings

- **MSCI.** Analysts and researchers at MSCI employ what they call a rules-based methodology to produce scores ranging from 1 to 10 on 37 different aspects of ESG performance. About 6,000 companies and 400,000 securities are then graded overall, using a scale that ranges from AAA to CCC. MSCI also employs artificial intelligence and machine learning to, as their brochure puts it, "increase the timeliness and accuracy of data collection and analysis."[12]

- **Refinitiv.** Part of the London Stock Exchange Group (LSEG), Refinitiv serves more than 40,000 customers in 190 countries. They provide ESG data and analysis on more than 11,000 companies, or over 80% of the global market cap. The firms are scored from 1 to 100, based on more than 500 indicators of ESG performance. Companies are also ranked in comparison to others; for example, a particular company might be ranked as fourth out of 350 in a particular industry.[13]

- **RepRisk.** In keeping with its name, the Zurich-based RepRisk offers ESG data and analysis with a particular focus on the question of risk. The company boasts that it has the "world's largest and most comprehensive database," covering not only public companies but also more than 170,000 privately held companies plus NGOs, specific projects, and emerging/frontier markets. With a variety of partners including the United Nations and the Sustainability Accounting Standards Board, RepRisk screens an enormous number of public and private sources and provides ratings ranging from AAA to D on about 100 ESG-related metrics.[14]

- **S&P TruCost.** A part of the S&P Global network, TruCost measures environmental and broader ESG factors for more than 15,000 companies to include datasets related to greenhouse gas emissions, land and air pollutants, waste disposal, water use, and revenue generation.[15] The company collects data from various sources to provide information that represents industry- and sector-specific data for such indicators as carbon and climate, supply chain water use, operational pollutants, and recycled waste.[16]

- **Sustainalytics.** A Morningstar company created after a 2008 consolidation of three European companies (AIS, DSR, and Scolaris), Sustainalytics has more than a thousand clients and a presence in 172 countries. It rates more than 20,000 companies on a scale of 1 to 100 based on key issues in the three pillars of ESG. The firm does not take a one-size-fits-all approach to scoring: how heavily a particular issue is weighed in an overall score depends on the particular industry. Sustainalytics also looks at a list of 70 indicators, which are divided into three themes: preparedness, disclosure, and performance (both qualitative and quantitative).[17]

- **V.E.** Formerly known as Vigeo EIRIS, V.E. was acquired by Moody's in 2019. Its history dates back to the EIRIS (Ethical Investment Research Services) Foundation, founded in 1983. V.E. assesses companies of all sizes, offering more than 70 index families, in which data is arranged according to particular themes. The company also performs risk assessments in areas such as climate impact and so-called controversial activities. Comprehensive reports from V.E. look at topics such as "company and sector performance," "management of risks and opportunities," and "carbon footprint and energy transition."[18]

When analyzing the methodologies of ESG rating agencies, it is helpful to classify them into general categories based on the type of data utilized in their respective examinations. The three categories generally used for this purpose are fundamental data providers, comprehensive data providers, and specialized data providers.[19]

Fundamental data providers offer a broad range of raw information that is widely available to the public, typically from company-generated reporting. Bloomberg and Refinitiv are examples of fundamental data providers. Bloomberg's annual evaluation includes company sustainability reports, annual reports, company websites, and a variety of other public sources.[20] Refinitiv's rating system likewise relies chiefly on public data sources such as annual reports, company websites, NGO websites, stock exchange filings, corporate social responsibility (CSR) reports, and news sources.[21]

Comprehensive data providers employ a combination of publicly available information with data curated by the provider's in-house teams.[22] Similar to fundamental data providers, they gather information from media sources, NGOs, and company reports and other public disclosures. However, they also rely on insights that they develop themselves using internal analysis. For example, MSCI collects macro data from academic, government, and NGO datasets such as Transparency International and World Bank.[23] Another comprehensive provider is V.E., which integrates qualitative and quantitative data into its ratings assessments, comprising management, performance, self-reported, and third-party data.

RepRisk is also classified as a comprehensive data provider, though the agency excludes company data that is self-reported from its assessment, because they believe entrusting a company to report on itself may not be the most reliable data approach.[24] RepRisk explains that they use AI and machine learning to "empower the size and scale of [their] dataset" and enhance human analysis.[25]

Specialized data providers focus solely on one or two aspects of ESG.[26] For example they may rate companies based only on activities in climate change and water. These agencies offer highly specialized and in-depth data within their expertise, making them very useful to investors who are interested in particular ESG domains. CDP is an example of a specialized data provider, because the organization addresses only specific environmental categories.[27] S&P Trucost, another specialized data provider, uses verified company information as well as media sources and direct company engagement to provide data on carbon and "brown revenues," which generally refers to revenues generated from fossil fuel activities.[28]

Whether we prefer one type of ratings provider over the others depends on what types of data we find most valuable. For example, an NGO user may want a deep dive into how specific companies are progressing water security policies and disclosure (specialized). However, an investor may want ratings that compare one company to its peers (fundamental and/or comprehensive). Ratings agencies specifically mentioned in this chapter have working relationships with top institutional investors, regardless of which category of data they use in their assessments.

Another useful way to think about different ESG ratings agencies is to consider the level of company interaction that goes into assessments. This can range from no communication at all, to the sharing of assessment information with the company for feedback and rebuttal. For instance, RepRisk invites companies to participate in a formal data verification process before publishing their ratings report.[29] MSCI, however, reaches out to companies as part of their standard data review processes but the agency does not send questionnaires, do interviews, or consider company-provided data that is not publicly available.[30] For their part, Sustainalytics doesn't involve companies in the initial preparations of their reports, but it does send draft reports to them for feedback and updated information.[31]

Although some ratings providers reject company input on the grounds that the firms may not offer unbiased information about themselves, others believe company interactions help drive comprehensive reporting and promote the use of accurate information. The ESG landscape can move quickly as companies manage their progress toward stated goals. By engaging via questionnaires and interviews, ratings providers can better ensure that they are reporting based on your firm's up-to-date data, which is extremely important to investors. Vast amounts of monetary transactions rely on ESG ratings, so these agencies want to present as accurate a picture as possible.

From a corporate perspective, interactions with ratings providers offer opportunities to perform audits and unearth valuable data, both positive and negative. Companies can use communications with ratings providers as opportunities to learn more about the criteria that go into their ratings. Gaining an understanding of the subcategories that make up ESG scores can help company leaders see what ESG really means in practice.

Getting feedback from ratings companies on how ESG functions in the real world can be quite an education for some firms. Consider for example the *S* in ESG: because it stands for *social*, a company may assume that it only refers to community relations and involvement with social issues that are external to the company. But in reality, there are plenty of internal factors—such as how managers interact with unions or subcontractors—that can also be part of what makes up the *S* in ESG. If you think about the *E* in ESG, a company may focus heavily on recycling in an attempt to improve its environmental scores but may not have a good handle on its water use. This may present equally high levels of risks and challenges for the firm. It incentivizes leaders to understand the many issues ESG ratings providers consider and to use the information they have collected for disclosure strategically. Rather than seeing ESG ratings as a burden, wise executives will view them as an opportunity to learn which areas of their operations are viewed as successful and which are not.

What Makes Up the Pillars of ESG?

As the preceding examples suggest, a wide variety of issues can fall under the broad umbrella of ESG. Ratings providers take a granular approach, analyzing the many facets of ESG. To understand how different rating providers function, it might be useful to compare the subcategories used by some of them for each of ESG's three pillars.

Environmental

Environmental scoring analyzes a variety of factors, including but not limited to a company's greenhouse gas emissions and its use of natural resources. Though no two ratings agencies are identical, when it comes to environmental assessments they do tend to focus on similar areas of concern. However, they might have different ways of measuring the same thing. For example, Refinitiv uses the categories of emissions, resource use, and innovation. They further break those categories down into themes. Emissions themes include waste, biodiversity, and environmental management systems. Resource use themes include water, energy, sustainable packaging, and the environmental supply chain. Themes that fall under innovation include product innovation and green revenues.[32]

V.E.'s environmental analysis includes subcategories related to carbon footprint, fossil fuel exposure, low carbon transition, and environmental strategy.[33] For each criterion, V.E. generates scores from 0 to 100 with lower scores indicating a poor level of assurance on a company's ability to manage a specific criterion.[34] They also provide up to 10 years of environmental back history for investment consideration.[35]

RepRisk's environmental set includes such factors as GHG emissions, global and local pollution, impacts on ecosystem, waste, animal mistreatment, and overuse of resources.[36] Though each agency uses different categories and names for the gathered datasets, they are somewhat similar in the general areas they cover.

Social

In comparison to environmental, the social pillar lends itself to a wider range of variations. Ratings providers vary significantly in the measures that they consider material to this ESG component. Although some focus mainly on the company's external actions with the community, society, and supply chain participants, other providers place substantial value on internal employee relations. Social scoring can encompass a company's business relationships with employees, suppliers, partners, and other supply chain participants. Ratings organizations may look at factors such as employee wages, factory worker conditions, and availability of sick leave. Social can however also encompass a company's charitable contributions, policy influence, and customer interactions.

V.E. considers a wide range of data points for its social pillar ratings.[37] The evaluation includes data related to social dialogue, employee participation, career development, supply chain standards, and philanthropy. Refinitiv divides the social pillar into the categories of community, human rights, product responsibility, and workforce.[38] Within the product responsibility category, the company considers more specific data points in regard to a firm's quality of product, responsible marketing, and data privacy. The workforce category is further divided into diversity and inclusion, health and safety, career development, and working conditions. RepRisk also divides the social pillar, but uses two broad categories: community and employee relations.[39] Community relations includes human rights abuses, community impact, local participation, and social discrimination. Under the employee relations category, RepRisk considers factors such as forced and child labor, collective bargaining freedoms, occupational safety, and working conditions.

Governance

Last, the governance pillar evaluates a company's compliance and board operations by looking at topics such as executive compensation and the racial, ethnic, and/or gender diversity of the board.

Though the variation for governance topics is not as great as the social pillar, some differences still exist. For example, MSCI separates the governance pillar into the two subcategories: corporate governance and corporate behavior.[40] Corporate governance is further broken down into ownership and control, as well as pay and accounting. On the other end of the spectrum, RepRisk divides governance into seven pillars, including tax evasion, fraud, misleading communications, and executive compensation issues.[41] They also look at issues related to violations of national legislation and internationally accepted business standards.

How Might Your Potential Investors Select Ratings Providers?

Alas, the simple answer to the question, "Which ratings provider do your investors use?" is . . . it depends.

There are a few things to know about what investors, NGOs, and other external stakeholders—we'll call them *users* in this context—consider when engaging with ratings companies to get more detail into your corporate sustainability practices.

Users Go Beyond Self-Reported Data

Users of ESG ratings are well aware that companies may present information in a way that isn't consistent with their peers. They might even assume a company's reporting to be biased and want to seek outside information. One way to get around that bias is to look at controversy scores based on news or social media. Controversy scores flag a company's potential external controversies by means of advanced technology and AI that, in theory, reduces bias. Sustainalytics, MSCI, and Refinitiv are examples of ratings

(Continues)

firms that provide this type of controversy insight.[42] However, critics point out controversy scores largely take into account acute activities like worker injuries, dangerous spills (e.g. oil spills into oceans), or even loss of life as a result of poor product design (e.g. car malfunctions), that might have occurred years in the past; the thought is that this might be a flawed way to measure controversy. The rationale is these past issues may have been dealt with by the company paying the fines, the restitution, and even removing management teams who oversaw the business during the acute event. At the same time, other companies that may have issues brewing are not called out with the current controversy-scoring model. In essence, they believe today's model puts tremendous focus on what happened in the past, as opposed to spotlighting trends that might lead to potential acute issues in the future.

Users Know What Information Is Most Important for Them

An investor who is interested in comparing workplace safety incidents and policies in the manufacturing sector may choose a different provider than one who is interested in understanding how water security is affecting the mining industry. In the first instance, an investor might look at the social subcategories of the various ratings providers to gauge which ones might provide a clear way to compare peers on workplace safety. However, in the second instance it might behoove the investor to look to the CDP to understand how a specific industry is faring in terms of water security and what needs to be done to improve the trajectory. To summarize, the stakeholders may first look at the company level information and then dive into the comparisons of the company with companies in the same industry.

Users May Seek to Enrich Proprietary Methodology

As mentioned previously, investors often have their own in-house methods for rating companies and making decisions on which security they will add or keep in their portfolios. They might look to external ratings providers to deliver additional insights or provide data for their own methodology. These users see ratings providers as being highly useful, but they don't rely on them solely. In keeping with that, many investors look to engage with several ratings providers to give them a broad perspective of companies' ESG standing.

Controversy Monitoring

Controversy monitoring is an important function of ESG ratings providers; it matters because a negative reputation can have lasting effects for a company, its stakeholders, and investors. Whether there are accusations of fraud, workplace discrimination, or harmful environmental incidents, company scandals can occur at any time, causing major financial and PR problems. Investors find controversy research valuable because it helps them better screen and compare companies when making investment decisions.

MSCI defines an ESG controversy as "an instance or ongoing situation in which company operations and/or products allegedly have a negative environmental, social, and/or governance impact."[43] Some controversies may involve actions that are clearly illegal, and others may just involve violating widely established norms. Examples of

ESG controversies include anti-competitiveness practices, discrimination, community protests, employee health and safety concerns, and spills and other accidents.

As discussed, different ratings agencies deal with controversies in different ways. At MSCI, research analysts assess controversies involving company operations and governance, as well as products and services that allegedly violate national or international laws and regulations. The controversies are given a level of severity ranging from very severe to minor.[44]

V.E. also integrates ESG controversies into their ESG assessments through daily monitoring.[45] All identified controversies are then assessed according to the severity of the event ranking from critical to minor, the frequency of the circumstance ranging from persistent to isolated, and responsiveness by the company. All this information is presented in the form of a company's controversy risk mitigation capacity, which can range from weak to advanced.

Refinitiv also uses a controversy scoring system. Their controversy score is based on 23 topics with categories that include community, product responsibility, management, human rights, resource use, shareholders, and workforce.[46]

The reality is most large businesses will likely have been part of a controversy at some point or another. Yours is no different. As a business leader who wants to improve the company's sustainability efforts and reputation, it is important to not deny, deceive, or mislead the public; instead, you should admit to the problem and—this is critical—share exactly what your company is doing to rectify the situation. This shouldn't just mean simply paying a mandated fine and remaining quiet; look for outside help where needed—such partnerships can be a valuable part of self-improvement. Examine what deeper actions are needed to prevent acute, potentially catastrophic problems. That may involve creating an internal shift in culture, putting more investment and funding into an external community, building stronger governance systems to combat corruption, or designing practices to ensure promotion and pay equity.

Transparency is essential: you should consistently release information on measurable, actionable progress. In practice, that might vary depending on the problem you face, whether that is reporting percentage increases in the numbers of diverse people in senior leadership in your annual reports as well as in quarterly calls with analysts, or expanding monitoring systems for supply-chain functions. Be specific: if we are to use the first example, this may include breaking down diverse categories and percentages of senior leaders in each category. Even if your firm suffered a major controversy, a genuine focus on fixing what is broken can slowly restore confidence of employees, investors, and consumers, while supporting your improved sustainability standing in the future.

Ongoing Consistency Challenges with ESG Ratings

ESG ratings are necessary tools to address the difficulties that investors have faced in finding data that is comparable and transparent when assessing sustainability performances.[47] The growth of the ratings provider landscape represents a positive evolution of the financial industry—but despite the many positives, the ESG ratings space still has some challenges to overcome. Critics of ESG ratings point to a lack of consistency among providers; as we have seen in this chapter, different ratings agencies approach their data in very different ways. The lack of comparability across ratings is arguably a barrier to the long-term value of ratings in the promotion of climate-related objectives.[48]

To understand these inconsistencies better, it is helpful to think about the method used to develop more traditional company credit ratings. These evaluations are chiefly done by three main agencies: Standard & Poor's (S&P), Moody's Investor Services (Moody's), and

Fitch IBCA (Fitch).[49] These agencies look at various factors related to business and financial risks. They then use their specific methodologies to come up with a credit score. This may sound extremely similar to the ESG ratings process, but there is an important difference: unlike ESG ratings, credit-ratings criteria are much clearer and uniform across the board because they have existed for longer. The reason ESG ratings can be so different is not only their relative infancy, but because different measurements may have different indicators; for example, a gender diversity rating might include pay parity or percentage of women on a board, or both, or something else.

Another challenge is the diversity of data-gathering strategies we discussed previously. With company-generated data, questions of transparency and veracity arise because it is in the company's best interest to present itself in the best possible way; this may lead to inaccurate claims, exaggerations, or empty gestures.[50] But data sources from outside the company need to reflect the most current information, as well as context of the company's situation. Further, although the quantitative aspect is important, it is also helpful for information gathering to include a company's qualitative approach and insight into how they are managing opportunities and risk that may affect their revenues, assets, and liabilities, and long-term reputation.

Another issue that can create problems, particularly for startup companies, is a one-size-fits-all model. For example, a particular methodology may fail to recognize the unique characteristics of a startup in the ESG space in comparison to an established corporation. Newer companies may not have had time to implement ESG policies, and they need ratings criteria that fairly take that into consideration.

The lack of transparency in the methodologies used by some firms is another key driver of these inconsistencies. They regard their methods as competitive elements that set them apart from their competition, and therefore, they are unwilling to offer full transparency about them.[51] However, it is this lack of transparency that negates the ability for investors and companies to adequately challenge the ratings.

An MIT Sloan working paper entitled "Aggregate Confusion: The Divergence of ESG Ratings" divides the ratings inconsistencies into three sources. According to the study, 53% can be attributed to measurement, where the providers measure the same ESG criteria with different indicators.[52] For example, the evaluation of company's labor practices may be based on employee turnover within one methodology and on the number of sick days in another.[53] The paper states that the scope of attributes represents 44% of the inconsistences: for example, greenhouse gas emissions are typically included under the environmental pillar, but only some agencies consider radiation emissions within their analysis. The final 3% of the inconsistency was attributed to the different weights that each rating company places on individual components when calculating an overall ESG score.

Do these inconsistencies make ESG ratings useless? Absolutely not. But they do demonstrate the complexities of measuring ESG performance, placing the onus on investors to dive deeper than simply looking at one company rating and acting on it. Investors need to understand the factors considered by the ratings agencies they choose to use. They must recognize what aspects of ESG are most important to themselves and their clients and do their homework to ensure that relevant criteria was considered.

Final Thoughts

Virginie O'Shea is the founder and CEO of Firebrand Research. In an interview with *ESG Investor*, she stated, "The securities industry needs more regulation to help reduce the disparity in ESG data sets and ratings methodologies via standardization. . . . At the moment, there is a lot of interpretation going on and it is reliant on a lot of manual processes." She explained that improved transparency will reduce some of the uncertainty that currently exists. "This is important as ESG becomes an integral and enduring part of the investment process, given the ongoing importance of climate and social change."[54]

ESG ratings regulation would require ratings providers to be fully transparent about their methodologies, which would allow investors a better understanding about the ways in which public data is translated into scores. These changes could work to improve reliability, build confidence, and promote accuracy. Minimum ratings standards for the requirement of disclosure, transparency, and quality may help investors through the creation of a consistent baseline for ESG ratings. They can then better choose ratings providers that use an approach that best matches their investment objectives and targets.

As an executive, the best way to manage the information that ratings providers share with investors is to understand what providers view as the most important components of the pillars making up ESG scores in your industry. Also, look to your peers. See where their focus is: which pillars are they outperforming you on and where are they underperforming. Likewise, never try to disguise where your company has performed poorly: instead, concentrate on the specific areas for improvement and share broadly how your firm will improve. Follow up on that communication with periodic updates in annual reports on how you're tracking against your goal. These can be shared more widely if needed. Go beyond simply trying to get good ratings in the immediate present and set up resilient structures, some of which may need to be partially independent to the rest of your business for the sake of impartiality, that are flexible to change.

Chapter 6 Takeaways

- The role of ESG rating entities is to deliver objective, transparent company insights that investors, asset managers, financial institutions, and other stakeholders can rely on when assessing ESG performances and building their respective portfolios.
- ESG ratings provide companies with valuable data on where they excel and where there is room for improvement. The metrics examined by ratings agencies can offer an outside perspective of a company's operations, processes, outreach, and governance.
- ESG ratings companies use a variety of methodologies when determining ESG ratings, but they all start with the collection of data that is either company-generated or pulled from outside sources. Some ratings providers monitor and assess ESG-related controversies to determine their potential impact.
- Inconsistencies among ESG ratings processes have created some challenges for the investors who rely on them, prompting calls for global regulation to promote transparency and reliability.
- ESG ratings—although not perfect—are valuable tools for investors, NGOs, corporations, and other stakeholders who are interested in providing capital, comparing data against peers, and getting insights into key areas for development to improve sustainability standing.

Notes

1. https://sustainserv.com/en/insights/esg-ratings-and-rankings-why-they-matter-and-how-to-get-started/.
2. https://insight.kellogg.northwestern.edu/article/esg-ratings-sustainable-investors.
3. Ibid.
4. Ibid.
5. https://www.sustainability.com/globalassets/sustainability.com/thinking/pdfs/sustainability-ratetheraters2020-report.pdf.
6. Ibid.
7. https://sustainserv.com/en/insights/esg-ratings-and-rankings-why-they-matter-and-how-to-get-started/.
8. Ibid.
9. Ibid
10. https://www.bloomberg.com/professional/dataset/global-environmental-social-governance-data and https://corpgov.law.harvard.edu/2017/07/27/esg-reports-and-ratings-what-they-are-why-they-matter.
11. https://www.cdp.net/en/info/about-us/what-we-do and https://www.esgtoday.com/cdp-releases-2021-company-environmental-scores-14-companies-achieve-leadership-rankings-across-all-categories. See also https://www.cdp.net/en/companies/companies-scores for recent grades.
12. https://www.msci.com/documents/1296102/21901542/MSCI+ESG+Ratings+Brochure-cbr-en.pdf and www.msci.com/esg-ratings.
13. https://www.refinitiv.com/content/dam/marketing/en_us/documents/methodology/refinitiv-esg-scores-methodology.pdf and https://www.refinitiv.com/en/about-us.
14. https://www.reprisk.com/ and https://corpgov.law.harvard.edu/2017/07/27/esg-reports-and-ratings-what-they-are-why-they-matter/.
15. https://www.marketplace.spglobal.com/en/datasets/trucost-environmental-(46).
16. https://www.spglobal.com/marketintelligence/en/documents/tucost_fi_brochure.pdf.
17. https://www.sustainalytics.com/about-us and https://corpgov.law.harvard.edu/2017/07/27/esg-reports-and-ratings-what-they-are-why-they-matter.
18. https://vigeo-eiris.com/solutions-investors/esg-assesments. See sample report at https://vigeo-eiris.com/wp-content/uploads/2021/07/MESG-Sample-ESG-assessment.pdf.
19. https://sustainserv.com/en/insights/esg-ratings-and-rankings-why-they-matter-and-how-to-get-started/.
20. https://corpgov.law.harvard.edu/2017/07/27/esg-reports-and-ratings-what-they-are-why-they-matter.
21. https://www.refinitiv.com/content/dam/marketing/en_us/documents/methodology/refinitiv-esg-scores-methodology.pdf.

22. https://sustainserv.com/en/insights/esg-ratings-and-rankings-why-they-matter-and-how-to-get-started/.
23. https://www.msci.com/documents/1296102/4769829/MSCI+ESG+Ratings+Methodology+-+Exec+Summary+Dec+2020.pdf/15e36bed-bba2-1038-6fa0-2cf52a0c04d6?t=1608110671584.
24. https://sustainserv.com/en/insights/esg-ratings-and-rankings-why-they-matter-and-how-to-get-started/.
25. https://www.reprisk.com/approach.
26. https://sustainserv.com/en/insights/esg-ratings-and-rankings-why-they-matter-and-how-to-get-started/.
27. https://www.esgtoday.com/cdp-releases-2021-company-environmental-scores-14-companies-achieve-leadership-rankings-across-all-categories/.
28. https://www.spglobal.com/esg/solutions/data-intelligence-esg-scores; https://www.ssga.com/investment-topics/environmental-social-governance/2019/03/esg-data-challenge.pdf.
29. https://corpgov.law.harvard.edu/2017/07/27/esg-reports-and-ratings-what-they-are-why-they-matter/#:~:text=ESG%20Report%2FRatings%20Summary%20Table%20%20ESG%20Report,A%20leading%20provider%20%204%20more%20rows%20.
30. https://www.msci.com/documents/1296102/4769829/MSCI+ESG+Ratings+Methodology+-+Exec+Summary+Dec+2020.pdf/15e36bed-bba2-1038-6fa0-2cf52a0c04d6?t=1608110671584.
31. https://corpgov.law.harvard.edu/2017/07/27/esg-reports-and-ratings-what-they-are-why-they-matter/.
32. https://www.refinitiv.com/content/dam/marketing/en_us/documents/methodology/refinitiv-esg-scores-methodology.pdf#:~:text=ESG%20scores%20from%20Refinitiv%20are%20designed%20to%20transparently,product%20innovation%2C%20human%20rights%2C%20shareholders%20and%20so%20on.
33. https://www.environmental-finance.com/content/guides/esg-guide-entry.html?planid=2&productid=311&editionid=3.
34. https://www.youtube.com/watch?v=1KJgJDxOz5k.
35. https://www.environmental-finance.com/content/guides/esg-guide-entry.html?planid=2&productid=311&editionid=3.
36. https://www.reprisk.com/approach.
37. https://vigeo-eiris.com/wp-content/uploads/2020/07/Best-EM-Performers-Ranking_07_2020_LL-AN.pdf#:~:text=RANKING%20METHODOLOGY%20Vigeo%20Eiris%20assesses%20and%20rates%20the,six%20key%20areas%20of%20corporateenvironmental%2Csocial%20and%20governance%20responsibility%2Cnamely%3A.
38. https://www.refinitiv.com/content/dam/marketing/en_us/documents/methodology/refinitiv-esg-scores-methodology.pdf#:~:text=ESG%20scores%20from%20Refinitiv%20are%20designed%20to%20transparently,product%20innovation%2C%20human%20rights%2C%20shareholders%20and%20so%20on.

39. https://www.reprisk.com/news-research/resources/methodology.
40. https://www.msci.com/documents/1296102/4769829/MSCI+ESG+Ratings+ Methodology+-+Exec+Summary+Dec+2020.pdf/15e36bed-bba2-1038-6fa0-2cf52 a0c04d6?t=1608110671584.
41. https://www.reprisk.com/news-research/resources/methodology.
42. See https://www.sustainalytics.com/investor-solutions/esg-research/ controversies-research, https://www.msci.com/documents/1296102/1636401/ ESG_Controversies_Factsheet.pdf/4dfb3240-b5ed-0770-62c8-159c2ff785a0, and https://www.refinitiv.com/content/dam/marketing/en_us/documents/ fact-sheets/esg-scores-fact-sheet.pdf.
43. https://www.msci.com/documents/1296102/14524248/MSCI+ESG+Research+Co ntroversies+Executive+Summary+Methodology+-++July+2020.pdf.
44. Ibid.
45. https://www.environmental-finance.com/content/guides/esg-guide-entry.html? planid=2&productid=312&editionid=3.
46. https://www.refinitiv.com/content/dam/marketing/en_us/documents/ methodology/refinitiv-esg-scores-methodology.pdf.
47. https://www.esginvestor.net/explainer-regulating-esg-ratings/.
48. https://www.eco-business.com/opinion/ the-inconsistency-of-esg-ratings-implications-for-investors/.
49. https://www.treasurers.org/ACTmedia/ITCCMFcorpcreditguide.pdf.
50. Ibid.
51. https://www.esginvestor.net/explainer-regulating-esg-ratings/.
52. https://www.eco-business.com/opinion/ the-inconsistency-of-esg-ratings-implications-for-investors/.
53. https://www.eco-business.com/opinion/ the-inconsistency-of-esg-ratings-implications-for-investors/.
54. https://www.esginvestor.net/explainer-regulating-esg-ratings/.

How Public and Private Partnerships Can Support ESG

One of the best ways to understand why corporate partnerships—whether with other corporations, governments, or NGOs—are such an effective tool in ESG settings is through a partnership story. This particular story is focused on finding a remedy for deforestation.

Solidaridad, the international organization focused on supply chain sustainability in partnership with Henkel, the German chemical and consumer goods company provides an example of working together for improved outcome for consumers and the environment. One of the aims of the partnership was to help small farmers produce greater amounts of palm oil without the need for using more land—which is costly—to do so. Solidaridad began providing farmers with training to help them yield more palm oil using less land, as well as helping them get their palm oil certified as "sustainable." Although critics point out the sustainability designation is far from perfect, certifications do support meeting requirements around production and responding to growing consumer demand around this level of sustainability.[1]

Henkel along with Solidaridad developed The Forum for Sustainable Palm Oil in 2013 to support not only elevating the message that palm oil could be developed in a way that did not include massively increasing the amount of land needed, which is the main thing contributing to deforestation, but also supported small farmers who historically haven't had the resources to learn and implement sustainable farming techniques.[2]

An indirect benefit of the partnership on Henkel's side is that the company can position itself as both an innovator in sustainable palm oil and an advocate for smaller farmers, who are often marginalized and lack access to technology and vital know-how to improve production.

As this example shows, strategic partnerships can create mutually beneficial relationships that address some of the world's most pressing ESG challenges. They help participants reach new markets, achieve sustainability objectives more efficiently, and dovetail with one another's previously established momentum. This chapter explores the various types of partnerships established among governments, the private sector, and not-for-profits. Properly leveraged, sustainable partnerships have the potential to introduce ESG-related principles into a variety of public and private economic structures.

Public-Private Partnerships

The public-private partnership (PPP; not to be confused with the pandemic-era PPP loan) is one type of partnership that has the potential to play a key role in the growing incorporation of ESG principles into the investment landscape. One area that showcases high PPP success rates is education, which is a key social tenet of ESG. This is unsurprising given the emphasis placed on learning and development as a means to combat poverty and establish a sustainable growth-oriented workforce. Transferring expertise via education to communities in need can be an extremely important tool for supporting social mobility.

The incredible challenge of advancing quality education for all requires an elevated level of innovation and funding, which can be accomplished through partnerships. Studies show that education-based

PPPs can result in numerous successes, including elevated program efficiency and expenditure transparency, improved service delivery to underserved populations, and greater resources to address public sector restrictions.[3] For example, in 2002, Caldas, Colombia, leveraged a PPP between the Luker Foundation and local government to adapt an improved school model for 38% of the public secondary institutions.[4] Through a program including governance modules for classrooms and self-paced studying, this PPP helped students see growth.[5]

A strong example of this is the district of Manizales, Columbia, which saw a notable improvement in schools with this scheme, in comparison to those that did not. As a result, PISA scores of students in the program were 15–20 points better in each subject in comparison with those who weren't and around 25–30 points higher than the Columbian average.[6] This scenario demonstrates how PPPs can help governments navigate current education issues and, to take this a step further, support the needs of tomorrow's workforce.

PPPs can also capitalize on green funding sources to further sustainable development around the globe.[7] The economic and political climate of the 2020s has inspired significant attention to environmentally and socially responsible projects that may mitigate unanticipated, acute events, such as pandemics or weather- and climate-related catastrophes. Planning for these types of events supports business resilience, which is a key aspect of good governance.

As a business owner, it is worth reaching out and considering which partnerships you can foster in order to bring in expertise in PPP. An example of this is Ceres. Ceres is a nonprofit organization working to transform the economy in furtherance of a more just and sustainable future.[8] The company leverages networks and global collaborations with investors, companies, and nonprofits to design and implement policy solutions. Its Investor Network involves more than 200 institutional investors that collectively manage more than

151

$47 trillion in assets.[9] Climate Action 100 is one of the partnerships of the Investor Network initiatives; more than 600 global investors participate in the program.[10] The goal is to pursue sustainable returns while working to ensure investors mitigate impact of physical climate risk, meaning risks that occur to physical sites, property, and land, and even business disruptions, as a result of severe climate and weather activity.[11] This shows how investment firms—through ongoing engagement with the companies in their portfolios—are helping to reduce physical climate risks. Some participating companies like Bayer, General Electric, BASF, Sasol, Duke Energy, BP, and others have made announcements on their plans and targets for decarbonization and zero emissions.

Sustainably minded infrastructure projects can unlock opportunities for short- and long-term economic gains, such as job creation, improved travel connectivity, and greater access to health care in developing nations. However, as discussed in Chapter 5, many regions of the world face economic risks that can hinder the implementation of costly large-scale projects. To navigate these financial obstacles, some global leaders are turning to PPPs to deliver expertise in fields they have not tackled before. Through these relationships, governments can outsource costs to the private sector while maintaining legal ownership of the projects. Business leaders, especially those who want to leverage partnership opportunities, may benefit from understanding how these partnerships work and what success looks like in terms of revenues and reputations.

Collaboration between the public and private sectors is our best chance to address environmental and societal challenges. Siloed thinking will not address the issues—we need collective problem-solving. Even if these partnerships are difficult to design, it is time for the public sector to think more like the private sector and for the private sector to think more like the public sector. From advancing diversity and inclusion to addressing climate change, these partnerships can be transformative if done correctly.[12] The public sector brings the expertise and understanding of the problems to be addressed and the private sector drives efficiency along with its financial backing.

But although PPPs can prove helpful, they are not foolproof. The practice of greenwashing—when a company boasts of its sustainable business practices but doesn't follow through in practice—can be a real problem. Customers, investors, not-for-profits, and other organizations are sometimes left to wonder whether private companies—particularly those that have avoided public scrutiny or been forced to adapt to new regulations—have the credibility needed to lead ESG efforts. Another concern is the possibility for greenwashing that can arise when one sector (be it public or private) dominates the problem-solving for a particular environmental or social issue without external input. By giving too much power to individual groups, we risk that their agendas may not reflect the agenda of the broader business stakeholders and society. They may be more concerned with crafting an image than actually working to create change.

In cases like these, one entity may have their own self-serving agenda for bolstering public relations, but other entities may have a more aspirational agenda for actually meeting environmental goals. Partnerships between the public and private sectors can prove challenging, particularly because each entity traditionally has different stakeholders with different objectives. To bring these variations into alignment, each side needs to understand and consider the goals and values of the other.[13] In other words, businesses need to think like the policymakers they hope to partner with and look after the public rather than their own interests, and policymakers need to think like businesses if they are to be ruthless and efficient in the execution of their policies. If both sides can focus on what they can do together instead of only on what they can do alone, much can be accomplished.

153

Contracts, Bids, and ESG in PPPs

Government regulation in the ESG arena can have a widespread impact on the private sector, forcing private partners to consider and manage ESG risks occurring throughout their own supply chains, potentially leading to the implementation of ESG into localized economic structures.[14] Yet even with these valuable opportunities, too many PPP arrangements still leave ESG as an afterthought. For example, when a PPP requires bidding on a government or private contract, ESG considerations may seem like a burden on the project as opposed to a benefit that may actually increase savings over the long term. That's because from a short-term perspective, winning bids depend on immediate costs, rather than long-term sustainability. Even when ESG is taken into consideration during the bidding process, governments often leave its implementation for the winning bidder to manage after the contracts have been executed. Unfortunately, this type of approach limits the government's ability to ensure a real commitment to ESG among its private partners.

To combat these issues, governments should include ESG criteria in their procurement processes from the beginning, making them a requirement for successful bids. For instance, the UK government has a procurement policy that requires that ESG elements account for at least 10% of proposal evaluation.[15] The policy applies to all contracts awarded by UK central government departments, their executive agencies, and nondepartmental public bodies.[16] It requires prospective bidders to carefully evaluate their ability to actually deliver on any ESG objectives included in their procurement. Those that are unable to verify ESG elements will be substantially disadvantaged when competing for public contracts. In addition, bidders that dare exaggerate or misrepresent ESG credentials may face severe penalties, including an exclusion from relevant procurement processes for three years.

Unfortunately, entities that award the bids can place so much emphasis on short-term goals that they may completely ignore the processes necessary to ensure long-term objectives. But it doesn't have to be this way: PPP criteria can be revised for better movement toward long-term goals and time frames with methodologies that are innovative and adaptive. For example, when private actors bid on Abu Dhabi Investment Office (ADIO) projects, they must include information to demonstrate how they will address ESG factors, as well as how they will use key performance indicators to report on their ESG activities. As H.E. Dr. Tariq Bin Hendi, director general of ADIO, stated in February 2021:

> While the "G" in "ESG" is often underrepresented, it is important that governance should be the starting point as it shapes the purpose of a company and defines opportunities in the long term. The integration of ESG standards and values into business and investment decisions helps to improve company performance, reduce risk and drive growth. By formally integrating ESG principles into ADIO's decision and investment process we aim to further support the development of Abu Dhabi's private sector.[17]

Thus, ADIO's policy looks to integrate ESG considerations into all of the decision-making, management, and operational processes of its partners. It actively solidifies the government's expectations that all partner companies center ESG goals and outcomes on widespread benefits. Future-focused businesses do not look at ESG as an exercise or a unit tangential to the business; rather, they include ESG considerations in strategy for every aspect of their business.

TRANSFORM: The United Kingdom Partners with Ernst & Young and Unilever

Governments can incentivize lasting change by building programs that spark demand and spur innovation toward long-term shared goals.

Policymakers should recognize that the private sector brings expertise and an understanding of market incentives that can help projects be more successful. This type of relationship is beneficial to both parties because each can bring their own specializations and unique resources to the table. A useful example is the United Kingdom's Foreign, Commonwealth & Development Office's collaboration with EY and Unilever to pilot new business models that serve the needs of low-income households in sub-Saharan Africa and South Asia.[18] By supporting entrepreneurs, the TRANSFORM partnership takes market-based solutions usually seen within private partnerships to address some of society's biggest development challenges.[19]

For example, the Kenya-based enterprise Mr. Green Africa (MGA) seeks to realize sustainable social, environmental, and economic impact through the collection, conversion and selling of postconsumer recycled plastic waste.[20] Unfortunately, the organization's efforts were stifled by the hesitance of East African consumers to separate their wastes and sell their plastics back for recycling. With support from TRANSFORM, MGA was able to implement a research-driven consumer model that elevated the collection of plastics. In this way, TRANSFORM helped Mr. Green Africa use data analytics to address a serious ESG challenge within its community.

Established in 2015, the initiative has supported 61 projects in 13 countries so far. One initiative in India is TrashCon, which helps solve the problem of waste management by implementing technologies and building machinery that segregates mixed waste into biodegradable and non-biodegradable components. With 90% efficiency, this innovation is proving to be a successful model that can possibly be replicated and scaled.[21]

Latin American Partnerships Framework

Latin America is another area of the world where large infrastructure investments are needed to address widespread environmental and social problems. Again, businesses can benefit from partnerships that generate solutions for the community while making profitable infrastructure investments.

More than 60% of Latin America's roadways remain unpaved. Sewage goes untreated and power outages occur due to outdated infrastructure.[22] Yet, even with these major problems, many Latin American countries spend only a small percentage of their GDP on infrastructure improvements. Their economies simply cannot support rolling out and financing projects promoting sustainable development and community empowerment.

To meet these needs, Latin America has increasingly relied on PPPs. For instance, the Argentina Investment and Trade Promotion Agency created a centralized PPP Unit within the Ministry of Finance, which has resulted in more than $169 billion of infrastructure investment, including $48 billion in roads and $34 billion in the energy sector.[23] Brazil's São Paulo Telecentres Project involved several PPPs working together to establish 128 community access centers, or telecenters, which offer free public access to facilities, technology, and training; residents participate in management of the centers, gaining valuable experience, and can also use the centers as venues for social organization.[24] In 2016 alone, PPPs in Latin America and the Caribbean attracted more than $33 billion in investment, accounting for 47% of private participation in public infrastructure globally.[25] In 2018, new PPPs were launched in Argentina, El Salvador, and Nicaragua, and countries such as Chile, Colombia, and Brazil have longer experiences with PPPs. Chile implemented 70 PPP projects prior to 2017, and Colombia had awarded almost 40 projects to the private sector. During the same time period, Brazil completed almost 270 PPP projects.[26] With the success of these projects, an increasingly wide range of stakeholders—from governments to recipients to business—see the value of PPP investment.

Businesses looking to scale while leveraging the expertise and intelligence of a partner can benefit from PPP engagement. But while

How Public and Private Partnerships Can Support ESG

these partnerships are essential for addressing environmental and societal challenges, business managers should be aware of the potential scrutiny they may bring. In addition to looking at clear criteria for ESG integration, be aware that any time you work alongside a partner entity—and especially if that partner entity is embroiled in scandal or corruption—there is a risk that your business' reputation could be tainted. That's why it is critical to understand the values of your business partner, as well as get clarity on the particular regulatory environment.

Financial Sector Partnership: Glasgow Financial Alliance for Net Zero

Banking institutions commonly provide the private financing for PPP projects. Today, banking and investment leaders are working toward furthering sustainability efforts by reducing financed emissions when they provide capital to emissions-intensive industries and projects.

Glasgow Financial Alliance for Net Zero (GFANZ) is one such group. Its goal is to bring together members of the financial services industry to accelerate emissions reduction. GFANZ has united 450 financial institutions around a "private-sector" plan to advance net-zero carbon emissions.[27] Banking participants include Bank of America, BlackRock, Goldman Sachs, Vanguard, and Wells Fargo, as well as various insurers, ratings agencies, pension funds, and financial service providers. Led by Mark Carney, a former Goldman Sachs executive and a former governor of both the Bank of Canada and the Bank of England, the alliance is said to have about $130 trillion at its disposal, representing the amount of assets coalition members—asset managers, asset owners, banks, and other institutions involved in GFANZ—are responsible for overall. Signatories to GFANZ agree to align with the Task Force on Climate-related Financial Disclosure (TCFD) framework, which helps companies report on financial-related climate information. Carney with businessman and former New York City mayor Michael Bloomberg helped to launch TCFD.) The signatories of GFANZ use the TCFD disclosure approach, such as climate stress testing their businesses, which involves getting insight into climate-related risks and discovering strategies for resolving and managing that risk.[28] They also commit to science-based transition plans and aligning their portfolios with net-zero goals.[29]

The $130 trillion in assets of the combined companies in GFANZ means having access to the resources to drive actions such as stress tests, quant modeling, and strategy development needed to reach net zero. Clearly, the influence and resources that come with this type of financial backing from the investment industry is unlike anything previously seen in the battle against climate change. Also, given Carney's and Bloomberg's formidable backgrounds and business savvy, this initiative shows tremendous promise with what they've already accomplished in onboarding the current group of investment industry partners. It gives hope as to what they are likely to accomplish in the future as we see greater emphasis on climate regulation and reporting.

That's not to say the GFANZ alliance hasn't raised concerns in some quarters. Critiques center on the absence of regulations to restrict investments in fossil fuels and/or require the enactment of reductions of absolute emissions.[30] Critics say the alliance is missing the point regarding fossil fuels. "An alliance on climate with no fossil fuel criteria in its guidelines is like an anti-smoking coalition which doesn't address cigarettes," Bill McKibben, author and cofounder of the grassroots climate campaign 350.org, said in a statement.[31] He noted that although the International Energy Agency (IEA) seeks to end support for fossil fuels, GFANZ has yet to address this issue at all. "For as long as the financial sector fails to heed the IEA's call to end support for new oil, gas and coal projects, its claims to climate leadership should be laughed out of the room."[32]

The 2015 Paris Climate Accord demanded that the flow of money from financial institutions to private businesses include a consistent commitment toward the reduction of greenhouse gas emissions and climate resilience. Therefore, when accepting pledges from banking institutions, the quality of their actual ESG commitments must be considered in addition to the quantity of their pledges. Experts say that this must include putting an end to the financing of new fossil fuel infrastructure systems.[33] While this example is most relevant to financial institutions, it is wise for any business that still relies heavily on or invests in fossil fuels, while maintaining other ESG targets, to be mindful of taking a holistic approach to their environmental footprint and sustainability commitments. In this case, the commitments financial institutions are taking are ambitious and a step in the right direction, but the work and output still appears to be minimal compared to the damage *still* being done by fossil fuels. Yet, it is a start.

Critical Considerations for PPP Success

A PPP to address Tanzania's major housing shortage provides an example of the inherent risks that can arise within PPPs without proper planning and precautions.[34] The Tanzanian government adopted PPP strategies to tackle its severe housing shortage; various joint-venture housing projects were undertaken throughout the country. Unfortunately, many of the Tanzanian PPP housing projects have experienced failures and early termination. The World Bank reported in 2016 that 15% of Tanzanian PPP projects terminated early, which is significantly more failures than the global average: 3.7% between 1990 and 2014.[35] Lack of awareness on risk management processes, lack of experience, and a lack of information are all given as the reasons behind these failures.[36] The World Bank suggests that governments should refrain from initiating infrastructure PPPs without adequate consideration of associated risks. Far too many governments lack the necessary level of risk management knowledge and capacity, which can hamper the success of PPPs.

The situation in Tanzania is certainly not the only example of when these partnerships don't progress as expected. A 2018 report by Eurodad examined 10 PPP projects in regions such as France, India, Indonesia, Spain, and Sweden.[37] The projects involved a variety of sectors, including education, energy, health care, transportation, water, and sanitation. Researchers found that every studied project resulted in higher than anticipated costs and excessive risks for the public sector. All of the projects were also found to lack transparency, with members of the private sector having little to no consult with members of the target community. In addition, each PPP project proved riskier for the state than it did for the private companies, largely due to the burden placed on the state to step in and handle excess costs when necessary.

Unfortunately, corruption can play a role in PPP failures, as demonstrated by the Queen Mamohato Hospital project in Lesotho. The hospital was built to replace an outdated hospital, but this new facility reportedly resulted in significant financial burdens on public funds. The private partner allegedly invoiced fees in amounts double the thresholds set by the government.[38] Needless to say, this had a profoundly negative effect on the most vulnerable populations of Lesotho.

In a PPP project in Jakarta, Indonesia, private business took over water distribution, which led to significant increases in monthly bills that were beyond the financial means of many impoverished residents. Private companies who do not keep their end of the deal on the unspoken social license to operate by increasing water bills or participating in corrupt practices can risk burdening taxpayers and losing the trust of communities. It behooves companies to ensure ethical business practices exist and will continue into the life of the partnership.

PPPs can be extremely valuable tools for advancing ESG goals, but they require thoughtful implementation and management. A takeaway to avoid unsuccessful PPPs is to ensure the mission and objectives of each entity are shared and aligned. Issues such as inflated invoices can be avoided if all partners specify what ethical practices are, commit to following them, and enforce penalties if one of the partners does not comply.

Citizens Recognizing the Role of PPP

A 2021 poll by the Center for American Progress found that the majority of American voters expect the government to take an active role in securing basic living standards for all people. They support policies that strengthen personal finances and financial growth opportunities for low-income people. American voters also view things such as access to clean water as basic human rights that governments should actively ensure.[39]

Growing numbers of citizens suspect there is an inability and/or unwillingness of some members of private sector to create a fully renewable economy when left to their own devices. For this reason, PPPs that include not-for-profits along with government and private businesses may be a way to build entities that gain public trust and support, while ensuring public agendas as well as private agendas are met. It is possible for public good goals *and* profitability goals to both be met simultaneously.

When looking at the scope of what PPPs can offer when implemented with the proper planning and alignment with a common agenda, I want to reiterate the potential they provide to small, mid-sized, and large private entities. PPPs create subcontracting opportunities for small and mid-sized companies in a variety of service areas, including civil works, electrical works, security services, facilities management, and cleaning services. By implementing strong policies and procedures in areas such as business ethics and compliance, ensuring the proper amount of resources are set aside for a project, and planning for unexpected (but perhaps costly) events during and after launch, companies can position themselves to add value for larger PPP private actors. Knowing the rules of the game helps smaller businesses earn the respect of larger businesses and governments when PPP opportunities arise. However, subcontracting or supplier services are not the only relationships where small business–large business partnerships thrive. Innovation labs are another area where both business sizes can benefit while simultaneously offering marketplace solutions that would be challenging for one entity to provide alone.

Innovation Labs and Partnerships

Generally speaking, innovation labs are spaces dedicated to creating, developing, and executing innovative ideas. Participants receive tools and resources to cultivate new initiatives while also forming valuable partnerships with established organizations. Some innovation lab models focus on more established firms supporting startups in exchange for an equity stake.

So, how might your business benefit from an innovation lab? It depends what you're looking to gain. Startups can gain mentorship, business guidance, and possibly financing; established businesses can benefit from a stake in a possible up-and-coming superstar business. This section looks at different types of innovation labs, including those that support products from external companies, as well as those looking to enhance their own internal production capabilities. These labs demonstrate how a company can support social innovation and foster diversity, both in the types of products on the market and the types of leaders who bring these products to market.

Private corporations such as Google, Amazon, Coca Cola, and Nike all sponsor innovation labs to create new solutions for current internal and external business challenges.[40] But many corporations also recognize the value that innovation labs can add when solving for various types of ESG-related issues. Although some of these innovation lab partnerships form between financial institutions and private business owners, others include public government actors.

The Morgan Stanley Multicultural Innovation Lab acts as an in-house startup accelerator that works to ensure underrepresented communities have the necessary resources for their startups and provides participants with access to capital for early-stage technology. They work with founders in regions including Europe, the Middle East, and Africa, and the lab also has a remit for supporting women and underrepresented people who, statistically, receive less capital for their ventures.[41]

COI Energy is an Innovation Lab project that demonstrates what progress can be made when financial services companies partner with sustainable startups. On being chosen to participate, Morgan Stanley's Multicultural Innovation Lab invested $200,000 into COI Energy, in exchange for which Morgan Stanley got an equity stake in COI Energy. Benefits also included mentorship and access to office space.[42] As this example shows, the recognition of the connection between technology and innovation creates viable opportunities for ESG conscious startups to implement new ideas.

Innovation labs can also serve goals that fall under the *S* plank of ESG. The Worker's Lab Innovation Fund works to expand and implement new ideas for the betterment of workers through investment, education, and information.[43] Since 2014, its Innovation Fund has invested more than $5 million in 78 innovators with new ideas about transforming systems and structures to ensure worker safety and security. The lab sponsors contests to identify these innovators, awarding them grants up to $150,000, in addition to offering mentorship, training, and organizational support. Early in the pandemic, before government financial assistance began, The Worker's Lab partnered with grassroots donors and with Steady, a mobile application platform that helps low-income individuals supplement their income, to disburse more than $2.5 million in emergency cash grants to workers facing unemployment and underemployment.[44]

Along with the numerous private companies that have adopted innovation labs, many governments in both emerging and developed countries have also crafted these partnerships to meet broad societal needs. The United Nations Development Program is focused on progressing decarbonization, equality, and improved levels of governance in a range of regions—from Serbia to Vietnam to the Caribbean.[45] Based in experimentation, these types of labs enable governments to test-drive new methodologies while establishing best practices. Government labs can be created at either the national or state level, and they develop partnerships with all types of private business leaders. For example, cities like Boston and Seattle operate variations of innovation labs.[46]

Various Canadian provinces also operate innovation labs, including Nova Scotia's GovLab, which develops policies and services to assist its aging population, and Toronto's MaRS program, which is aimed at working with a wide range of stakeholders, including those at the community level, who want to participate in environmental and social change solutions.[47] Its Mission from MaRS program works with a focus on the areas of real estate, transportation, and energy. Stakeholders involved include suppliers, investors, and others with the goal of developing best practices and steps for accelerating the adoption of greenhouse gas (GHG)–reducing innovations.[48]

In addition, the Canadian government partners with a variety of other governments, organizations, and private entities to drive innovation that benefits and empowers the most vulnerable members of society, with an emphasis on women and girls.[49] A partnership with

165

Grand Challenges Canada supports identifying and implementing new ways to deal with maternal and newborn health challenges.[50] It also engages the private and not-for-profit sectors in developing and rolling out tools and practices that can make operations more sustainable. For instance, the Canadian government partners with the organizations Mennonite Economic Development Associates, which implements partnerships to eradicate poverty,[51] and Convergence, which focuses on routing business and philanthropic investment funds to sustainable development projects.[52]

The United Kingdom's Behavioral Insights Team works with stakeholders ranging from charities to governments to businesses for the purpose of identifying and contributing to improvements to policy and public services.[53] The lab commonly uses controlled testing and small-scale implementation tactics to identify viable solutions before governments waste large amounts of funding on ineffective policy ideas. To date, the organization has completed more than 1,000 projects in dozens of countries, including those aimed at addressing gender-based violence, where hotlines were established to help women access survivor services in Eastern Europe and Latin America.[54] The team has also conducted experiments to measure the potential for heat pump adoption in the United Kingdom, aimed at the adoption of greater residential heating options.[55]

Innovation labs can also be found among developing nations. For example, the Global Innovation Lab for Climate Finance (The Lab for short) recognizes that India is not just one of the fastest-growing economies in the world but also one of the most polluted countries in the world.[56] Launched in 2015, The Lab is bringing together public-private players to craft, develop, and advance solutions for renewable energy, infrastructure, and other sustainability channels.[57]

The Indian Ministry of New and Renewable Energy is one partner in The Lab, as are Shakti Sustainable Energy Foundation, the Swedish Development Corporation, both capital providers, and the UK Department for International Development. One nonprofit/investor partnership initiative responds directly to India's reputation as being one of the most polluted countries globally: electric rickshaws. The program includes an initiative to deploy more electric auto-rickshaws in cities throughout India while improving the livelihoods of auto-rickshaw drivers through 100% debt financing and opportunities for driver ownership.[58] Meanwhile in Indonesia, Pulse Lab Jakarta uses data and artificial intelligence to inform policy and develop programs such as managing information on natural disasters and monitoring SDG progress across the country.[59]

Private and public innovation labs can provide small and mid-sized companies with valuable opportunities for investment, mentorship, and collaboration while working on issues that drive ESG ratings and boost investor confidence. They can provide larger companies with the opportunity to expand into new markets, learn more nimble solutions, and support new businesses and entrepreneurs.

Partnerships are a central way to access resources that different types of organizations have—from private company capital to governmental or not-for-profit research—to create change across climate and social areas. Governments and businesses have different strengths and resources, and pooling their capabilities can support quantifiable changes in the lives of employees, communities, and citizens. As we see greater focus on pandemic management, climate solutions, and worker safety and engagement, PPPs that combine investment dollars with intellectual capital can continue to result in short- and long-term economic gain for governments, industries, and communities.

Chapter 7 Takeaways

- Business leaders, especially those who want to leverage partnership opportunities, may benefit from understanding and using PPPs.
- When bidding on projects that involve private and public sector engagement, it is increasingly important to frame ESG considerations as part of the project's scope.
- Entities must be clear about potential risks, which include higher than anticipated project costs, lack of experience among project leaders, and national/global crises. The pandemic is an example of a macroeconomic crisis risk that some partnerships faced.
- When government partners require businesses to improve their operational sustainability—and that of their suppliers—ESG can become a core part of the organization's infrastructure and planning.
- Sustainability-focused firms are seeing success engaging with innovation labs, some of which provide financial support in exchange for a stake in the company.

Notes

1. https://www.henkel.com/spotlight/2021-03-23-it-makes-no-sense-to-stop-using-palm-oil-1163402 and https://www.solidaridadnetwork.org/news/the-power-of-a-palm-partnership.
2. https://www.henkel.com/spotlight/2021-03-23-it-makes-no-sense-to-stop-using-palm-oil-1163402.
3. https://www.thedialogue.org/blogs/2019/09/public-private-partnerships-ppp-in-education.
4. https://www.thedialogue.org/blogs/2019/09/public-private-partnerships-ppp-in-education/#_ftn4.
5. https://www.thedialogue.org/blogs/2014/01/pisa-2012-some-good-news-from-colombia/.

6. https://www.thedialogue.org/blogs/2014/01/pisa-2012-some-good-news-from-colombia/.
7. https://greenbeeinsights.com/esg-in-public-private-partnerships-a-vehicle-for-sustainable-development.
8. https://www.ceres.org/about-us.
9. https://www.ceres.org/networks/ceres-investor-network.
10. https://www.climateaction100.org/whos-involved/investors/.
11. https://www.climateaction100.org/business-case/.
12. https://www.greenbiz.com/article/how-harness-transformative-potential-public-private-partnerships.
13. https://www.greenbiz.com/article/how-harness-transformative-potential-public-private-partnerships.
14. https://greenbeeinsights.com/esg-in-public-private-partnerships-a-vehicle-for-sustainable-development.
15. https://greenbeeinsights.com/esg-in-public-private-partnerships-a-vehicle-for-sustainable-development.
16. https://www.mondaq.com/uk/government-contracts-procurement-ppp/996282/esg-in-uk-public-procurement-taking-social-value-seriously.
17. https://www.mediaoffice.abudhabi/en/economy/adio-launches-esg-policy-to-foster-long-term-sustainable-growth-in-abu-dhabi/.
18. https://www.transform.global/about-transform/.
19. Ibid.
20. https://www.transform.global/news/how-transform-helped-mr-green-africa-get-under-the-skin-of-consumers-to-tackle-stigma-around-plastic-waste-in-east-africa/.
21. https://www.transform.global/where-we-work/?.
22. https://www.dlapiper.com/en/us/insights/publications/2018/12/ppp-projects-in-latin-america/.
23. https://blogs.worldbank.org/ppps/portrait-ppps-latin-america.
24. https://ppp.worldbank.org/public-private-partnership/library/case-study-sao-paulo-telecentres-project.
25. AKE. "Special Report: Public-Private Partnerships (PPPs) in Latin America." (September 2017). https://akegroup.com/wp-content/uploads/2017/09/AKE-Special-Report-PPPs-in-Latin-America.pdf.
26. https://infrascope.eiu.com/wp-content/uploads/2017/02/EIU_IDB_INFRASCOPE_2017-FINAL-1.pdf.
27. https://www.oliverwyman.com/our-expertise/insights/2021/nov/glasgow-financial-alliance-for-net-zero-report.html.
28. https://www.forbes.com/sites/davidcarlin/2022/01/09/climate-stress-testing-is-here-4-ways-your-firm-can-prepare/?sh=14f1b5c11996.
29. https://www.forbes.com/sites/jillbaker/2021/11/08/mark-carneys-ambitious-130-trillion-glasgow-financial-alliance-for-net-zero/?sh=985717b3a312.

169

How Public and Private Partnerships Can Support ESG

30. https://www.cnbc.com/2021/11/03/cop26-climate-finance-pledges-missing-the-point-on-fossil-fuels.html.
31. Ibid.
32. Ibid.
33. Ibid.
34. http://article.sapub.org/10.5923.j.ijcem.20180702.04.html.
35. http://www.worldbank.org/tanianla/economlcupdate [Accessed 10 January 2016].
36. http://article.sapub.org/10.5923.j.ijcem.20180702.04.html.
37. https://d3n8a8pro7vhmx.cloudfront.net/eurodad/pages/508/attachments/original/1590679608/How_Public_Private_Partnerships_are_failing.pdf?1590679608.
38. https://d3n8a8pro7vhmx.cloudfront.net/eurodad/pages/508/attachments/original/1590679608/How_Public_Private_Partnerships_are_failing.pdf.
39. https://www.americanprogress.org/article/americans-want-federal-government-help-people-need/.
40. https://builtin.com/corporate-innovation/corporate-innovation-labs.
41. https://www.morganstanley.com/about-us/diversity/multicultural-innovation-lab/.
42. https://www.morganstanley.com/ideas/coi-energy-multicultural-innovation-lab.
43. https://www.theworkerslab.com/about-us.
44. https://www.theworkerslab.com/the-workers-fund.
45. https://acceleratorlabs.undp.org/content/acceleratorlabs/en/home/about-us.html.
46. See https://www.boston.gov/departments/new-urban-mechanics and http://www.seattle.gov/innovation-and-performance.
47. See https://novascotia.ca/govlab/ and https://www.marsdd.com/partner-with-us/.
48. https://www.missionfrommars.ca/.
49. https://www.international.gc.ca/world-monde/issues_development-enjeux_developpement/priorities-priorites/development_innovation-innovation_developpement.aspx?lang=eng.
50. Ibid.
51. https://www.meda.org/what-we-do/.
52. https://www.convergence.finance/.
53. https://www.bi.team/about-us/who-we-are/.
54. https://www.bi.team/blogs/gender-based-violence-helplines/.
55. https://www.bi.team/blogs/how-much-are-we-willing-to-pay-to-make-home-heating-greener/.
56. https://www.climatefinancelab.org/the-labs/india/.
57. https://www.climatefinancelab.org/the-labs/india/.
58. https://www.climatefinancelab.org/project/low-carbon-auto-rickshaws/.
59. https://pulselabjakarta.org/ourwork#Platforms.

Partnership, Philanthropy, and the Pursuit of Social Good

The first order of business for firms wanting to engage with ESG is to weave sustainability concerns into their daily operations. A second potentially fruitful path is to develop partnerships with other entities, such as non-governmental organizations (NGOs). Businesses that engage with partners may find themselves with increased resources and expertise, especially as it relates to delivering climate and community-focused solutions as part of their company strategy. Successful partnerships between corporations and NGOs can result in better products, more effective philanthropy, and improved outcomes in arenas such as social justice and environmental protection. Understanding how collaborative ventures can play a role in your overall strategy is a good first step toward developing partnerships that support your ESG ambitions. Before we review the benefits of partnerships and how they operate, let's look at different types of organizations that partner with businesses.

Important Definitions

Philanthropy involves efforts made by an individual or organization to further an altruistic desire to assist others in some way. Businesses sometimes form private foundations to facilitate their philanthropy.

NGO is a broad term used to classify organizations not under government control. These entities generally address social, environmental, and political concerns. Though they operate as nonprofits, NGOs may maintain operating budgets in the billions or even trillions; they are largely funded through private donations and government contributions.

Private foundations are charitable organizations funded by a single primary donation from an individual or corporation. Rather than soliciting smaller periodic donations, private foundations generate revenue by investing a large initial donation. They often distribute investment income into other charitable initiatives.

Not-for-profit organizations, or **nonprofits**, are organizations that do not operate for the purpose of gaining profit. Instead, they commit their funds to furthering social causes and public benefit, and as such, they are granted tax-exempt status by the IRS. A variety of organizations are designated as not-for-profits, including those related to religion, science, charity, and public safety.

Today, the charitable sector includes more than 1.5 million organizations, and their philanthropic efforts have proven extremely effective within the ESG space.[1] Many philanthropic investors and donors hold ESG in high regard; they want to place their money with NGOs, foundations, and nonprofits that can further those interests. One of the most valuable attributes of nonprofit organizations is their critiques and challenges of the trends and practices set by the private sector. It is this outside perspective which is so valuable. Increasingly, corporate boards are following nonprofit boards in incorporating climate and other environmental concerns, social justice, and ethical business into their cultures and missions. Similarly, innovative nonprofit organizations have been expanding the list of concerns that they consider as part of their operations.

When private companies partner with philanthropic entities, they can increase their impact on society in all areas of ESG while also benefitting themselves. Businesses can experience such advantages as increased employee engagement inspired by a shared purpose, a boost in sales and reputation as consumers recognize the company's efforts, and increased shareholder returns.[2] Katherine McDonald, cofounder of Radiant ESG, calls this the "halo effect."[3] Speaking specifically about NGOs, she explained that private businesses and philanthropic organizations learn a lot from one another through partnership.

> I think what's [most important] is the learning that goes on for the company and for the NGO; it becomes this kind of virtuous cycle. The company needs to understand the true breadth of threats and opportunities that are associated [with their business], whether it is logging or biodiversity or mining practices, things like that. These public-private or public-NGO partnerships are effective so long as there's an earnestness and an authenticity that goes with it.[4]

Nonprofits can likewise benefit from working relationships with for-profit firms through expanded donor lists, new business connections, increased funding, and improved brand recognition. Nevertheless, once again, poor donor reputation can lead to rejected donations or public backlash, and thus it is important to not simply try and cleanse your reputation through NGO engagement. In 2021, Keep Scotland Beautiful suffered massive reputational damage after they accepted funding from an arms dealer called BAE Systems for their campaign to clean up plastic pollution.[5] Although that is an extreme example, the lesson is clear: nonprofits must be thoughtful about who their "friends" are perceived to be.

173

The broad nature of ESG opens the door to effective collaboration because environmental sustainability, social responsibility, and corporate governance are applicable to every industry in a variety of ways.[6] Through partnerships, for-profit and nonprofit organizations can combine their resources to better meet internal and ESG objectives, while also meeting stakeholder demands in an efficient and cost-effective manner. Partnerships promote information sharing, best practices, and conversations with influential stakeholders. They also increase access to capital, sparking innovation and technology regarding ESG goals.

How Businesses Partner with Organizations

Philanthropic organizations and businesses can work together in a variety of ways. One of the most-common forms of partnerships is through providing a nonprofit with a substantial financial donation that is earmarked for a specific ESG purpose.[7] These are commonly referred to as direct donations, and they can also come in the form of in-kind donations, which are non-monetary physical items or professional services. Businesses may also choose to donate a percentage of sales to the organization or match funds raised and donated by employees.

Other partnership options include corporate sponsorships in which businesses sponsor a specific event held by the organization. Perhaps a nonprofit is holding a tree-planting event or a recycling initiative; in exchange for financial support, the business's name and logo are displayed on event or advertising materials, promoting a positive brand association. Corporate partners can also encourage employees to volunteer with the organization or set up a workplace giving program to match all employee monetary donations to the organization. With partnership fundraising, the business helps the philanthropic organization develop a fundraising campaign in which a percentage of particular proceeds are donated or customers are asked to contribute in some way. These options offer valuable opportunities for businesses and philanthropic organizations to benefit from partnerships while also making positive contributions toward established ESG goals.

Many companies establish private foundations to address their philanthropic ESG objectives.[8] This type of organization enables businesses to formalize these efforts, reducing the potential for wasting time and resources on ad hoc, haphazard giving. Forming a private foundation provides various benefits, including tax savings, enhanced visibility, and a formal structure for philanthropy efforts. Here are just a few examples of corporations that have established foundations:

- The Sanofi Foundation for North America is a philanthropic arm of multinational health care company Sanofi S.A., which is headquartered in France. With a mission to reduce inequities in health care, the organization awards monetary and nonmonetary donations to various medical causes,: providing no-cost products to the uninsured and partnering with nonprofits and NGOs in their emergency relief efforts.[9]

- Spain's Banco Santander created the Banco Santander Foundation, which aims to build a more equitable, inclusive, and sustainable society by developing projects related to culture, environment, and research, and social action.[10]

- The United Kingdom's Barclays Foundation is sponsored by the London-based Barclay's financial corporation. Started in 2020, the foundation initially focused on supporting vulnerable populations against the spread of COVID-19.[11] It will be interesting to track how (and if) the remit of the foundation changes over time.

In addition to foundations, there are other financial tools that can be created to support vulnerable populations. Low incomes and little collateral result in people in poverty being unable to access loans that can support new businesses that may keep those in the community employed and out of poverty.

Grameen Bank has created a structure that enables this population access to loans, largely based off a trust system, which includes removing collateral requirements usually needed to borrow money.

The Grameen family of organizations offers numerous examples of successful corporate and philanthropic partnerships. At its base lies the Grameen Bank, also referred to as the Bank for the Poor, supporting people in Bangladesh with community-based programs.[12] The institution makes microloans to impoverished borrowers without requiring collateral.

Building on that foundation, Grameen also created the Grameen Trust, a nonprofit NGO established in 1989 to expand on the Grameen Bank approach of using microcredit as a tool for poverty reduction.[13] Operating in countries around the world, Grameen Trust trains and educates other entities that are interested in duplicating their structure to support communities who could benefit from microloan systems as a way to combat poverty.[14] With initiatives spanning key markets in sub-Saharan Africa, Asia, and Latin America, Grameen brings "diverse partners into strategic alliances; harnesses technology for improved data and decision-making; uses evidence to deliver results and impact; places poor women and their households at the center of design, and forges business solutions for scale and sustainability."[15] Professor Muhammad Yunus and Grameen Bank received the Nobel Prize for the work done in this area.

In one of its most notable collaborations, Grameen partnered with the French-based Danone Group to create Grameen Danone Foods Ltd., a social business enterprise (We discuss social enterprise B Corps in greater detail in Chapter 2) dedicated to providing children in Bangladesh with an affordable supply of nutrient-rich yogurts and other fortified dairy products.[16] To the partnership, Danone brought expertise in design, production, quality, and nutrition, and Grameen contributed its highly developed network of established branches throughout Bangladesh's rural communities.[17] The partnership has been widely regarded as a success, helping to address the nutritional needs of Bangladesh children and families while also providing an income stream for local farmers who provide milk to the company.

Business executives can look at this partnership as an aspirational model, even if the product and service your business produces falls outside of the traditional ESG realm. If your firm and your employees have a strong interest in a particular segment—be it health, nutrition, climate, etcetera—there may be an opportunity to share resources such as human capital, funding, or even program management support with organizations that have the necessary expertise (like Grameen in this case). The keys to successful partnerships are: 1) an understanding of which organizations have a record of success in specific areas, and 2) clarity on alignment between you and the organization on goals, metrics and what success looks like.

Going back to our example, in addition to furthering its corporate ESG goals, the partnership benefits Danone in a variety of other ways. For instance, Grameen is a well-regarded brand throughout the developing world, where Danone seeks to expand its business. "We can take the mission into territories where we couldn't previously go," says former Danone CEO Emmanuele Farber.[18] In addition, the partnership provides Danone with a type of testing ground for product innovation. During the development stage, Danone discovered an enzyme that can preserve unrefrigerated milk for up to four hours. Although it is currently being used only in Bangladesh, the enzyme could eventually be used in wider capacity. In this case the testing ground had a positive outcome, but it's imperative that companies not test potentially harmful products on populations; this is unethical and clearly can result in reputational damage, repelling customers, employees, and shareholders.

Although Grameen Bank has a reputation for collaborating to eradicate poverty, the Global Fund is known for collaboration on eradicating health problems and diseases. The Global Fund is an international partnership designed to accelerate the end of AIDS, tuberculosis, and malaria. Collaborating with governments, technical agencies, the private sector, and people affected by the diseases, the organization pools global resources for strategic investments. Since its founding in 2002, the Global Fund has disbursed more than $50 billion across more than 155 countries, which makes it one of the world's largest funders of global health. The organization describes its partnership method as centering on a collaborative and nimble approach to solving these health issues.[19] They bring together public and private innovators to deliver essential medicines to people in need. Grant funding supports quality-of-life programs for those living with the diseases.[20]

As of 2021, the private sector has contributed more than $2.7 billion to the Global Fund; clearly, these partnerships are critical to the organization's success.[21] One of the most successful partnerships was the internationally recognized (RED) campaign, where brands such as Apple, Montblanc, Salesforce, and Starbucks sold (RED)-branded products and experiences to support the fight against AIDS.[22] The concept grew from a partnership between the Global Fund and a private marketing company called Product Red. When consumers purchased products with the (RED) logo, a percentage of profits were donated to the Global Fund.[23] Since its inception in 2006, (RED) has generated more than $600 million through the Global Fund.[24] But in addition to this substantial financial gain for such an important cause, participating companies benefitted from the promotion that their products received as well as the enhancement of their social image.[25]

Other notable partnerships include Ecobank, a leading pan-African bank that partnered with the Global Fund in 2014 to support malaria programs in Mozambique and Nigeria.[26] On the private business side, the partnership involved financial contributions, in-kind support, providing financial training for partners, as well as identifying new financing techniques and solutions. Ecobank also engaged its employees and customers in supporting the Global Fund's mission. In 2017, IBM partnered with the Global Fund and the India HIV/AIDS Alliance to pilot a tablet-based mobile app in India aimed at improving quality of care for people living with HIV and TB.[27] They each contributed their strength and expertise, and all partners benefited.

Cynics might argue that many companies are more invested in improving their public image than making a contribution for the greater good. However, as discussed throughout this book, a company's reputation within the ESG space has become a critical component of maintaining its public license to do business. Although today's consumer recognizes the value of a campaign such as (RED) and others like it, they are less trusting than they once were and are more likely to hold a business accountable if they fail to deliver or are not transparent.

What does this mean for you? It means communicating clearly and publicly what you plan to accomplish, then sharing milestone goals—for example, for a three-year goal, ensuring that you track and update progress every six months—outlining how you are progressing. Sometimes you will need to report failure but at least this is honest. This type of information can be shared simply as blog-posts when discussing milestone achievements, as well as formally in your annual sustainability report.

With all of that said, keep in mind that the best results can be seen when efforts are integrated in the daily operations of the business, rather than done as isolated activities. That will not just help your business with its social license to operate but also boost staff morale by increasing employee engagement and collaboration—resulting in increased productivity.

Social Change as Business Strategy: TOMS and Bombas

B Corporations, as we discussed in Chapter 2, have established themselves in the market: (1) as a way to stand out from competitors and really be seen as genuine change agents and (2) because they believe changing the way we do business is the way to change the trajectory of the environment and social issues we grapple with today. TOMS and Bombas provide examples of B Corps from a real world operational perspective. Your company may not be seeking to transition to a B Corp. However, a view into a B Corp's operations, goals, and even their challenges can provide business leaders with valuable case studies around risks and opportunities.

TOMS is a for-profit business that offered a One for One® giving model, meaning that the company gave away one item for every item sold.[28] Though it started out in 2006 as a shoe company, TOMS expanded relatively quickly to also offer sunglasses, bags, and apparel, which may be indicative of its products' quality and the success of its giving model. Through its partnership with IMA World Health, TOMS has distributed hundreds of thousands of shoes to children in Haiti since 2011. The company has also partnered with other nonprofits on initiatives related to sight restoration, the provision of safe water, and supporting safe childbirth. The company's revenue rose to more than $625 million within eight years of its formation, arguably thanks to its reputation as a socially and environmentally conscious corporation.

However, social good is not a replacement for innovation and market-leading products. Although a company may have an admirable social focus, it still needs to maintain strong business fundamentals, such as attention to innovation and product mix, understanding when to diversify, keeping an eye on competitive forces, and knowing what elements affect costs. Business strategists say that TOMS relied too heavily on their shoe products for too long. Once companies began to copy those shoes and sell them for less, TOMS lost its luster.[29] By 2019 the company was struggling financially and ended up being taken over by its creditors.

But TOMS's giving-centric business model and its association with social impact may support the company's rebound. TOMS shifted their strategy to donating one dollar for every three dollars it makes and refocusing its product range to reflect greater materials' innovation and a greater focus on environmental issues and sourcing. This is a key lesson on how allocating a portion of your company's revenue to those in need may provide more flexibility to pivot your giving strategy if the needs of your recipients change. Similarly, donated shoes are of far more limited use to charitable organizations than currency. TOMS may turn out to be one of the best examples of a social impact–focused company course correcting and acting on lessons learned to be able to help even more people and generate even more customer demand.

New York–based apparel brand Bombas is another company that uses a one-for-one donation strategy; for every item purchased the company donates one piece of clothing to a person in need.[30] Through partnerships with shelters, nonprofits, and organizations dedicated to helping at-risk communities, Bombas has donated more than 50 million items of clothes across every state in the union. By placing social giving at the center of its business model, Bombas has crafted a viable plan to assist at-risk populations while still making a profit. It also centers employee satisfaction within its business plan, with a variety of internal communities aimed at fostering employee well-being, such as their system for investing in employee growth and including employees in retooling performance management through comprehensive training programs.[31] Initiatives like this start charity at home and make employees feel valued.

These ESG goals appear to be having a positive effect: according to *Forbes*, only seven people resigned from Bombas as of 2020.[32] In addition, answering widespread calls from consumers, the company expanded its production from socks to other apparel. In a 2019 interview with Yahoo Finance, Bombas cofounder David Heath stated, "I think when we look at the future, we could easily be a billion-dollar brand in revenue in the next 5 to 10 years." He added, "We're not necessarily thinking about, how we're maximizing value for ourselves and our shareholders. We're really thinking about how we build a brand that is going to be around for our grandkids."[33]

Building for the future starts with the people in your organization. Your business' competitive advantage must include fairly compensated, dedicated talent who feel confident their leadership teams and businesses will support their innovation and creativity. Creating a firm that nurtures that confidence can start with steps such as the ones discussed here—that includes investing in employee training and development and gathering employee input in performance platforms.

Battling Controversies while Pursuing Social Good

Although longevity and steady growth is how Heath gauges value for his social change–focused business, it is important that you qualify and measure public criticism and negative press with the same rigor you measure business successes. Even for businesses with strong policies and guidelines in place, sometimes mistakes are made. It is thus important for a business to not only appropriately address this criticism, but to ensure that these impacts are measured.

Unfortunately, negative impacts can also be challenging to fully comprehend. While you can measure revenue or carbon emissions with charts and data, how do you determine the level of negative social impact your business has had on communities?

Robert Blood is the founder and managing director of Sigwatch, an independent data source for reputational and ESG monitoring. In his work, Blood identifies important topics for activists and analyzes trends that lead to those topics becoming real-life controversies that companies must address. He explained how NGOs play a role in dealing with and measuring controversies in context of business outcomes. Controversies typically manifest themselves as either a lack of awareness or deliberate malpractice. Both require an internal shake-up if a business is to move forward. When these controversies occur across multiple media outlets, or if a business is consistently in the press for mishaps, this can lead to a company having a negative controversy score that may damage its overall ESG standing. "NGOs operate to raise controversies or raise concerns about controversies, which then companies and politicians have to respond to. So inevitably, a lot of the work in this area is basically criticism."[34] Hiring expertise from outside your company to help understand where you went wrong can be vital if you are to shake up your practices.

A partnership between the H&M clothing brand and the Asia Foundation demonstrates how joint ventures may help repair damage from a company's past controversies. In 2018, H&M had faced widespread backlash for a racist image they used on clothing and in advertisement campaigns.[35] The advertisement featured a Black child wearing a shirt with the words "coolest monkey in the jungle." As stores were vandalized and celebrities broke ties with the brand, H&M's stock plummeted. Further adding to H&M's problems was a report by Global Labour Justice that named H&M suppliers among factories abusing female garment workers.[36] H&M accepted full responsibility, removed the ad, and investigated the incident, where they found a lack of diversity and cultural awareness at the decision-making level being partly to blame for the advertisement moving forward.

There was a clear need to rectify these wrongs. In 2020, the H&M Foundation joined with the Asia Foundation to address the immediate and long-term impacts of the COVID-19 pandemic in Bangladesh, home to some of the world's leading garment manufacturers and exporters. The Asia Foundation is a nonprofit international development organization committed to improving lives across Asia.[37] Working across the region, the organization focuses its efforts on good governance, women's empowerment and gender equality, inclusive economic growth, environment and climate action, and regional and international relations. According to an Asia Foundation press release, the goal of the H&M partnership was to "address the longer-term needs, welfare, and livelihoods of Bangladesh's female garment workers by supporting their successful adaptation to an automated and digitized 'future of work.'"[38]

Critics may point to this as H&M leveraging the Asia Foundation partnership to counter some of the backlash they'd faced pre-pandemic. Clearly, there is still a long way to go, but some of H&M's efforts may be paying off. They've been able to withstand the challenges of the pandemic while reporting a nine-fold increase in profit for 2021 rebounding sales to pre-pandemic levels.[39] The company has also partnered with the nonprofit Buy from a Black Woman organization to support Black women–owned businesses.[40] In 2022, H&M teamed up with UNICEF to launch the "Be Inclusive" global campaign aimed at raising awareness about children with disabilities.[41]

This demonstrates how a company can build a strategy on supporting key social issues in a way that supports them regaining their reputational footing. However, this is a gradual process: if you are called out, rebuilding trust requires time and cannot be rushed.

Philanthropic Support of Climate Change Initiatives

Although supporting social change is on the rise, we also see efforts to use corporate and philanthropic dollars to affect climate issues.

Climate change has led to the increased severity of natural disasters around the world, increasing the frequency and intensity of storms, floods, droughts, and of course intense heat. What's more, the effects of climate change are worsening many of the societal challenges that were already the focus of philanthropic efforts.[42] Problems in education, health, human rights, and food security have been exacerbated, and the likelihood is that these challenges will worsen in the years to come unless greenhouse gas emissions are drastically reduced worldwide.

Even with these looming problems, philanthropies generally assign a relatively small percentage of their giving to climate issues. According to a McKinsey & Company research article, US-based grant makers disbursed almost $64 billion in 2020 with only about $320 million allocated for climate change.[43] Even the $1.4 billion in additional funds allocated to environmental priorities such as air, land, and water conservation were small when compared to social matters. As a business leader, where you choose to direct your firm's philanthropic resources and capital may help move the needle.

According to the World Health Organization, climate change is expected to cause approximately 250,000 additional deaths per year between 2030 and 2050, due to problems such as heat exposure, malaria, and childhood malnutrition.[44] Racial and ethnic minorities, low-income communities, and less-developed countries tend to be more exposed to climate hazards. For example, African farmers face significant vulnerabilities around rainfall and temperature fluctuations.[45] Research by the McKinsey Global Institute also indicates that the extreme heat resulting from climate change will reduce working hours in poorer countries at a higher rate in the Southern hemisphere than in the Northern.

Social and climate benefits are not necessarily intertwined, but they frequently can be—particularly within certain industries. Farm Africa is an NGO dedicated to the reduction of poverty in the eastern part of the continent.[46] Working in Democratic Republic of the Congo, Ethiopia, Kenya, Tanzania, and Uganda, Farm Africa works to help farmers accomplish a number of goals: increasing the quality and quantity of their products, accessing broader markets for increased sales, and improving the sustainable management of local ecosystems.[47] In furtherance of this mission, Farm Africa has partnered with a variety of private firms. For example, ALDI UK funded their three-year program to support young farmers in Kenya.[48]

UK-based chef Heston Blumenthal and his company, Dinner, has been a flagship supporter of Farm Africa. Through its Dine for Good fundraising campaign, diners can make a donation to the organization when paying for their meals. Other private partners include Oscar Meyer, UK's Barfoots, and Ireland-based Thompsons. Farm Africa's partnership with grocery stores and packaged goods companies is an example of working with suppliers and important partners in a company's supply chain and operative framework (in this case, farmers who supply foods) to ensure you are supporting those partners and communicating the importance of their role through promoting their growth and knowledge.

However, it is notable that while this system has to some extent been successful, any charitable giving aiming at specific populations can have negative consequences. AGRA, a charitable initiative established by the Bill & Melinda Gates Foundation and the Rockefeller Foundation, aimed to improve food security; instead, there has actually been a 30-percent increase in malnutrition within AGRA's 13 focus countries, in part due to a focus on a small number of crop types such as maize.

Here we see that charity can fail if it seeks to bring forward changes that the donors wish to see in communities, rather than actually addressing their wants and needs.

Philanthropic funding of climate change and adjacent areas lags behind funding of other areas and has not increased as quickly.

US philanthropic grant funding, by subject area, $ billion

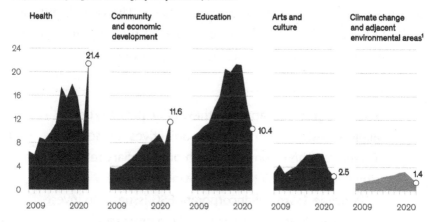

¹Includes funding for climate change, sustainable agriculture, sustainable forestry, forest preservation, environmental education, environmental justice, air quality, energy resources, land resources, water resources, solid-waste management, environmental and resource rights, and atmospheric sciences.
Source: Candid

Source: https://www.mckinsey.com/business-functions/sustainability/our-insights/its-time-for-philanthropy-to-step-up-the-fight-against-climate-change

Principles for Responsible Investing

Although financial services are responsible for much of the funding for carbon-intensive industries, in their day-to-day operations financial services are comparatively removed from the frontlines of environmental impact. In the modern era, this apparent detachment does little to shield the industry from the public desire to know that those who invest our money—for example, 401Ks, pensions, and so on—do so with responsibility to people and environment in mind. This is most relevant for financial services, but other industries that don't have a strong environmental footprint may nevertheless

Partnership, Philanthropy, and the Pursuit of Social Good

provide services to firms that do. If that sounds like your firm, you may benefit from guidance as to how you can support reducing the carbon intensity of the companies you provide services to or who are in your supplier network.

To that end, the Principles for Responsible Investment (PRI) offers business and investors a selection of possible actions for incorporating ESG issues into investment practice.[49] The overall purpose of the PRI is to promote ESG issues as part of the investing process when investors analyze securities for their portfolios.

[We] recognize that applying these Principles may better align investors with broader objectives of society. Therefore, where consistent with our fiduciary responsibilities, we commit to the following:

- Principle 1: We will incorporate ESG issues into investment analysis and decision-making processes.
- Principle 2: We will be active owners and incorporate ESG issues into our ownership policies and practices.
- Principle 3: We will seek appropriate disclosure on ESG issues by the entities in which we invest.
- Principle 4: We will promote acceptance and implementation of the Principles within the investment industry.
- Principle 5: We will work together to enhance our effectiveness in implementing the Principles.
- Principle 6: We will each report on our activities and progress towards implementing the Principles.[50]

Developed by an international group of institutional investors, the PRI offers specific examples of potential actions that can be taken to implement the principles. For instance, regarding Principle 1, the PRI advises investors to address ESG issues in investment policy statements and assess the capabilities of internal investment managers to incorporate ESG issues. Regarding Principle 4, investors are advised to communicate ESG expectations to investment service providers and revisit relationships with service providers that fail to meet ESG expectations.[51] As of early 2021, over 2,700 financial institutions participate in PRI by becoming signatories to the six key principles and then filing regular reports on their progress.[52] These organizations manage total assets of over $100 trillion. One benefit of PRI is that it sends a clear message to the market in general and to specific investors, while holding the investment team in charge of the ESG integration accountable.[53] Although PRI supports organizations developing ESG metrics, they don't specify metrics, progress tracking, and milestones. This perhaps highlights a common flaw within the ESG space: agreeing to adhere to principles on their own isn't enough to ensure enforcement. Thus it is important to ensure rigorous data collection is in place alongside mutual, accurate reporting.

Plastics Partnership Initiative: Tackling Product Packaging

From concern about health consequences of consuming chemicals from packaging to surges in demand for biodegradable plastics, public interest in waste and sustainable packaging is greater than ever. Consumers and other stakeholders are looking to companies who rely on product packing to solve these issues.

Led by international charity the Ellen MacArthur Foundation, New Plastics Economy Initiative is helping to drive change with a commitment to creating a "circular economy" that can address challenges such as climate change and biodiversity loss.[54] The program aims to reduce waste and pollution by keeping products and materials in use rather than in landfills or oceans. Businesses, governments, and regions commit to aligning on clear reporting and 2025 goal setting.[55] Even with clear programs and targets set by the organizations, challenges like lack of regulation, lack of awareness on broader issues, and lack of detailed technical expertise can create hurdles.

In November 2020, through a partnership with World Wildlife Federation and the Boston Consulting Group, the organization called for a UN Treaty on plastic pollution, accompanied by a business manifesto signed by 45 leading companies.[56]

Additionally, the Ellen MacArthur Foundation, along with the UN Environment Programme, established "The Global Commitment" in which 500 companies, who account for 20% of global plastic production, aim to reduce plastic pollution. Mars, Inc., the Switzerland-based food and beverage company, is one of the partner companies. They have committed to reduce its use of virgin (meaning new) plastic by 25% by 2025, while also moving away from single-use and toward reusable packaging.[57] Interestingly enough, in the same year that Mars endorsed the commitment, they secured a spot on the Reputation Institute's Global RepTrak® 100, which is an annual ranking of corporate reputations.[58] Mars also made the list in 2019, landing at number 69. This is no coincidence: when a company engages a strategic partner on improving sustainability efforts in a meaningful way—in this case, reducing its contribution to plastic pollution—consumers and media stakeholders take notice. Partnerships support targeted goals and developing operations and strategies to meet those goals.

Although this is movement in the right direction, business leaders should have a clear sense of just how large the plastics challenge is as they partner with others or set goals to help solve it beyond their organizations. Roughly 90% of ethical packaging pledges are predicted to fail by 2025. Goals are all well and good, but they need to be attainable; otherwise they are just pipe dreams. That's why campaigning for changes to regulation can be an extremely important tool in creating industry standardization and changing supply chains—in banning single-use plastics in most circumstances for instance innovation is forced.[59]

If you are looking to improve your firm's ESG profile, don't just look at what products your company makes—look at what you wrap those products in and how you ship them. Firms such as Mars and Unilever are taking the lead in sustainable packaging as one route to improving their environmental practices. Although sustainable packaging may not be mandated by law (yet!), it is clear that industry is moving toward reducing plastics use. Including this reduction in your business strategy just makes good business sense. Small and mid-sized businesses that believe they can't immediately pivot in this way benefit greatly from partnering with organizations that focus on similar issues. Business and NGO partnerships can effectively share resources and help each other develop a path forward on ESG improvements.

Academia and Business: How Universities Are Preparing Tomorrow's Leaders

For businesses to integrate ESG into their strategy and daily operations, they need employees who understand the intricacies of sustainable operations and have the skills to strategically implement programs that successfully address the company's goals and challenges in innovative ways. That is why recruitment and hiring within these areas of expertise have steadily increased. Academia is meeting the need by equipping new business leaders with ESG knowledge and implementation skills. Business and academia may not be in a formal partnership, but schools are attempting to respond to marketplace demand for equipping students with the necessary skills. This includes a rebalancing of business school curricula that includes not just traditional topics such as banking or mergers and acquisitions but also includes sustainable business. This results from the demand from business for strategic thinking about the climate and social impacts their businesses have on communities, as well as the opportunities and risks.

Training is crucial and often overlooked. Business managers should not expect entry-level employees and even some more senior staff to come through the door with comprehensive knowledge in all fields. This is especially applicable to ESG. Training new employees on your company's overall mission—and on how social and environmental purpose fits into that mission—is vital if you want to build a talent pipeline and increase the diversity of hires. Experience can be as much a sign of privilege as it is competence and thus training is essential in achieving the S section of ESG.

We spoke earlier in this chapter about the need for employees to feel confident about having the support of their leaders. This goes doubly so for employees who might be directly out of school or transitioning into a new industry. Equip new employees with training programs that include hands on work with mentors who can guide and supervise, while enabling new hires to express their own individual perspectives. Even at entry level, it could well be they know something you do not.

The demand for ESG knowledge and skill will continue evolving. Businesses need executives who understand how to finance sustainable programs as well as think through the social and climate risks involved. Asset managers need analysts to identify the ESG risks and opportunities of a security or a portfolio. But recruitment for these roles can prove challenging because only a small number of professionals have worked in sustainable finance for long periods of time. As Richard Oldfield, global markets leaders at PricewaterhouseCoopers, said, "There are not enough people today that know about ESG challenges to meet the demand that exists."[60] This is where directly investing in your employees' knowledge can create a competitive advantage.

Of course, starting salaries and the burden of student debts do still play a significant role in career choices. With extensive education debts, recent graduates may understandably seek the highest compensation options—options which do not necessarily foreground ESG. But this tide may be turning. An unpublished Yale School of Management survey of more than 2,000 students across 29 business schools found that 51% of respondents would accept a lower salary for employment with an environmentally responsible organization.[61]

Final Thoughts

As stated by Kathryn McDonald, cofounder of Radiant ESG, the future will bring a desire for greater collaboration for advancing improvements to the environment and society in general.

> We have historically put corporations over here in one corner, governments [in one corner] and NGOs [in another corner]. I think that there's now an acknowledgement, probably precipitated by the existential threat that is climate change, that we must have greater collaboration between all of these entities, if we are really going to get something done. I believe that there's a very, very strong role for corporations to play when it comes to mitigating climate risk but corporations are not going to solve the problem alone.[62]

Whether it's working with government, NGOs, investors, or academia, the case for collaboration is clear. No single business—regardless of its resources, financial backing, and even desire—can force swift changes in the use of natural resources, investment allocation, or even delivering sustainability education to employees at the same rate and scale that a partnership can. Partnerships provide access to diverse influencers, capital, intelligence, and perspective. When there is alignment in the value and the goals of the collaboration, there is success.

Chapter 8 Takeaways

- Beyond the products and services they offer, businesses can contribute to society through philanthropic giving, as well as foundation development, where they can direct resources and capital toward advancing progress in specific areas such as poverty reduction and health care.
- A good first step to building a potential business partnership is understanding which goals you'd like to contribute to; UN SDG's provide one framework for that. Then seek out examples of successful government or private collaborations that you might emulate.
- Partnerships can come in various forms: direct corporate giving, building a foundation, creating a social enterprise, or giving your energy savings to underserved communities who are in need.
- Even when social change is at the heart of business strategy for companies such as TOMS and Bombas, business leaders shouldn't neglect analyzing market demand, competitors, and product diversification when seeking to grow and compete.
- Education for students and continuous education for those who are currently corporate leaders is the way to ensure today's businesses can improve issues related to climate, social justice, and becoming ethical, well-managed businesses.

Notes

1. https://www.fidelitycharitable.org/content/dam/fc-public/docs/3rd-party/what-makes-an-effective-nonprofit.pdf.
2. https://www.nonprofitpro.com/post/infographics-stats-facts-partnerships-essential-nonprofits/.
3. Kathryn McDonald interview with the author (24 January 2022).
4. Ibid.
5. https://www.thenational.scot/news/19921535.keep-scotland-beautiful-urged-reject-cash-arms-dealers-bae-systems.
6. https://financialservicesblog.accenture.com/meet-the-challenges-of-esg.
7. https://www.volgistics.com/blog/nonprofit-corporate-partnerships/.
8. http://www.valorcsr.com/blog/why-would-you-want-a-corporate-foundation#:~:text=Companies%20generally%20start%20foundations%20%28or%20alternatives%20to%20corporate,main%20reasons%20that%20companies%20start%20their%20own%20foundations.
9. https://www.sanofifoundation-northamerica.org/.
10. https://www.fundacionbancosantander.com/en/foundation.
11. https://philanthropynewsdigest.org/news/barclays-launches-foundation-covid-19-community-aid-package.
12. https://grameenbank.org/introduction/.
13. https://grameentrust.org/about/.
14. https://grameentrust.org/about/.
15. https://grameenfoundation.org/partners.
16. https://www.gca-foundation.org/en/organisation/grameen-danone-foods-ltd/.
17. https://knowledge.essec.edu/en/business-society/a-social-business-success-story.html.
18. https://www.forbes.com/sites/csr/2010/05/21/danone-and-grameen-bank-partners-in-csr-and-marketing/?sh=66f4e1145a38.
19. https://www.theglobalfund.org/en/partnerships/.
20. https://www.theglobalfund.org/en/private-ngo-partners/.
21. https://www.theglobalfund.org/en/private-ngo-partners/.
22. https://www.theglobalfund.org/en/private-ngo-partners/resource-mobilization/red/.
23. https://www.globalcitizen.org/en/content/7-surprising-pairs-of-nonprofits-and-corporations/.
24. https://www.prnewswire.com/news-releases/on-behalf-of-the-private-sector-red-increases-global-fund-replenishment-pledge-by-50-commits-to-generating-usd-150-million-to-fight-aids-over-the-coming-three-years-300936385.html.
25. https://www.globalcitizen.org/en/content/7-surprising-pairs-of-nonprofits-and-corporations/.

26. https://www.theglobalfund.org/en/private-ngo-partners/delivery-innovation/ecobank/.
27. https://www.theglobalfund.org/media/8708/publication_privatesectorempower project_focuson_en.pdf?u=637066556880000000.
28. https://imaworldhealth.org/toms-partnership.
29. https://www.businessinsider.com/rise-and-fall-of-toms-shoes-blake-mycoskie-bain-capital-2020-3.
30. https://bombas.com/pages/giving-back.
31. http://www.theuncommonenterprise.com/issues/how-bombas-is-making-social-impacts-with-a-revolutionary-business-model-369204 and https://www.cultureamp.com/case-studies/bombas.
32. https://www.forbes.com/sites/kathycaprino/2020/03/30/bombas-how-this-mission-driven-organization-remains-profitable-and-impactful-even-in-crisis-times.
33. http://www.theuncommonenterprise.com/issues/how-bombas-is-making-social-impacts-with-a-revolutionary-business-model-369204.
34. Robert Blood interview with the author (January 28, 2022).
35. https://stockton.edu/diversity-inclusion/h-and-m-marketing-controversy.html.
36. https://goodonyou.eco/how-ethical-is-hm/.
37. https://asiafoundation.org/about/.
38. https://asiafoundation.org/wp-content/uploads/2021/09/Investing-in-the-Future-of-Asia.pdf.
39. https://dailytimes.com.pk/876300/hm-profit-soars-as-sales-return-to-pre-pandemic-levels/.
40. https://social.hm.com/en_US/hm-and-bfabw-partnership.
41. https://www.unicefusa.org/supporters/organizations/companies/partners/hm.
42. https://www.mckinsey.com/business-functions/sustainability/our-insights/its-time-for-philanthropy-to-step-up-the-fight-against-climate-change.
43. Ibid.
44. https://www.who.int/news-room/fact-sheets/detail/climate-change-and-health.
45. https://www.mckinsey.com/business-functions/sustainability/our-insights/its-time-for-philanthropy-to-step-up-the-fight-against-climate-change.
46. https://www.farmafrica.org/us/what-we-do/our-work.
47. https://www.farmafrica.org/us/what-we-do-1/our-strategy.
48. https://www.farmafrica.org/corporate-support/our-partners-1.
49. https://www.unpri.org/about-us/what-are-the-principles-for-responsible-investment.
50. https://www.unpri.org/about-us/what-are-the-principles-for-responsible-investment.
51. Ibid.
52. https://www.unpri.org/annual-report-2020/how-we-work/building-our-effectiveness/enhance-our-global-footprint.

53. https://miranda-partners.com/principles-for-responsible-investment/#:
~:text=Signatories%20publicly%20commit%20to%20responsible%20invest
ment.%20The%20biggest,resources%20for%20signatories%20%28like%20
reports%2C%20data%2C%20events%2C%20etc.%29.
54. https://pacecircular.org/new-plastics-economy.
55. Ibid.
56. Ibid.
57. https://ellenmacarthurfoundation.org/mars-incorporated.
58. https://www.3blmedia.com/news/mars-earns-spot-reputation-institutes-global-
reptrak-r-100-second-year-row.
59. https://www.packaginginsights.com/news/failure-looms-as-industry-
environmental-sustainability-pledges-slip-away-reveals-gartner.html.
60. Gross, Jenny. "M.B.A.s Are Embracing E.S.G." *New York Times.* (November 13,
2021).
61. Ibid.
62. Kathryn McDonald interview with the author (January 24, 2022).

ESG Frameworks and Voluntary Standards

A wide variety of stakeholders, from investors to NGOs, depend on corporate sustainability reporting for a number of reasons: one is to assist with decision-making for providing capital; another is to learn about challenges and opportunities in the ESG space. Interest in ESG investing has sparked the growth of numerous organizations, all working to meet the need for reliable and consistent data.[1] Various standards and frameworks facilitate the disclosure of information about corporate ESG actions and plans for improvement. Business leaders are usually familiar with *where* sustainability info is reported: annual reports and sustainability reports are pretty simple to find. Understanding *what* to report is the thing that usually gives executives pause.

If you are confused as to which organizations are supposed to help with which element of your sustainability reporting, you are not alone. Many professionals in corporate and investment sectors bemoan the "alphabet soup" of organizations with acronyms for names. And if professionals occasionally become frustrated with the sheer number of organizations, sorting through them all can be extremely daunting for those without a background in the sustainability field. Nonetheless, executives at every level need to understand which framework or standard provides what level of detail.

This chapter will give you some background on some of the commonly used standards and frameworks and how they can help you with your corporate reporting. For a clear understanding about the differences and relationship between standards and frameworks, we'll start with a brief explanation of why reporting standards are important, and how standards and framework organizations collaborate. Then, we'll review each organization to outline what they specifically bring to the table to support reporting on your firm's current sustainability situation and your improvement plans.

Why Is Consistent Corporate Reporting Important?

Businesses of all sizes and industries should be interested in ESG standards and frameworks because they give valuable insight on what data should be disclosed and how to disclose it. Investors looking to base investment decisions on ESG need to understand how a particular firm incorporates sustainability into their operations. The environmental component of ESG may demand reporting about the use of renewable energy for the reduction of long-term costs. The social criteria for ESG reporting may disclose the firm's efforts to be a good steward of human capital and resources, such as through employee health programs or community-awareness campaigns. Board diversity and retention rates are examples of elements that investors are keen to know about the companies in their portfolios. Investors leverage this data to identify companies that are the best fit for their portfolios.

We can also see how this same information could be helpful for corporate leaders. Understanding your industry's progress around metrics such as the usage of renewable energy and stewardship of human capital provides insight into where your peers are when it comes to ESG issues. This is yet another metric to compete on and should not be overlooked. Industry and peer data of this nature can help you determine if you are a leader or a laggard in your efforts: which areas you might need to bolster, and even how you can measure your own progress year to year. Furthermore, if you have this data on other companies, so do NGOs, regulators, and other stakeholders; they may use this data to determine which companies are not progressing on climate, employee well-being and boosting community investment as they should. These insights into which firms *aren't* keeping up may ultimately become obstacles to the firms maintaining their social license to operate.

In addition to providing important transparency, ESG reporting helps companies from a marketing perspective, providing a pathway for publicly taking credit for their positive advancements.[2] Disclosures enable companies to brag about themselves a bit by highlighting their most impressive plans and accomplishments. This may not only strengthen investor relationships, it can also promote consumer confidence (furthering credibility in social license). That being said, business leaders should be mindful to not treat ESG reports as primarily boasting exercises; doing so would be counterproductive for their relationship with their investors and customers. These reports provide an opportunity for you and for your stakeholders to give honest assessments of current progress, while describing plans to make long-term improvements. In this context, reporting what is needed to improve in the future is just as important as what you have done right in the past.

For companies that have underperformed on key ESG areas, such reporting can quickly be seen as a disadvantage—no one enjoys sharing news of poor performance with investors and consumers. In these cases, it's important to consider whether "progress" might look different depending on long-term versus short-term time frames: sometimes investments in innovation simply take time to pay off. A perceived lack of progress may only be temporary.

Shortfalls and lack of progress is one thing, complete indifference is another. In the case of indifference or constantly being the focus of ESG-related controversies, these can no longer be hidden from investors or the public as easily as they once could. We live in a digital age

201

where consumers can quickly download lists like "top companies for diversity" or "most eco-friendly brands" and use those lists to decide which businesses to support. Negative information affects purchasing decisions and, in severe cases, may even lead to government regulatory problems. Clearly, this is not the position you want your company to be in, and this is not a road to success. However, even companies that haven't met goals and performed poorly in the past may use corporate reports to explain those past errors and present their turnaround plans to course correct sustainability efforts.

Stakeholders like company boards, the financial community, and supply chain business partners also utilize ESG reporting to supplement traditional corporate-reporting activities and assess both tangible and intangible business risks and opportunities.[3] For instance, brand value, corporate resiliency, risk, and growth potential can all be highlighted or called into question through these reports. Armed with this information, stakeholders can make more informed decisions about forming and maintaining business relationships with companies.

Indeed, these stakeholders increasingly expect access to comprehensive, quality, and comparable ESG reporting. And they don't just expect it from large corporations: it is imperative for small and mid-sized companies to implement best ESG disclosure practices to promote their growth and reputations. In addition, large corporations are beginning to spread their ESG goals and expectations to their supply chain partners, which creates an obligation for smaller companies to engage in ESG reporting in order to demonstrate their efforts to comply with the larger corporation's criteria.[4]

One way for a company to think about how to approach corporate reporting is to look at competitors in the industry who are doing it well. Ask a series of questions about their reporting such as:

- Are they providing an annual web-based sustainability report?
- Do they follow a specific framework or standard, or do they combine approaches of various frameworks and standards?

- Which ESG topics do they report on? Where are they outperforming or underperforming?

- What types of policies do they have in place to improve in the future?

- How are they managing their most important ESG issues?

Another thing to consider for your company report, is that it should entail input from various stakeholders inside and even outside your firm. For example the infrastructure technology team may compile data security intelligence, legal may be involved in sharing how successful your firm has been in meeting regulatory compliance, and HR may deliver on worker safety metrics over the last year. Suppliers may also contribute by inputting the number of workplace injuries their workers sustained or their energy and water consumption while working as your firm's vendor.

It's important to have support from your board, internal accountability, and a commitment to transparency even when unearthing ESG results you do not like. Clearly, with so many members of a firm being involved in compiling reporting data, things may be a bit unwieldly. Guidance from standards and frameworks are in place to ensure clarity of approach and that you include the most relevant information that delivers transparency of your operations and policies, while using standard metrics so that it enables easy comparison with other companies in your industry.

Frameworks and Standards Unite

As mentioned in Chapter 5, when the framework and standard-setting organizations (SASB, IIRC, and CDSB) announced their collaboration in forming the ISSB, their aim was to craft a comprehensive and connected reporting system that incorporates financial accounting and sustainability disclosure. The organizations also highlighted the need to present information in ways that are usable by a broad array of stakeholders—not just investors but also NGOs and policymakers—who need clarity on key sustainability challenges. These other stakeholder groups are quite often not included in designing information for traditional financial reporting.[5] But, today's ESG reporting seeks to take them into account. The alliance seeks to provide a sustainability disclosure solution that addresses data needs for diverse audiences who use information in diverse ways; their goal is to include all the elements necessary for a comprehensive corporate reporting system, encompassing traditional financial accounting and sustainability disclosure.

An important part of these organizations working together is the collaboration itself. Collectively, these organizations guide the majority of quantitative and qualitative sustainability disclosures, so this joint commitment demonstrates an important moment in the ESG landscape at a time when businesses, regulators, NGOs, and others are coming together to progress reliable, decision-useful, and comparable corporate reporting data.[6]

It's important to recognize that at the outset—before the announcement about a collaboration—each of the individual organizations were originally designed to address the concerns of specific stakeholders, but they also offer complementary perspectives. The key takeaway for business leaders here is that companies can use aspects from each of these organizations as building blocks for a specifically tailored disclosure system that serves their communications objectives and meets the unique needs of their stakeholders.

Standards and Frameworks in Corporate Reporting

In the context of corporate reporting, frameworks offer principles-based guidance on which topics should be covered and how that information is structured and prepared. By contrast, standards offer

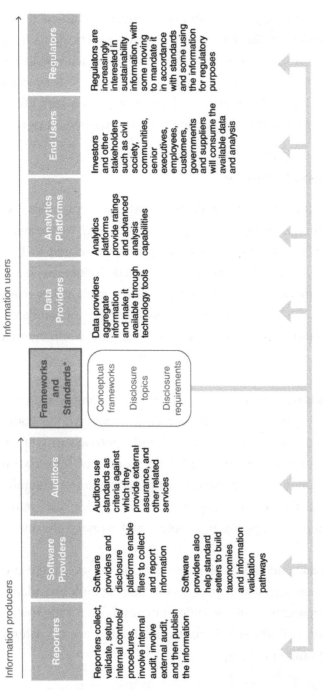

Information producers

Reporters	Software Providers	Auditors	Frameworks and Standards*	Data Providers	Analytics Platforms	End Users	Regulators
Reporters collect, validate, setup internal controls/procedures, involve internal audit, involve external audit, and then publish the information	Software providers and disclosure platforms enable filers to collect and report information Software providers also help standard setters to build taxonomies and information validation pathways	Auditors use standards as criteria against which they provide external assurance, and other related services	Conceptual frameworks Disclosure topics Disclosure requirements	Data providers aggregate information and make it available through technology tools	Analytics platforms provide ratings and advanced analysis capabilities	Investors and other stakeholders such as civil society, communities, senior executives, employees, customers, governments and suppliers will consume the available data and analysis	Regulators are increasingly interested in sustainability information, with some moving to mandate it in accordance with standards and some using the information for regulatory purposes

Information users

Underpins all information

* **Framework:** A set of principles and guidance for "how" a report is structured; **Standards:** Specific, replicable and detailed requirements for "what" should be reported for each topic

Information producers and information users.

Source: "SASB Standards & Other ESG Frameworks." SASB Standards. https://www.sasb.org/about/sasb-and-other-esg-frameworks/

ESG Frameworks and Voluntary Standards

specific requirements for what should be included within each topic, including metrics. In the words of the Sustainability Accounting Standards Board (SASB), "standards make frameworks actionable, ensuring comparable, consistent, and reliable disclosure."[7] They complement one another and are meant to be used together. Let's take a look at the individual standards, starting with an explanation of GRI.

Global Reporting Initiative

The Global Reporting Initiative (GRI) Standards help companies report on environmental, economic, and social data, such as the number of women in senior roles[8] to specific standards related to ESG issues like energy, waste, or biodiversity[9] to stakeholders who are interested in a company's impacts on those issues, such as investors, policymakers, and governments.[10] GRI uses three types of standards, which enable a company to report details about their company in a way that is easily comparable and transparent:

Universal Standards. All companies wanting to comply with the GRI Standards must use the three Universal Standards: the Foundation Standard outlines the principles and approach to GRI reporting; the General Standard guides disclosures of information about the company such as their activities, governance structure, and so on; and the Material Topics Standard guides disclosures about the company's approach to select and manage the material topics.

Sector Standards. GRI has a plan to cover 40 sectors; there are standards that are specific to your sector. For example, standards for the banking sector would be different than those for the forestry sector because of different impacts they might have on natural resources and human capital.

Topic Standards. Disclosures under these standards provide explanations of the important information on the different environmental, social, and economic topics that the organizations should collect to report fully on specific topics. For example, for a standard such as waste, you'd include the amount of waste generated and how your company is handling environmental impacts of that waste.[11]

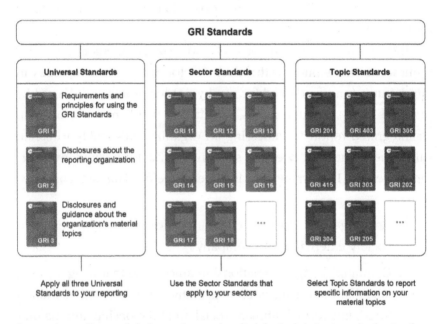

Source: https://www.globalreporting.org/media/s4cp0oth/gri-gristandards-visuals-fig1_family-2021-print-v19-01.png

Value Reporting Foundation: SASB Meets IIRC

In response to growing calls for simplification and clarity in the ESG reporting landscape, in June 2021 the International Integrated Reporting Council (IIRC) and the Sustainability Accounting Standards Board (SASB) merged into the Value Reporting Foundation. The nonprofit foundation aims to help businesses and investors understand the creation, preservation, and erosion of enterprise valuation through a comprehensive suite of resources.[12] To best understand the value of the foundation, let's explore the tenets of the two original organizations.

SASB provides 77 industry specific standards for organizations to meet the needs of their providers of capital. The industry specific standards provide disclosures and topics that are financially material to the organizations.

IIRC represents the framework side of the merger. The IIRC framework was written with private sector, for-profit companies in mind, but it can be adapted for use by not-for-profits and the public sector as well. Although it lists information that can be included in an integrated report for assessing an organization's ability to create value, the framework does not set benchmarks for a company's performance. The IIRC framework includes three fundamental concepts:

1. Creating value for the company and for environment and society external to the company

2. Communicating the relationship among the following six capitals that the organization constantly uses: financial, manufactured, intellectual, human, social and relationship, and natural capital

3. Informing on how company value is created or eroded over time[13]

One important thing to note is that this framework was designed for different stakeholders of the organization—from the providers of capital to customers, local communities, and employees. The framework assists in understanding how these interests all map into how to report information in a way that is useful to this audience range. This integrated report approach includes guiding principles that companies should keep in mind when producing a report, such as conciseness, materiality, consistency, and comparability. Additionally, there should be content elements in an integrated report to categorize significant information. These include organizational overview and external environment, risks, and opportunities.[14]

The Value Reporting Foundation also uses the integrated thinking principles, which guide board and management planning and decision-making.[15] Representing a leadership philosophy centered on value creation over time, the principles are rooted in integrated thinking that leads to integrated decision-making. They promote the collective work of an organization's various departments to create lasting value across financial, manufactured, human, social, and natural capital.

Case studies from the Value Reporting Foundation's Integrated Thinking and Strategy Group demonstrate the real-world benefits that can result from application of the three principles.

It is important to look at real world examples. The BMW Group is one of the world's most successful manufacturers of premium automobiles and motorcycles in the world. It has utilized this framework in pursuing its sustainability goals, placing them at the core of its corporate strategy and decision-making.[16]

In 2020, the company published a report aiming for a greater than 40% reduction of CO_2 emissions by 2030.[17] By 2022 it had accelerated those aims to 50% due to early success. It also targeted its own manufacturing plants for the reduction of CO_2 emissions by 80%, plus a 20% reduction through its supply chains. To do this, BMW's integrated approach includes harmonizing the same business components that most industries and companies have, but making them more efficient. By listening to and leveraging ideas from their workforce, supplying dedicated training programs for employees, dispersing financial capital, including investing in R&D, and clarity in supply chain materials and costs and energy consumed to produce a vehicle, they are able to increase the pace of their innovation. This perspective gives insight into who the stakeholders are: employees, suppliers, and environmental NGOs among others.

Also, this approach shows how the company is affected by external events—for example, how a shortage of supplies can affect production. This also shows how the company can directly affect its external environment, such as emissions from producing the cars. There is tremendous interconnectedness in business: one thing can easily affect another and cascade to affect the entire operation. An integrated-approach mindset helps leaders think through how to mitigate negative impacts and influence positive ones.[18]

The Climate Disclosure Standards Board

The Climate Disclosure Standards Board (CDSB) is a group of businesses and environmental NGOs focused on helping companies report their risks and opportunities in the area of environmental capital.[19] With a focus on developing reporting that puts environmental concerns on par with financial concerns, CDSB provides a framework for reporting environmental data with the same thoroughness as financial.[20] Their offerings not only benefit businesses and investors but also provide regulators with the compliance-ready materials they are increasingly expecting.[21] Released in 2010, its first framework centered on the opportunities and risks that climate change brings to a business strategy and financial condition. That was followed in 2015 by the release of the CDSB framework for reporting environmental and climate change information, and an update in 2018 to align with recommendations on other organizations' key reporting requirements aimed at helping more companies. (This again points to the importance of collaboration to generate data that are more useful for a wider range of stakeholders.)

Evolving user demands led to an expansion of the CDSB framework to include social data as well as environmental, resulting in the

2022 release of the CDSB framework for reporting environmental and social information. We can take this development as evidence that many business stakeholders who are committed to rigor in climate and environmental reporting are adopting the same commitment toward reporting on social elements such as workforce, community, and human rights.

Framework development is overseen by the CDSB Technical Working Group, which consists of representatives from the largest accounting firms, reporting organizations, companies, and academia. Objectives of the CDSB framework include these actions:

- Help businesses communicate the long-term value that comes from their sustainability communication.

- Deliver alignment between an organizations' sustainability performance and its overall strategy, while equipping investors with transparent, consistent company data.

- Streamline the reporting process while adding valuable insights to reports.[22]

In addition, this framework promotes compliance with current and developing regulatory requirements for sustainability reporting, such as the EU Non-Financial Reporting Directive.[23]

Note that the CDSB announced their sunsetting after their collaboration with Value Reporting Foundation to form ISSB.[24]

Carbon Disclosure Project

Though we briefly mentioned the CDP in Chapter 2, it is worth taking a more in-depth look at what the organization contributes to the reporting landscape. Originally called the Carbon Data Project, CDP is an international nonprofit organization helping companies effectively disclose their environmental impact. Their purview is broad in that they engage companies, cities, states, and regions on measuring and reducing environmental impacts.[25] With funding support from a wide range of sources, CDP gathers data on climate risks and low-carbon opportunities from the world's largest companies. This matters in context of the breadth of CDP's scope; they work on behalf of over 680 institutional investor signatories with a combined $130 trillion in assets. These investors rely on CDP to get an understanding of a company and their operation's environmental impacts.[26]

The process begins with a questionnaire that is sent to a particular a company or city; CDP uses responses from that questionnaire to generate a score.[27] Many times this information is reported voluntarily because investors request the information, as might be the case with other frameworks and standards as well. After all, if investors want something, companies are wise to provide it.

Forest conservation and water security are examples of CDP's interests. The organization provides companies with a framework of action to measure and manage forest-related risks, report on progress, and commit to proactive goals aimed at the restoration of forests and ecosystems.[28] In 2019 the organization also began collecting data about the biodiversity impacts, risks, and opportunities present throughout the mining sector.

Though the sustainability reporting structure has grown and expanded, no single standard exists for companies to comprehensively report data related to natural, social, and human capital. That is why efforts to create unified reporting standards are so important. With inadequate information, investors and financial institutions lack what they need to truly account for environmental and social factors in their decision-making.

An absence of reliable information can lead to problems with greenwashing, where companies go through the motions of "greening up" but don't fundamentally change anything that matters. Ironically, poor transparency benefits organizations that just talk about making changes but don't act: they can benefit from their false claims and never back them up. Meanwhile organizations that are truly making progress can get penalized, due to an inability to communicate their work amidst a climate of decreased trust. This is why leaders of small and large businesses alike eagerly await one unified approach to sustainability reporting, as discussed in Chapter 5.

A deeper dive into the newly established ISSB showcases the major impact this development will have within the ESG reporting space. With an objective to put sustainability reporting on the same footing as financial reporting, the initiative will use a building block approach using global sustainability reporting that national and regional jurisdictions can build on to establish supplemental standards tailored to their specific jurisdictional needs.[29] From the perspective of those who provide capital to businesses, investor-focused ESG disclosure, along with the standards they adopt, will be just as consistent (in theory) as the investor-focused accounting data that corporations provide.

Potential metrics and protocols released by the board's task force include data relevant to capital expenditure, financing, or investment in climate-related risks and opportunities; the price for each metric ton of greenhouse gas emissions from internal operations; and the proportion of executive compensation affected by climate-related considerations.[30] Although rapid adoption of ISSB standards is expected in jurisdictions such as the United Kingdom, the speed of adoption is less clear in the United States, where it is taking longer to establish required ESG disclosures at the federal level.[31] However, support for forming ISSB does exist across various governments including Mexico, Saudi Arabia, Singapore, Nigeria, Paraguay, and Jamaica.[32] As such, companies worldwide can and should prepare for the ultimate implementation of these proposed standards.

Valerie S. Grant, managing director and portfolio manager at Nuveen, a TIAA company, spoke about the use of what she termed a "materiality map" to examine the sustainability of individual companies.

> We started with the SASB framework, but then customized it based on the input of our industry analysts who cover these companies globally so we have an idea of what we believe to be most important from an ESG perspective, by sector, and then by industry. Then we look at individual companies [to determine] what's really important for this company. What's really going to have an impact overall on the company's financial performance and its relationships with stakeholders.[33]

Grant went on to say that it gives her confidence when a CFO knows ESG numbers off the top of her head, because "these are things that he or she is tracking in their overall oversight of the company. That's what I mean when I say [ESG] needs to be integrated."[34] She also discussed some of the specific factors that she looks at when reviewing reports across various business sectors. For instance, labor management is a major factor in the retail industry; labor management includes salary, opportunity for advancement, and employee perception. According to Grant, "[If] the company's been telling us that they're doing all these wonderful things, but we [don't] see it show up in the data from what the employees are actually experiencing, then we don't really give them the credit. But when we see the combination of the two, that's usually an indication that things are on the right path."[35] For the utility sector, Grant highlighted the evolution toward renewable energy sources, not just in theory but in practice, saying that it comes back to the CFO again. "A command of both the numbers as well as the strategy . . . that's what gives us confidence."[36]

The Council for Inclusive Capitalism

The concerted effort toward a unified approach to corporate reporting shows business leaders that more rigor around reporting is imminent. But there are other indicators of this trend. Business leaders should be attentive to other organizations—beyond standards and frameworks—that take the pulse of how global society views corporate engagement with climate, environment, governance, and communities. One example showing us ESG demands from the public is only increasing is the Council for Inclusive Capitalism.

The council was established in late 2020 with the backing of the Vatican and the moral guidance of Pope Francis and Cardinal Peter Turkson, who leads the Dicastery for Promoting Integral Human Development at the Vatican.[37] The council has partnered with some of the world's largest business leaders, inviting these organizations to join as stewards and make "their own commitments, scaling actions to improve outcomes for people and the planet."[38] As of January 2022, the council had over 502 commitments and 225 organizations. Its core group of leaders, referred to as "Guardians for Inclusive Capitalism," meet annually and represent more than $10.5 trillion in assets under management, companies with a market capitalization of over $2.1 trillion and with employees located in over 163 countries.[39] Speaking to the guardians, Pope Francis said, "An economic system that is fair, trustworthy, and capable of addressing the most profound challenges facing humanity and our planet is urgently needed. You have taken up the challenge by seeking ways to make capitalism become a more inclusive instrument for integral human well-being."[40]

CEOs from investment and business powerhouses such as Mastercard, Bank of America, BP, Salesforce, and others are taking part in the council and its expressed goal of making capitalism a greater force for sustainability. Through its participation with the coalition, German pharmaceutical company Bayer AG has committed to a 30% reduction in greenhouse gas emissions in major agricultural markets by 2030, and also a 30% reduction in the environmental impact of plant-protection products.[41] Mastercard has committed to 100% renewable electricity for all global operations and planting 100 million trees over five years, along with other coalition initiatives.[42] Shinhan Card Co., Korea's largest credit card company, committed to the reduction of its own carbon emissions by 46% in 2030 as well as in its asset portfolio by 38% in 2030 and 69% in 2040.[43] The company also pledged to convert 30% of its vehicles into zero-emission cars in 2025, 70% in 2028, and 100% in 2030.

Another impressive and telling aspect of the Council for Inclusive Capitalism is its placement of social and governance on the same level as environment within the ESG paradigm. Its priority areas entail "planet, principles of governance, people and prosperity."[44] Some of its people-related initiatives include a commitment from Rwandan tech company ARED Group, Inc., which pledges to bridge the digital and energy gap that exists in Africa through the provision of digital and energy access to more than 10 million people a month, potentially leading to the indirect creation of more than 10,000 micro-entrepreneurs in the next five years.[45]

These commitments to improving the well-being of those who live and work in the communities where we do business proves that we can "walk and chew gum" when it comes to promoting climate and environmental efforts, including actions and reporting those actions.

Final Thoughts

It is in the best interest of companies to quantify their ESG work, such as how much they've reduced CO_2 emissions or lowered the amounts of water used in their operations. But it's also important to go beyond the numbers. Especially in cases where the company's ESG progress is not up to par, framing an explanatory narrative may help demonstrate how you plan to address areas where you may be lacking. For example, if you don't have underrepresented groups on your board of trustees, explain your plan for changing that in the near term. Or, if you've had data security issues that resulted in lawsuits, describe what your company has done to improve security.

Whether an investor or a policymaker is viewing your report, this type of information helps them get a full picture of what your company is doing to improve your impacts on planet and people while also giving them insight into your strategies for mitigating issues that affect your business, such as the effect climate risks have to your business locations. A good reporting structure—complete with proper use of frameworks and standards—can help you deliver your numbers, as well as provide commentary about your strategies for future improvement. With general standards in place, companies can evolve from climate-centered reporting to the inclusion of broader social issues, including workplace issues and wider community concerns.

Chapter 9 Takeaways

- Standards and frameworks are used by corporate leaders, governments, NGOs, employees, and others. They can be used to complement each other to show how nonfinancial information (e.g. sustainability data) may affect a company or how a company is affected by issues such as climate change and the social happenings where that business operates.
- Reliable, useful, and comparable corporate reporting benefits a host of users. For example:

ESG Frameworks and Voluntary Standards

- Investors who are examining the risks and opportunities associated with firms in their portfolios
- Company leaders who want to understand where their peers and their broader industry rank in ESG, determining whether they are lagging behind and how to improve their efforts
- Companies of all sizes need to maintain—or create, if they haven't done so—reporting processes related to their sustainability goals and efforts.
- Successful business should tune into industry organizations, NGOs, and others to check public sentiment about ESG. Understand the issues these organizations are responding to and how they are prioritized.
- Savvy business leaders are looking beyond environmental issues and strategizing how to improve their social standing in areas such as diversity and inclusion, employee engagement, and community relationships.

Notes

1. https://www.sasb.org/about/sasb-and-other-esg-frameworks/.
2. https://www.inogenalliance.com/blog-post/what-esg-and-sustainability-reporting-and-why-it-important.
3. https://www.inogenalliance.com/blog-post/what-esg-and-sustainability-reporting-and-why-it-important.
4. Ibid.
5. Ibid.
6. https://www.sasb.org/blog/progress-towards-a-comprehensive-corporate-reporting-system/.
7. https://www.sasb.org/about/sasb-and-other-esg-frameworks/.
8. https://www.globalreporting.org/standards/media/1020/gri-405-diversity-and-equal-opportunity-2016.pdf.

9. https://www.globalreporting.org/about-gri/news-center/2020-05-22-agriculture-and-fishing-project-working-group/.
10. https://www.globalreporting.org/media/wtaf14tw/a-short-introduction-to-the-gri-standards.pdf.
11. https://www.globalreporting.org/media/wtaf14tw/a-short-introduction-to-the-gri-standards.pdf.
12. https://www.valuereportingfoundation.org/about/.
13. https://www.iasplus.com/en/resources/sustainability/iirc.
14. Ibid.
15. https://www.valuereportingfoundation.org/resources/resources-overview/.
16. https://www.integratedreporting.org/wp-content/uploads/2022/01/VRF_Case_BMW-final-to-publish-28.1.2022.pdf.
17. https://www.integratedreporting.org/case-studies-from-the-business-networks-integrated-thinking-strategy-group/.
18. https://www.integratedreporting.org/wp-content/uploads/2022/01/VRF_Case_BMW-final-to-publish-28.1.2022.pdf.
19. https://www.cdsb.net/our-story.
20. Ibid.
21. https://www.cdsb.net/what-we-do/reporting-frameworks/environmental-information-natural-capital.
22. https://www.cdsb.net/what-we-do/reporting-frameworks/environmental-information-natural-capital.
23. Ibid.
24. https://www.cdsb.net/.
25. https://www.cdp.net/en/info/about-us.
26. https://www.cdp.net/en/climate.
27. https://www.cdp.net/en/guidance; https://www.cdp.net/en/scores.
28. https://www.cdp.net/en/water; https://www.cdp.net/en/forests.
29. https://home.kpmg/xx/en/home/insights/2021/11/sustainability-reporting-climatechange-issb.html.
30. https://www.theimpactivate.com/new-international-sustainability-standards-board-aims-to-unify-esg-metrics/.
31. https://home.kpmg/xx/en/home/insights/2021/11/sustainability-reporting-climatechange-issb.html.
32. https://www.theimpactivate.com/new-international-sustainability-standards-board-aims-to-unify-esg-metrics/.
33. Valerie Grant interview with author (December 12, 12022).
34. Ibid.
35. Ibid.
36. Ibid.
37. https://newsroom.bankofamerica.com/content/newsroom/press-releases/2020/12/the-council-for-inclusive-capitalism-with-the-vatican--a-new-all.html.

219

38. https://www.inclusivecapitalism.com/.
39. https://newsroom.bankofamerica.com/content/newsroom/press-releases/
2020/12/the-council-for-inclusive-capitalism-with-the-vatican--a-new-all.html.
40. Ibid.
41. https://www.inclusivecapitalism.com/organization/bayer-ag/.
42. https://www.inclusivecapitalism.com/organization/mastercard/.
43. https://www.inclusivecapitalism.com/organization/shinhan-card/.
44. https://www.inclusivecapitalism.com/commitments/.
45. https://www.inclusivecapitalism.com/organization/ared-group-inc/.

Challenges of Today and Tomorrow

B oth dialogue and action concerning ESG has progressed significantly over the last couple of decades, but there is no denying
that strides made in environment and climate change spaces have
far outpaced those made in the social space. Still, thanks to inter-
sectionality between environmental rights and social rights such as
water and food security, we are seeing benefits spilling into social
aspects of doing business. This is also a result of changing priorities among consumers and investors. In this chapter, we'll discuss
what the future of ESG will look like—primarily as the social aspect
progresses—and how businesses can evolve in response.

That said, this chapter does not neglect climate and environment.
Rather it focuses on the new terrain companies will encounter—
and need to master—if they hope to succeed in tomorrow's ESG
landscape.

Social Issues Ascendant

Michael Posner served in the Obama administration as the Assistant
Secretary of State for Democracy, Human Rights and Labor.[1] He explained that although ESG has been around for 15 to 20 years, the
focus has almost exclusively been on the *E* and the *G*. "There's a couple of reasons for it. One is, it's harder to come up with a common

definition of what is social. Second, even if you come up with a definition, it's probably going to be different in different industries."[2] He offered labor rights as an example of this point. "If you're talking about labor rights in a supply chain for manufacturing, that's very different than privacy or disinformation for a technology company. And that's different, again, from the social issues relating to mining practices in a conflict zone. And all of those things are different from issues of diversity and inclusion. So there's many, many definitions of what S is."[3] Posner added that the S can be extremely difficult to measure and quantify, before concluding with the fourth reason that S lags behind. "I would say in most instances . . . if you drill deep on the S and figure out how to correct the inherent operation challenges that actually resolve the S, it requires time and money."[4]

In the past, the goal of revenue generation often trumped any responsibility to respect the rights of the citizens in the communities where they did business. For instance, sometimes firms refused jobs or service to people on the basis of race, or they offered poor working conditions, or they released toxins into the air and water. In the future, considering the continued strength of activists and social media, the ease of retail investing, and the power of active consumers alternatively boycotting and buycotting products, firms must operate in a space of greater respect for and partnership with communities where they do business. Business leaders that fail to champion this model will be replaced by leaders more willing to partner with their communities.

The following are some examples of companies that have handled social challenges well, alongside companies that have room for improvement. We will also see cases in which the overlap exists within the ESG space. For instance, some social issues have governance concerns and many have environmental concerns.

When Companies Understand Women's Rights are Human Rights

Companies that pledged support to women's reproductive health-care after the June 2022 Supreme Court decision are promoting a 'social' aspect of ESG in its most basic sense. Women make up about half the population. Progressive business leaders are working hard to ensure those numbers are represented in their workplace. Creating an environment for half of a corporate population to thrive includes creating an environment where women feel they are protected; they feel their company has their backs even when other establishments don't.

In June 2022, Nike released the statement:

"No matter where our teammates are on their family planning journey — from contraception and abortion coverage, to pregnancy and family-building support through fertility, surrogacy and adoption benefits — we are here to support their decisions,"

In the past, corporations have benefited from being on the "right" side of civil rights or marriage equality; likewise, companies that stand up for reproductive healthcare will be celebrated for their rational and compassionate support of their workforce.

(*Source:* https://www.cbsnews.com/boston/news/dicks-star-bucks-among-companies-to-cover-employees-abortion-related-travel/)

Indigenous Rights and Corporations

In 1990, the UN Global Consultation on the Right to Development declared that "the most destructive and prevalent abuses of Indigenous

Challenges of Today and Tomorrow

rights are the direct consequences of development strategies that fail to respect their fundamental right of self-determination."[5] Though Indigenous peoples' rights have progressed since that time, the sentiment remains more relevant than ever. Corporate actions worldwide consistently threaten Indigenous populations—governments and companies almost always place the value of the resources on these lands above the rights of those who inhabit them. Too often, companies ignore the cultural connections that these populations have to their lands, as well as the extent to which they depend on the land for their livelihoods. Activities such as mining, deforestation, oil drilling, and water appropriation are routinely carried out on Indigenous lands, in spite of protection programs that intend to prevent those activities.[6] Today, company managers can no longer be ignorant of the fact that Indigenous peoples' knowledge of land, water, and air— and how to protect them—is rooted in generations of expertise as caretakers of their environment. Business leaders must understand that firms should not attempt to wield their power over them during negotiations and conversations about use of the land. You must seek the guidance of the community and genuinely work with them, not ignore them or shout over them.

As Michael Posner explained in our interview, the corporate valuation of land—predicated on what can be extracted and sold—is in tension with the ways Indigenous communities value the same spaces. "And so it's often the case that people are evicted as the lands are exploited in ways that hurt Indigenous communities and their ability to live and farm and exist."[7] He said that these controversies happen often and in a variety of industries, "but in any industry where you're trying to get something out of the ground that's valuable, there's likely to be a conflict and there's likely to be a high potential of infringement on an Indigenous population that's in those places."[8] Displacement, food scarcity, and the decimation of traditional livelihoods jeopardize the public health and communities of Indigenous people where land is a source of economic, spiritual, ancestral, and cultural connection.[9] Business leaders must understand that land has value beyond its ability to generate a revenue for their firms. Abusing land because the practice suits your firm fiscally is not good social or sustainability practice; such activities are unlikely to be tolerated by future investors, employees, and consumers.

The palm oil industry provides a useful example. Today, palm oil plantations constitute 10% of all permanent crop land.[10] Though the exportation of palm oil has sparked economic improvements within many countries with large Indigenous populations, it is a labor-intensive industry that has been embroiled in numerous controversies. In 2021, violence ensued in Guatemala as community members fought the expansion of the palm oil industry onto their traditional lands.[11] In an effort to reclaim the area, they built homes on the disputed tract, which led to eviction notices and a vast enforcement presence that resulted in deadly violence. The rapid expansion of palm oil plantations has sparked hundreds of conflicts over lands and natural resources across the country. The Roundtable on Sustainable Palm Oil, a palm oil industry group, asserts that nearly two-thirds of all palm oil produced in Guatemala is certified as sustainable by international standards.[12] However, global activists routinely characterize this as a meaningless classification, pointing to incidents around the world where palm oil production is linked to environmental destruction within Indigenous communities and labor rights abuses. Certifications should be chosen wisely, looking at how they contribute to resolving the issue. They should definitely not be seen as an alternative to a company's reporting on ESG performance. The companies should be looking at striking the right balance between managing the ESG issues internally as well as getting their processes certified.

Wilmar is another example of a business potentially threatening Indigenous cultures' way of life. The Singapore-based agri-business

225

runs numerous palm oil plantations in Indonesia; they supply oil to the likes of Unilever, Nestlé, and Procter and Gamble.[13] Communities in West Sumatra and West Kalimantan say the palm oil company is seizing their lands.[14] Amnesty International conducted an investigation into human rights allegations against the company and reported numerous findings related to the exploitation of Indigenous workers.[15] Wilmar has also faced accusations of destroying the homes of natives in the Sumatra Islands and forcing them away from their land for the purpose of using the space for additional palm plantations.[16]

This perhaps points to an important but little talked about facet of ESG, which is knowing when to walk away from a deal because ethical business practices can simply not be written into it. Local political will to use a Westernized economic model is often not very prevalent on Indigenous lands, where community rights to land and shared wealth are more important. Not every opportunity can be exploited, and it is vital to know this limit. You can make an offer that seeks (to the best of your abilities) to help those on the land by entering into a partnership that protects their right to primacy and control over it; but if they turn this down (which they have every right to do), to force it through in any way is to participate in deeply unethical behavior, land theft, and potentially even serious violations of international law. Given that Indigenous peoples currently act as stewards for a large swath of the world's remaining biodiversity, there is much that can be learned from them about ESG, such as a lack of prioritization of financial gain and measuring success by metrics beyond the financial.

Many companies still attempt to steamroll over the will of Indigenous people, in spite of protest. The oil and gas sector in particular is notorious for violating the rights of Indigenous people. In fall 2016, Native Americans and their supporters staged a mass protest at the Standing Rock Sioux reservation in North Dakota against the Dakota Access Pipeline.[17] Energy Transfer Partners (ETP) was the company behind the pipeline, and tribal members said they were not given the opportunity to engage and give their input on the route. They said that the construction would disrupt their water supply and would damage sacred sites near the Missouri River in violation of established treaties.

Although it's fair to say that financial losses should not be a priority when considering such egregious ethical breaches, it's worth noting that ETP did sustain large losses as a result of their policy of Indigenous dispossession. To be blunt, such policies don't just create misery, but they increasingly make poor financial sense. A 2018 case study by University of Colorado Boulder examined the financial costs suffered by the company and its backers in relation to their business practices and protests against the pipeline.[18] Researchers concluded that ETP's stock not only decreased in value during the controversy, but that declining stock values remained after project completion. "In fact, from August 2016 to September 2018, ETP's stock declined in value by almost 20% whereas the S&P 500 increased in value by nearly 35%."[19] The case study estimates ETP and others that participated in the Dakota Access Pipeline deal had costs that stacked up to more than $7.5 billion. Although the precise number is impossible to state, there's no doubt that some of those losses resulted from stakeholder dissatisfaction with how the project's outcomes affected the local community.

There were additional costs to banks that financed the project. The report suggests that money losses came in part from people or organizations closing accounts with the banks because of their role in the Dakota Access Pipeline project. The study goes on to address the social costs, which researchers said reached beyond the financial investors into the local communities, and even the governments of the tribes, who often have limited resources to dispute these types of projects. As the report states, "These communities often bear the financial burden when companies fail to obtain consent from Indigenous peoples regarding projects that impact."[20] Lastly, the report points to the tremendous amount of support that the Standing Rock Sioux tribe received from Indigenous people and their allies around the globe, largely based on the commonality of the challenges brought about by the Dakota Pipeline.

The DAPL controversy pushed these issues to the forefront, but the themes underlying the wider social movement continue to simmer in Indigenous communities around the world.[21] As Indigenous communities become more active voting blocks, expect these issues to become more prevalent.

Of course, not all projects will be as intrusive—or as controversial—as a major oil pipeline. Still, there are important steps to take if you wish to engage in business in proximity to Indigenous land. Here are a few:

- Consult with appropriate tribal community members—listen rather than dominate.

- Adhere to government policies on these issues—do not try and operate on the edge of what is legal, instead simply be more considerate.

- Perform due diligence as it relates to cultural consequences around your business actions; understand that local valuations of the land may differ from yours and must be respected.

A lack of communication and consultation is quite justifiably seen as a lack of respect for the people on the land.

Many of these principles can extend beyond just Indigenous peoples, to all underrepresented people. Whether it's building a grocery store in a food desert where not a single employee lives within a five-mile radius, or participating in infrastructure planning to build a freeway that will cut through the middle of a neighborhood, people are affected, but many times not considered. Your business expansion may be profitable for your business, but recognize there are people and communities involved who want to see a benefit for *themselves*. A true win for the business should not come at the expense of people's livelihoods and homes, especially when they have not received the opportunity to give input. A win for the business really comes when the community has the opportunity to thrive and benefit from a partnership. Shareholders, media, and customers will recognize your business's intention toward inclusivity and collaboration, and other companies in your industry may even begin to follow suit with you leading the way.

Think about it this way: any short-term costs you incur from time and resources it takes to establish relationships will hold less weight than intangibles such as improved reputation, and industry standing. This is the future of incorporating social change—as a part of ESG—into business strategy. If your long-term play is to lead your industry and gain market share, being attentive to social engagement in the communities where you do business is the right approach.

Indigenous Community Engagement

As ETP learned the hard way, companies that infringe on the rights of the Indigenous communities where they operate can face financial and social backlash. It's essential to engage proactively with local communities and actively respond to their concerns. Companies, banks, and investors must perform inclusive due diligence and be transparent about company operations and any potential harm. Through practical steps, such as hiring individuals from the communities and effectively addressing their concerns, companies can better engage with Indigenous communities to identify, prevent, mitigate, and account for the human rights impact of their activities. One of the most important decisions you can make as a business leader is knowing when to walk away from a deal. In this context,

229

Challenges of Today and Tomorrow

discontinuing a project because it can't be done without infringing on others is a valuable, strong, and wise decision to make.

Repsol S.A. is a Spanish energy company based in Madrid. To combat infringement on the rights of Indigenous populations, the company leverages outside reports that incorporate local and community feedback to understand best practices for working with the people there.[22] In another example, Colombia's Cerrejón coal mine offers training to their staff to ensure knowledge about local culture, norms, and a deeper dive into the Indigenous Wayúu language, ethnicity, and their perspectives on and interactions with nature.[23]

Transparency as well as ongoing measurement of progress is another way to build trust between businesses and communities where they do business. BHP Billiton is an Australian-based mining, metal, and petroleum company operating globally.[24] It undertook remediation efforts after receiving complaints from Indigenous communities regarding a copper mine in Peru. The company's plan to establish open lines of communication with the affected community included collaborations with local and international NGOs. BHP also voluntarily participated in a commission of multiple stakeholders established to investigate and resolve concerns pertaining to environmental impact and human rights. The resulting agreement established a community development fund accompanied by ongoing monitoring of environmental impact.[25]

Words without Deeds

It's important to note that corporate actions in the arena of community engagement should not be just for show. They need to be genuine in substance, not just appearance. For instance, in response to highly publicized protests against their natural gas

---

pipeline on First Nations land, Canadian oil and gas companies have reportedly put significant resources and effort into advertising campaigns that portray themselves as advocating for the rights of Indigenous people.[26] These fossil fuel companies spend tens of thousands of dollars on hundreds of targeted Facebook and Instagram ads pushing support for their oil and gas projects.[27] The companies' ads include strategic buzzwords such as *defender*, *eco-colonialism*, and *reconciliation* to imply that their project outcomes actually promote the interests of Indigenous groups and that their economic development potential is necessary for the alleviation of Indigenous poverty. Critics accuse these companies of "Indigenous-washing," saying this activity is comparable to greenwashing except with Indigenous communities instead of climate.

Product Design and ESG

When companies think about product design, the first ESG component that comes to mind tends to be the environment. They ask questions such as, how can our products be made more sustainably or how can they be recycled more effectively? That's all important, but there is an *S* component to product design as well, which has to do with accessibility, in context of including marginalized groups with physical differences. Companies that build accessibility into their product design strategy will have a competitive advantage as a future industry leader that has inclusivity and equity at the heart of their business.

When companies leave a subset of the population out of their product designs, the results can be challenging, or even dangerous, for those not taken into consideration. This typically occurs because companies have historically defaulted to white, able-bodied males when designing and developing products for use within the mass

Challenges of Today and Tomorrow

marketplace. Although this design decision may not have an impact on the use of some products, others can cause significant problems.

Machine learning algorithms, particularly those involving facial recognition systems, offer prime examples of racially biased product development. In 2015, a software engineer discovered that his African American friends were being categorized as gorillas when their images were evaluated by Google Photos.[28] After making his findings widely known, Google responded inadequately, by simply removing gorillas from the dataset instead of taking the time and effort to modify the algorithm. This raises questions about Google's lack of representation within its product development processes— further exacerbated by the company's meager number of Black employees overall (only about 4% as of 2021).[29]

Another example comes from the automotive industry, where poor product design can prove physically dangerous. Automotive design has traditionally been based on the physical traits of males, which means that seatbelts have been designed and manufactured to fit the height and weight of an average-sized male, which left out a variety of body types and sizes.[30] As such, studies have found that female drivers, and particularly pregnant female drivers, have been at a substantially higher risk of injury when involved in an automobile accident. It was not until 2011 that the industry started requiring the additional use of test dummies modeled after the average-sized woman.

Individuals with varying levels of abilities often have to use products not designed with them in mind. In 1990, the Americans with Disabilities Act established accessibility standards for areas of public use.[31] As a result, society saw increased accessibility in the design of stores, government buildings, parking lots, and bathrooms. But these regulations did not extend to the products, tools, and devices that companies offer to their consumers. This gap in the legislation results in less effort undertaken by businesses to ensure product accessibility. Business executives should leverage their research and development (R&D) teams to get an understanding of who uses their product currently and what changes in design they can make to enable others—who aren't currently using it—to be able to use it easily. For the most success in doing this, include diverse voices in your R&D and product testing efforts. As a savvy business executive who wants to lead their industry into the future, innovate before regulations force you to innovate. Be led by your customers and cater to their needs.

As we've seen over and over in the course of this book, pursuing positive change in ESG is not just about "doing good"—it can also be about "doing well." After all, adults with disabilities have an estimated combined purchasing power of about $490 billion, including $21 billion in discretionary funds.[32] This net-worth would be greater if there was adequate support within products. When companies fail to consider these consumers in their design process, they are marginalizing people with disabilities and missing out on a number of fronts—yes, on valuable revenue, but also on valuable customers. They also send a subliminal message that they do not *want* to provide products or services for this population of consumers to use.

One area where accessibility has become a major concern is in the design and functionality of business websites. In 2017, a court ruled that grocery chain Winn Dixie violated the ADA by not providing access to online shopping for the visually impaired.[33] The court found that Title III of the ADA required equal accessibility, classifying the store as a public accommodation. The ruling was later overturned in the states of Alabama, Florida, and Georgia, based on the 11th Circuit Court of Appeals opinion that the Winn Dixie's website was not a public accommodation. Nevertheless, the initial decision brought wide attention to a serious social issue. Many businesses across all industries began paying attention to the accessibility of their websites and made appropriate changes. Website accessibility tests such as accessibilitychecker.com and accessibility tech companies saw their use skyrocket as businesses of all sizes sought help for improving the accessibility of the websites.[34] Coca Cola, Jenny Craig, Disney, eBay, and Porsche are just a few of the corporations that have sought outside assistance for improved website accessibility.[35]

Diversity and Inclusion in Product Design

Product development discrimination often indicates a lack of diversity within a company's design and manufacturing ranks. Investors are increasingly pointing to diversity as a key consideration and discussion point with firms in their portfolios. As investors focus on building a more just society, corporate attention to this S part of the ESG pillar is critical for businesses to connect with a variety of customers and ensure innovation that comes from an inclusive approach to employee engagement. Diversity and inclusion are key pieces to this puzzle, and every step of the product development can benefit. Companies need people who can speak to diversity concerns from the design table to the board room. Firms also need to start thinking beyond their ideal consumer when designing their products and consider a larger demographic as potential customers. After all, doesn't it benefit your firm to offer your product or service to as many potential buyers as possible?

Sarah Gordon is the CEO of Impact Investing Institute. She spoke about the fact that, though many companies make a lot of noise about equity, diversity, and inclusion, they don't actually have to meet any minimum standards. There are no formal disclosures or standards that insist companies demonstrate their "commitment" and how it is translated into genuine action.

A taxonomy is only as useful as what it's used for, but its usefulness would be in holding businesses much better to account for their claims, saying what social issues should be included in the *S* of ESG. Then, they need transparency so that investors, individuals, and all stakeholders, whether it's the government, whether it's customers or clients, can have much better transparency over how businesses are performing in this regard.[36]

Several companies are making efforts to get it right by taking steps to encourage diversity within product development. For instance, in 2019, The Gap, Inc. was named by the Refinitiv Diversity & Inclusion Index as one of the world's most diverse and inclusive companies for the third consecutive year.[37] Its product diversity commitments include True Hues, an initiative of the company's Color Proud Council. This an internal organization was started by employees to advance diversity and inclusion across the company's product development process, including design, merchandising, and marketing.[38] The Gap also held a Product Inclusion Summit to "explore how to grow the company's capacity to serve all those who want to work for and shop with them."[39] The event included a brainstorming session about inclusive design for diverse types of women—not only those with disabilities but also those who are breastfeeding or are non-binary.

Business executives need decision-makers who have different world views. Gone are the days when one "diverse" person in the executive suite was responsible for understanding and communicating the needs of all marginalized groups. This habit was not only unrealistic, it was exhausting for employees and often led to burnout.[40] To successfully build inclusive design for products, you must have an inclusive business team. The more diverse perspectives you include—and the more team members are empowered to make real decisions—the less shallow your actions to improve workplace culture will be.

Tech giants Microsoft and Logitech have also been making headway with accessible product design. They have each designed accessible controllers and other accessories designed to interact with their game consoles.[41] In 2019, Logitech introduced its Adaptive Gaming Kit, which lets gamers configure the components in ways that they find most accessible.[42] The Switzerland-based company worked closely with the Microsoft Inclusive Tech Lab to design and develop the product.[43] They also partnered with various accessibility groups and enlisted feedback from users with disabilities during the product design and development phases.

Decades ago, we didn't see a strong focus on inclusivity in product design. That was at our peril. Today, customers and investors are driving the conversation about the need for diversity at every level. Successful companies of tomorrow are listening to these stakeholders and delivering products accordingly.

Customer Privacy and Data Security

Companies have a responsibility to respect the privacy of their customers and protect their personal data—this is not just good practice, it's the law. Businesses of all sizes need systems in place to ensure consent for data collection and proactively prevent its unauthorized disclosure. Policies and systems to support this help reduce the litigation we see so frequently today in this space. Lawsuits not only hit a company's financials today, but they can increase the cost of capital—or the cost to borrow money, such as an interest rate—for years to come. Clearly, this situation would not bode well for a company's reputation, much less its sustainability and ESG standing.

In 2022, Meta, the parent company of Facebook, agreed to settle a decade-old privacy lawsuit for $90 million.[44] Claims included accusations that the company continued tracking users' internet activity after they had logged out of Facebook. The lawsuit alleged that

Meta's actions violated federal and state privacy and wiretapping laws. Additional accusations asserted that Facebook then sold the users' browsing data to advertisers. The case was previously dismissed in June 2017, but a federal appeals court overturned the dismissal in April 2020 and reinstated the case. Since that time, Meta has made numerous—but unsuccessful—efforts to have the case thrown out.[45] Though the company still denies any fault or wrongdoing, it reportedly settled in order to mitigate the costs of litigation and the negative commentary that would accompany a potentially adverse court ruling. Meta spokesman Drew Pusateri said that settling was "in the best interest of our community and our shareholders and we're glad to move past this issue."[46] This lawsuit amount may seem small for a company of Meta's scale, but the company is increasingly seeing reputational consequences in the public sphere as a result.

So, how long will it take for the court of public opinion to move past the issue? Tech companies that can access personal data continue to weigh on the minds of regulators, as well as consumers, who want to progress policy changes that keep our data safe. In addition to the possibility of impending regulation, lawsuits from data mishaps can do irreparable damage to the trust companies need to establish with users in order for them to be dominant in the future. Operational costs that can come as a result of compliance with regulation, as well as revenue challenges accompanying user distrust, must be addressed. Further, companies need to demonstrate and commit to internal policies, as well as actions and people dedicated to enforce those policies, in order to retain investor interest and investor dollars.

These issues are increasingly international. In 2021, China saw its first facial recognition privacy ruling when a visitor to Hangzhou Safari Park sued the establishment for collecting facial data without obtaining consent from visitors.[47] This controversy began when the complainant purchased an annual pass. He agreed to let the park collect his fingerprints and photo for admission. When the park later

Challenges of Today and Tomorrow

notified him that the old entry system had been replaced with facial recognition technology, the visitor became worried about identity theft and filed suit. The court ordered the defendant to delete the plaintiff's facial recognition data and pay a small amount of monetary compensation.[48] The case was the first since China published a draft law on personal data protection in 2020, which was intended to prevent the illegal collection and sharing of personal information.

This issue matters to business leaders who are pursuing strong social strategies because of the prevalence of data protection laws over recent years. From Europe's General Data Protection Regulation to China's new data privacy law, now known as Personal Information Protection Law, regulations are more commonplace globally, and they are being enforced. Businesses that operate in different parts of the world need to be aware of and have policies to comply with relevant laws. Thoughtful executives will also try to understand the motivations behind these laws, as well as the general regional climate and the priorities of the governments involved.

As stated by Omer Tene, a partner specializing in data, privacy, and cybersecurity at the law firm Goodwin, "If European data protection laws are grounded in fundamental rights and US privacy laws are grounded in consumer protection, Chinese privacy law is closely aligned with, and I would even say grounded in, national security."[49]

As we've seen throughout this chapter, failure to comply can have immediate-term consequences as well as longer-term consequences.

The future points strongly to increased regulation globally. Knowing why a specific region imposes regulations and their current priorities is a first step in understanding what impending regulations could be imposed and how to prepare for them. This will prevent being caught flat footed and risking litigation and reputational issues down the road, while also putting you ahead of the game in tomorrow's ESG-focused business environment.

Whether you're a startup tech firm or an established one, there are ways to get data security right. Consider Apple, which according to security.org, is a tech company that gets it right when it comes to the security of user information.[50] In a 2022 study, the cybersecurity organization concluded that Apple ranks highest among big tech companies for keeping user data private. Awarding the company an A+, researchers concluded that Apple collects relatively little information compared to companies such as Google, Facebook, and Twitter. Although they do keep track of device use, they only maintain the information that is necessary to the maintenance of subscriber accounts. They also refrain from selling the personal information of their customer to third parties. The importance to businesses is this: Apple is an industry leader and the company's standing as it relates to data security shows how an industry leader should behave.

Of course, markets change over time. Cyber-criminals become more sophisticated. Competitors become more nimble and agile. Even established leaders need to keep doing the work to stay prepared. In order to keep data secure, comply with regulations, and prevent litigation, businesses will need to understand their regional environment and prepare themselves for impending rules through compliance and forward-thinking policy. One simple yet practical step your team can take is to track and monitor obsolete products to prevent data breaches from manifesting there. Firms of all sizes who want to be good stewards with strong ESG focus are future focused, taking into consideration their environment and their customer needs, not just today but for tomorrow.

Commitments to Customer Welfare

Customer welfare is another ESG issue that may increasingly confront companies and investors in the future. A notorious example of corporations ignoring customer welfare is of course the tobacco industry, which faced significant backlash during the 1990s as numerous antismoking organizations joined together in their protests.[51] Activists used a variety of tactics—including media campaigns, boycotts, and lawsuits—to publicly shame cigarette makers. These efforts went a long way to diminish the tobacco industry's social license to do business. In 1998, 46 states and five of America's largest tobacco companies entered into the largest civil litigation settlement in US history to that point. The "Master Settlement" sharply restricted the companies' ability to create pro-tobacco advertising, and it required them to pay $246 billion over the course of 25 years.[52]

The issue of customer welfare isn't limited to companies that make obviously dangerous products. It needs to be top of mind for any company creating products for consumption, especially in the consumer packaged goods space. Concerns about unhealthy products extend to alcohol companies, gambling, producers of sugary and salty foods and beverages, and pretty much anything sold specifically to children.

Controversies about potentially harmful products exemplify how interrelated these issues can become, affecting businesses, consumers, and governments. In 2005, the Center for Science in the Public Interest, a consumer advocacy agency, filed suit against the Food and Drug Administration (FDA) for failing to regulate the amount of salt in the food supply.[53] As justification for the suit, the group pointed to the consumption of dangerously high levels of salt by Americans. In response, the FDA published guidance for food manufacturers and chain restaurants regarding voluntary sodium reduction in processed, prepared, and packaged foods.[54] In 2013, the city of New York issued what came to be known as "the soda ban," which prohibited restaurants, movie theaters, and food service establishments from serving sugary drinks in sizes larger than 16 ounces.[55] (The regulation was not applicable to drinks sold by grocery and convenience stores, which fell under state regulations.[56]) Not all progressive policies last.

Beverage companies such as PepsiCo campaigned heavily against the limit and eventually joined a suit in opposition to it. The New York Court of Appeals, overturned the regulation in 2014, ruling that the New York City Board of Health exceeded its authority.[57] Many consumers were delighted—a poll published by the *New York Times* had found that 6 in 10 residents opposed the ban.[58]

This points to a key issue about customer sentiment on social issues; not every customer will have the same view. Customers are not a monolithic group and should not be treated as such. As businesses consider how to progress their ESG agenda, they will need to establish connections between themselves and their customer base. This can be done via focus groups, employee resource groups, or customer roundtables who can share opinions around your product—even if those opinions contradict each other. These groups can help you gain insight into how to improve customer welfare while also equipping customers to act as advocates for your business, while equipping you to act as advocates for the customers' welfare. As we've stated in the book, this type of partnership is important for demonstrating ESG leadership in the future.

When companies provide goods that people consume, they need to be aware of the litigation and long-term costs that can arise when the products might be perceived as harmful. Even without regulation, consumers may still recognize the risks involved in the product and refuse to consume it, and even work collectively to force changes in the product. The list of lawsuits in this arena is long and includes the following:

- In 2002, a 56-year-old man filed a class-action lawsuit against a number of fast-food companies, including KFC, McDonald's, Burger King, and Wendy's over their unhealthy food. The lawsuit alleged that the restaurants failed to properly disclose all ingredients included within their foods.[59] The suit was ulti-

mately dismissed, but not before costing the restaurants significant litigation expenses and sparking numerous other similar
actions.[60]

- In 2008, McDonald's Corp. was sued by a California mother
and the Center for Science in the Public Interest for "exploiting
very young California children and harming their health by
advertising unhealthy Happy Meals with toys directly to them."[61]
This suit was also dismissed by the courts.[62]

- The following year, a man filed suit against Kellogg's for leading him to believe that the Froot Loops cereal contained actual
fruit.[63] The lawsuit was dismissed for legal technicalities, but
again, it required the company to pay out legal expenses and
sparked additional lawsuits from citizens.[64]

- As of March 2022, more than 700 school districts nationwide
have joined in an ongoing lawsuit against Juul Labs, Inc., a
nicotine vape manufacturer.[65]

Although many of these types of lawsuits prove unsuccessful,
they can still be costly in terms of high legal fees, lost company time,
and a general hit to a company's social reputation. Additionally, companies often find themselves increasing marketing costs to counter
bad publicity and win their customers back.

Business managers in the food and beverage sector should be
aware of the prospect of greater regulations around reducing quan-
tities of certain ingredients—especially sugar, sweeteners, and salt.
Firms may struggle to replicate the expected flavors and textures in
this new, more health-conscious environment. In the United Kingdom, Public Health England (PHE) has demanded that food manufacturers reduce calories by 20% before 2024.[66] It has also called for
stricter guidelines regarding the advertisement of unhealthy foods to
children. Several companies have agreed to make relevant changes,

including Kellogg's, which revealed plans to reduce the amount of sugar in its children's cereals sold in the United Kingdom by 40%.[67] Major drink manufacturers such as AG Barr and Britvic have also significantly reduced the amount of sugar in their products. Whether you produce food or cleaning products, the well-being of your customers will weigh heavily as it pertains to your sustainability performance.

Nothing is easy, but getting ahead of these trends and becoming an industry leader can have its benefits. The Seventh Generation household product line makes sustainable products with a focus on promoting health and wellness.[68] With a mission to make the world more sustainable for the next seven generations, the company uses plant-based formulas to create products such as household cleaners, which have historically been dangerous to the environment as well as to users. The company also operates with full ingredient transparency to further promote wellness and ensure that consumers are fully informed about the products they are using. Seventh Generation designed a laundry pack that meets the strict criteria of the EPA Safer Choice program. It also removed all boric acid from its products in response to concerns about its toxicity.[69] In terms of specific metrics, Seventh Generation committed to goals that included reducing virgin plastics in packaging by 75% and cutting their total plastic use in half, all by 2025. Their 2020 sustainability report stated that in 2018, 30% of their packaging used virgin plastic and in 2020, they admitted that their total plastics use had increased. A note to business leaders is that it is admirable that Seventh Generation not only publicized their goals, but also stated publicly when they fell short.

Supply Chain: Labor Issues and Human Rights

For many companies, the supply chain is where most of their social impact challenges arise. This is largely due to the failure of business leaders to closely examine the operations of all suppliers in their chains. Others may have policies against certain behaviors but no process for identifying and addressing noncompliance. Still others have no policies in place and move forward under the assumption that their suppliers operate within acceptable social parameters. Supply chain issues arise in a number of ways, but the exploitation of labor is one of the most common.

Conscripts are individuals who are enlisted into working for a particular organization by force. Though we often hear the term *conscript* in relation to military service; in areas of the world with high rates of worker exploitation, vulnerable individuals can be conscripted into oppressive labor-intensive situations by governments or private businesses. Forced labor became a huge problem for the Canadian firm Nevsun Resources when it partnered with the Eritrean government to build the country's first modernized mining operation.[70] When building commenced in 2008, Nevsun put little to no human rights protections in place. Company leaders also made minimal effort to research labor practices within the country or prepare for possible human rights violations. At the government's insistence, Nevsun engaged Segen Construction Company as a local contractor. According to Human Rights Watch, evidence suggests that Segen routinely exploits conscript workers assigned to it by the government of Eritrea.[71] Some workers interviewed at the mine site disclosed that they had been conscripted by the government. Human Rights Watch also found that many of Segen's workers were forced to endure horrendous conditions, including inadequate food and unsafe housing. It is a moral imperative to not be involved in such practices—in other words, something that transcends business priorities entirely.

Human Rights Watch prepared a report about the situation in 2013, characterizing Nevsun's response—or lack thereof—as "a situation of deep concern." They explained that Nevsun officials seemed uncertain about the use of conscripts and that attempts to investigate were blatantly denied. According to Human Rights Watch, Segen refused to allow Nevsun to interview mine workers; "Nevsun appears to feel that it has no power to confront its own politically connected contractor about allegations of abuse at its own mine site. Instead its response to Segen's stonewalling has been one of quiet acceptance."[72] In 2016, Nevsun was faced with the legal repercussions of their willful ignorance when three Eritrean workers filed a lawsuit against the company, stating that they were forced under threat of imprisonment to work in harsh conditions, without adequate pay or access to food.[73] In an affidavit filed with the case, one worker described the death of a fellow conscript. According to Amnesty International, Nevsun settled the lawsuit in October 2020, following years of unsuccessful attempts to have the courts throw out the case.[74] Although the exact settlement amount was undisclosed, sources described it as "significant."[75] Company leaders must be aware that these sorts of violations are increasingly likely to bring legal and financial punishments, even if the violations happened in the past.

Child labor exploitation is another risk that companies face within their supply chains. It is estimated that almost 152 million children globally suffer at the hands of forced labor and its crippling effects on their health and overall well-being.[76] International Labour Organization defines child labor as work that "is mentally, physically, socially or morally dangerous and harmful to children; and/or interferes with their schooling by: depriving them of the opportunity to attend school; obliging them to leave school prematurely; or requiring them to attempt to combine school attendance with excessively long and heavy work."[77] The majority of the countries with the worst records on child labor are located within the continent of Africa, where an estimated one-fifth of all children fall into some category of child laborer. Countries in Asia and the Pacific follow Africa, with an estimated 62 million children forced into labor.[78] These countries generally suffer from high rates of poverty, and little is done to enforce

245

Challenges of Today and Tomorrow

what few labor laws do exist. As such, children are sometimes taken from their schools and forced into farming work. Students who resist may face threats to themselves and their families, or risk financial destitution.[79]

Western companies should expect to be held accountable for their contributions to the demand for global child labor. The companies Mars, Nestle, and Hershey were among the defendants named in a 2021 lawsuit brought by human rights firm International Rights Advocates on behalf of former child workers in the Ivory Coast of Africa.[80] Eight children claimed that they had been subjected to slave labor practices on cocoa plantations that existed as part of the companies' supply chains. They accused the corporations of aiding and abetting the illegal enslavement of thousands of children. In 2022, in response to global backlash, Nestle announced it would improve compensation for African farmers, with the intention of keeping their children in school instead of working as child laborers. Nestle's CEO Mark Schneider said the initiative "focuses on the root cause for child labor."[81]

Nestle's actions might seem like good practice, but here we can see how a deeper dive casts the genuineness of these actions into doubt. The company had to be pushed into these changes by massive negative publicity. Significantly, they have taken steps to remove themselves from independent bodies designed to regulate pay and labor—such as Fairtrade—to set up their own, non-independent body, eschewing scrutiny.[82]

In contrast, the Dutch B Corp called Tony's Chocoloney has embedded its exploitation-free stance into its branding. They've been intentional about rooting out child labor in the production of their products, and in 2020 identified 87 cases of illegal child labor in their supply chain.[83] Although they are still working on the problem of illegal child labor, they are seen as a chocolate industry disruptor. In 2021, net revenues went from 88.4 million Euros to 109.6 million Euros, demonstrating increasing support from consumers.[84] Furthermore, because they make their commitments public and are fully transparent about work they have yet to do, the company is seen as a model of ethical business among its peers.

Looking beyond chocolates, US-based retailer Patagonia has taken an interesting approach in its efforts to prevent child labor within the garment industry.[85] One aspect of their plan is similar to Nestle's: the company seeks to increase farmer revenue and create a communitywide approach to preventing child labor. But additionally, Patagonia has been surprisingly transparent about the potential for fair labor violations within its global production chain.[86] The company's leaders admit to the virtual impossibility of treating each and every worker well at every single point along the production process, even when the company is genuinely committed to that goal.

In response to this reality, Patagonia instituted a remediation plan for instances in which acts of forced labor, slavery, or human trafficking activities are identified within the supply chain.[87] On receiving allegations of forced labor, slavery, or human trafficking, Patagonia's corporate responsibility and sourcing teams activate the investigation and remediation protocol, which includes a review of local laws to identify gaps that need to be filled, communication with the source of the report, communication with factory management, a full investigation, and reporting of the incident to appropriate authorities. Once findings are finalized, Patagonia works with the factory to develop sustainable corrective action plans and timelines, with continuous monitoring. Though the company still contends with occasional allegations and concerns about potential child labor within its supply chain, its commitment to transparency and substantive change went a long way to repair its reputation in the eyes of the public. In January 2015, the company was asked to share its experiences and responses to child labor at the White House Forum on Combating Human Trafficking in Supply Chains.[88] In 2019, the Ethical Fashion

Report awarded Patagonia a grade of A+ for its ethical business practices, transparency, and traceability.[89]

To prepare for a future where sustainability is embedded into your corporate strategy, not as an afterthought, leaders should pay close attention to their supply chains to make sure advocacy for human rights is a part their policies and are embraced by their vendors.

Human rights violations will threaten a company's reputation. Today, they are already a sure way to earn the ire of NGOs, consumers, and regulators. But tomorrow, in a business environment that's increasingly focused on a just society, ignoring human rights will be a genuine competitive disadvantage. In the future, leaders in sustainability will increasingly be market leaders as well.

Recession, Inflation, and ESG

With inflation in the US hitting close to 9%[90] in May 2022, it is an often neglected, but nevertheless important concern that investments not contribute to inflationary pressures. As inflation squeezes wages and increases the cost of living, these pressures can harm workers' quality of life, and thus inevitably fail the "social" element of ESG.

In the near term, investors may still be expected to increase profits in an inflationary environment, while remaining committed to clients' ESG preferences.

In their discussion of ESG, Inigo Fraser Jenkins and Alla Harmsworth, co-authors of the white paper "The Intimate Linkage of ESG and Inflation," speak to the notion that pursuing ESG strategies in an inflationary environment is a part of ongoing and complex market changes that investors can expect as part of their business.

"Any mode of investing must continually evolve as it encounters the vagaries of the investment landscape and changing investor preferences. ... ESG is no different, and we think a sustained resurgence of inflation will bring changes in people's definitions of ESG. One thing seems certain: ESG investing is here to stay".[91]

Simply put, inflation may add another layer on top of what may already be considered a delicate dance of increasing revenues, while continuing to prioritize investments that benefit climate and society.

Example of Supply Chain Success

There are many examples of companies successfully monitoring their supply chains for social violations and putting policies in place to strengthen their partners. One way to go about this is to embrace suppliers' growth through formal opportunities to learn together.

Mary Jane Melendez is chief sustainability officer for General Mills. In Chapter 2, we discussed her company's commitment to investing in the farmers that comprise their supply chain. On the topic of regenerative agriculture efforts, she says,

It starts from close to home because we're learning as we're stepping into this for the very first time and investing in helping farmers to step into the regenerative agriculture process and in moving their lands to be more regenerative. It was really important that we think about these in terms of learning laboratories. So the farm all of a sudden becomes this really powerful classroom where we have been bringing leaders to learn and understand what the farmers are seeing, the differences between soil on a piece of land that is *not* managed regeneratively versus what soil looks like when it is.[92]

The future of sustainably-focused businesses includes high levels of innovation. Whether you're in the consumer packaged goods or agricultural industry, the best way to innovate is to educate and train employees and suppliers about how to operate and bring communities goods they care about, with environmental efficiency in mind.

Size *Doesn't* Matter: Businesses and Social Progress

Businesses—even small and mid-sized ones—are well positioned to support social improvements. In addition to serving their customers, businesses have the power to improve the well-being of their employees and the economic conditions of the regions where they operate. Larger global companies have resources, finances, and human capital. Their leaders may also have relationships with other industry leaders, those who head their vendor companies. Bigger firms also have substantial capital they can allocate to community projects globally. However, multinationals may have a long timeline to put social improvement plans into effect, because more people usually equals more red tape.

Small and medium-sized enterprises (SMEs), by contrast, may only have regional or even just local reach. Founders of SMEs usually have intimate relationships with local communities that were sometimes forged before the business was even developed. People who are considered friends, who work alongside you, or even buy from you are more incentivized to partner with you on programs to improve the communities where, not coincidentally, their employees also live.

Employees may not only have their fingers on the pulse of social issues that can impact your business, but they are also your business' most important partners. When you create a company culture that focuses on the mental and physical well-being of your staff, equitable and fair pay and promotion practices, and inclusion at all levels, your teams are not only happier, but they are more creative and innovative. No matter the size of your firm, empowering employees to make decisions about the culture and even about your ESG strategy can support your employees' growth. Employee Resources Groups (ERGs) encompass teams of employees who are empowered to source funding, intellectual resources, and human capital toward engaging the firm in issues such as community relations, sustainability, and even cultural awareness of historically underrepresented communities. Leverage, encourage, and compensate ERGs to support your ESG efforts. They will be valuable in holding you to account.

How to Get Started

Across the last ten chapters, we have seen how efforts aimed at all facets of ESG are important and rightfully so. Similarly, we have seen that due to their relationship to complex earth, cultural, and management systems, ESG is not a simple tick-box exercise and requires ongoing investment of funding, effort, and research. We've shown through examples about supply chains, product development diversity, Indigenous rights, and consumer privacy that businesses can play a role in improving the world around them. In many cases, this can be a catalyst to improve resources inside the firm. Get ahead of the curve by first reviewing the information provided in the Appendix. It will help you organize your initial thoughts as you begin to solve issues inside and outside your firm with both workers and suppliers.

Once a company takes the steps to strengthen its social standing, it can benefit from improved relationships and support within the communities where they operate and do business. This can have a direct effect on the company's reputation, which can further translate into the financial benefits of increased revenue and investments. An improved reputation can also increase a company's standing within its peer group because it serves as an example to competitors. They can also leverage these programs to build employee morale as they empower the workforce to innovate, driving revenue and market solutions. In the Appendix, I will provide a practical guide to balancing social tenets within your ESG strategy, applying my industry knowledge attained from interviewing C-suite executives, institutional investors, and real-world consultancies.

Now we're moving into some key considerations for business leaders who want to contribute to society and see their business grow as a result. Executives, board members, managers, and individual contributors should ask themselves and their colleagues these questions:

- Where are our firm's resources?
- Where do the interests of our employees lie?
- What is top of mind among current and potential investors?
- How do I engage potential partners, including community members, to work with them on these issues?

For business leaders who need greater clarity when considering the *S* in their ESG planning, the UN Sustainable Development Goals provides a valuable starting point. In this section, and the Appendix that follows, we're calling out issues that are important now and will only become more critical in the months and years ahead. Note here how the *S*, is often very much connected to the *E*. You are going to want to examine the impacts of these topics on your business, your business's locations, and your workforce:

- **Climate migration.** Understand how changes in population size will affect economic environment. Clarity on how this affects your business can help you develop tools to support the people who will feel the economic effects of having to change locations—and change jobs—due to climate issues such as flooding and droughts.

- **Weather-related physical climate risk.** Although your company's headquarters or other buildings may not be exposed now, expect that to change. If you have a global supply chain or have offices located in areas that are experiencing severe weather, now is the time to partner with NGOs, peers, and other organizations in those regions to determine how your business can help the people and the environment.

- **Human trafficking.** Work hand-in-hand with your supply chain to develop the right policies to prevent this from even happening.

- **Pandemics.** Engage with NGOs to support research, contribute financing, and even volunteer. Again, understand what resources your business has and how to make the biggest impact.

- **Food/water scarcity.** Understand where food and water shortages are likely to be most severe, then leverage your resources to deliver resources for research, contribute financing, or even volunteer. This is a simplified approach, but it is important to first understand the issue.

- **Well-paying jobs and leaving no employee behind.** Develop training programs to support ongoing learning among your employees (e.g. preparing employees to work in new/green industries) while maintaining a high level of innovation at your firm to ensure you and your employees remain competitive.

For practical guidance on how to be an industry leader in dealing with risks and opportunities of tomorrow's social issues, see the Appendix that follows this chapter.

Chapter 10 Takeaways

- Though the ESG space has traditionally focused on *E* first and *S* to follow, there is a noticeable shift occurring where worker/supplier elements of the *S* in ESG are just as critical as climate and other *E* elements.

- Business leaders and boards, even on the small and mid-sized scale, can and should create and implement an ESG agenda. Do this by looking at product design, customer welfare, and even how to prevent cybersecurity disruptions.

- Enforce and adhere to practices in environmental and community preservation. These actions will not only support the company's future growth and revenues but also shareholder value and the growth and health of the communities where they do business.

- Supply chain health is a critical element of any business. Work with suppliers to establish policies as well as educational programming on hot-button issues. It's a way to develop a competitive advantage while improving relationships.

- Companies that neglect social issues may experience negative legal, social, and financial consequences. But if handled correctly, the process of addressing these problems head-on can actually be beneficial. Companies can solve for important social issues while meeting the expectations of their consumers, boosting standing among peers and attracting increased investment.

Notes

1. Michael Posner interview with the author (February 9, 2022).
2. Ibid.
3. Ibid.
4. Ibid.
5. https://www.culturalsurvival.org/publications/cultural-survival-quarterly/corporations-and-rights-indigenous-peoples-advancing.
6. Ibid.
7. Michael Posner interview with the author (February 9, 2022).
8. Ibid.
9. https://www.culturalsurvival.org/publications/cultural-survival-quarterly/corporations-and-rights-indigenous-peoples-advancing.
10. https://www.theguardian.com/news/2019/feb/19/palm-oil-ingredient-biscuits-shampoo-environmental.
11. https://www.aljazeera.com/news/2021/10/15/guatemala-growing-palm-oil-industry-fuels-indigenous-land-fight.
12. Ibid.
13. https://www.facing-finance.org/en/database/cases/palm-oil-in-indonesia.
14. https://www.farmlandgrab.org/26679.
15. https://www.amnestyusa.org/reports/the-great-palm-oil-scandal-labor-abuses-behind-big-brand-names.
16. https://www.facing-finance.org/en/database/cases/palm-oil-in-indonesia.
17. https://www.npr.org/sections/thetwo-way/2017/02/22/514988040/key-moments-in-the-dakota-access-pipeline-fight.
18. https://www.colorado.edu/program/fpw/DAPL-case-study.
19. https://www.colorado.edu/program/fpw/sites/default/files/attached-files/social_cost_and_material_loss_0.pdf.
20. Ibid.
21. Ibid.
22. https://www.americasquarterly.org/fulltextarticle/business-responsibility-to-respect-indigenous-rights/.
23. Ibid.
24. https://www.bhp.com.
25. https://www.americasquarterly.org/fulltextarticle/business-responsibility-to-respect-indigenous-rights/.
26. https://www.theguardian.com/environment/2022/mar/10/canadian-pipeline-groups-spend-big-to-pose-as-indigenous-champions.
27. Ibid.
28. https://towardsdatascience.com/racial-bias-in-software-772d6e949269.
29. https://www.theverge.com/2021/7/2/22560628/google-diversity-report-departures-black-women.

30. https://techcrunch.com/2016/11/16/when-bias-in-product-design-means-life-or-death/.
31. https://www.mckinsey.com/business-functions/mckinsey-design/how-we-help-clients/design-blog/drive-innovation-with-accessible-product-design.
32. https://www.mckinsey.com/business-functions/mckinsey-design/how-we-help-clients/design-blog/drive-innovation-with-accessible-product-design.
33. https://arstechnica.com/tech-policy/2021/04/appeals-court-rules-stores-dont-need-to-make-their-websites-accessible/.
34. www.accessibilitychecker.com.
35. https://userway.org.
36. Sarah Gordon interview with the author (January 17, 2022).
37. https://www.gapinc.com/en-us/values/sustainability/social/talent-management/equality-belonging.
38. Ibid.
39. https://www.gapinc.com/en-us/articles/2020/02/gap-inc-product-inclusion-summit-welcomed-guests-f.
40. https://www.diversityinc.com/experts-warn-of-burnout-within-corporate-diversity-workforce-one-year-into-new-social-justice-era/.
41. https://www.mckinsey.com/business-functions/mckinsey-design/how-we-help-clients/design-blog/drive-innovation-with-accessible-product-design.
42. https://www.logitechg.com/en-us/products/gamepads/adaptive-gaming-kit-accessories.943-000318.html.
43. https://irishtechnews.ie/logitech-g-adaptive-gaming-kit-accessibility-needs.
44. https://www.natlawreview.com/article/facebook-to-pay-90-million-to-settle-data-privacy-lawsuit.
45. Ibid.
46. https://www.msn.com/en-us/news/politics/facebook-settling-privacy-lawsuit-for-90m/ar-AATTcVE.
47. https://news.cgtn.com/news/2021-04-10/China-s-first-lawsuit-on-facial-recognition-made-verdict-ZlvYRrL2la/index.html.
48. Ibid.
49. https://www.wired.com/story/china-personal-data-law-pipl/.
50. https://www.security.org/resources/data-tech-companies-have/.
51. https://onlineexhibits.library.yale.edu/s/sellingsmoke/page/big-tobacco-big-lawsuits.
52. https://news.harvard.edu/gazette/story/2021/08/applying-lessons-learned-from-the-tobacco-settlement-to-opioid-negotiations/.
53. https://www.webmd.com/food-recipes/news/20050224/lawsuit-asks-fda-to-regulate-salty-foods.
54. https://www.natlawreview.com/article/fda-issues-guidance-voluntary-sodium-reduction.
55. https://www.nycourts.gov/reporter/3dseries/2013/2013_05505.htm.

56. https://www.reuters.com/article/us-sodaban-lawsuit-idUSBRE92A0YR20130311.
57. https://www.nycourts.gov/ctapps/Decisions/2014/Jun14/134opn14-Decision.pdf.
58. https://www.nytimes.com/2012/08/23/nyregion/most-new-yorkers-oppose-bloombergs-soda-ban.html.
59. https://abcnews.go.com/US/story?id=91427&page=1.
60. https://money.cnn.com/2003/01/22/news/companies/mcdonalds/.
61. https://www.latimes.com/archives/la-xpm-2010-dec-15-la-fi-mcdonalds-lawsuit-20101215-story.html.
62. https://www.foxnews.com/politics/california-judge-dismisses-happy-meal-lawsuit.
63. https://www.loweringthebar.net/2010/04/yet-another-lawsuit-claims-no-fruit-in-froot-loops.html.
64. https://melmagazine.com/en-us/story/crunch-berry-cereal-lawsuit.
65. https://clarksvillenow.com/local/cmcss-joins-700-other-school-districts-in-national-mass-action-lawsuit-against-juul-vape-manufacturers/.
66. https://www.reutersevents.com/sustainability/how-big-brands-are-helping-consumers-shift-healthier-eating-options.
67. Ibid.
68. https://www.seventhgeneration.com/blog/how-we-work-seventh-generations-principle-precaution.
69. Ibid.
70. https://www.hrw.org/report/2013/01/15/hear-no-evil/forced-labor-and-corporate-responsibility-eritreas-mining-sector.
71. Ibid.
72. https://www.hrw.org/report/2013/01/15/hear-no-evil/forced-labor-and-corporate-responsibility-eritreas-mining-sector#.
73. https://qz.com/africa/794955/eritrean-workers-are-suing-nevsun-resources-a-canadian-mining-company-for-using-them-as-forced-labor/.
74. https://www.business-humanrights.org/en/latest-news/nevsun-lawsuit-re-bisha-mine-eritrea/.
75. Ibid.
76. https://www.compassion.com/poverty/child-labor-quick-facts.htm.
77. https://www.compassion.com/poverty/child-labor-quick-facts.htm.
78. Ibid.
79. https://ec.europa.eu/international-partnerships/stories/are-clothes-you-are-wearing-free-child-labour_en.
80. https://www.theguardian.com/global-development/2021/feb/12/mars-nestle-and-hershey-to-face-landmark-child-slavery-lawsuit-in-us.
81. https://africa.businessinsider.com/local/markets/following-child-labour-backlash-nestle-proposes-to-pay-african-cocoa-farmers-to-keep/63bbvd2.

82. https://www.fairtrade.org.uk/media-centre/blog/nestles-kitkat-will-stop-being-fairtrade-faq/.
83. https://www.confectionerynews.com/Article/2021/02/16/Tony-s-Chocolonely-rejects-modern-slavery-allegation-in-its-cocoa.
84. https://www.confectionerynews.com/Article/2021/12/06/Tony-s-Chocolonely-sees-revenues-pass-100M-revenue-mark-driven-by-UK-sales.
85. https://www.theneweconomy.com/business/how-businesses-can-avoid-buying-into-child-labour.
86. https://www.theatlantic.com/business/archive/2015/06/patagonia-labor-clothing-factory-exploitation/394658/.
87. https://www.patagonia.com/static/on/demandware.static/-/Library-Sites-PatagoniaShared/default/dwb48d6b02/PDF-US/human_trafficking_child_labor.pdf.
88. https://www.inc.com/anna-hensel/patagonia-pledges-to-implement-higher-standards-in-factories.html.
89. https://media.bhrrc.org/media/documents/files/documents/FashionReport_2019_9-April-19-FINAL.pdf.
90. Trading Economics US inflation Rate https://tradingeconomics.com/united-states/inflation-cpi
91. Alliance Bernstein https://www.alliancebernstein.com/americas/en/institutions/solutions/insights-and-solutions/the-intimate-linkage-of-esg-and-inflation-esg-and-the-hegelian-dialectic.html#:~:text=ESG%20is%20a%20cause%20of,investors%20need%20to%20deal%20with.
92. Mary Jane Melendez interview with the author (March 10, 2022).

Appendix: ESG Analysis for Beginners

Measuring and decreasing the effects of climate change on communities and businesses is of paramount importance for regulators, NGOs, investors, and corporations, but there are many other social problems competing for attention. A steady stream of employment data numbers suggests that pools of potential employees are shrinking, and scathing stories about the "great resignation" suggest the reasons why. People of color continue to be underrepresented at senior levels of management. Meanwhile, there is a perception of inconsistency in return-to-work safety protocols. In the post-COVID era, we're seeing a resurgence of rigid management structures that force conformity around when and how we work (many of which gave rise to the great resignation in the first place). Given all this churn in the employment sector, measuring worker engagement and safety is swiftly rising in terms of importance. Lack of engagement and poor safety protocols often coexist with inequity. Money and status dictates where people live, which in turn impacts the quality of land, air, and water they can access. It is this limited access which becomes a reality for marginalized people at lower ends of the pay and worker safety spectrum.

Strong and enforceable policies around worker engagement are a must for corporations big and small. But strong policy isn't necessarily about a show of force by the firm. It is about being resolute in your determination to support workers in the way they want to be supported—be that within the formal office setting or not. It is about giving them a say in how products are built, and the way they interact with and give back to the communities where they live and work. Strong and enforceable policy involves an honest assessment and accountability structure around building an inclusive executive leadership team; it starts with a strong commitment to the people in your firm. Remember, we are in a workers' economy: in a post-COVID world, employees wield considerable power in determining where they work, how they work, what they earn, and how they are treated.

Your firm may not have been called out by negative media reports about working conditions. You may not have experienced employee lawsuits around lack of D&I, or NGO queries on supplier oversight. Not yet, at least. But just because your firm might be small or mid-size, that doesn't mean you are immune from either financial penalties or reputational damage if your practices go against society's view of what is acceptable workplace conduct.

It benefits your firm to have policies in place *before* stakeholders, like customers, investors, and NGOs, call out unacceptable conduct or perceived violations. Also, you need sound worker and supplier engagement and policy footing *before* formal regulations are brought to bear. Remember, when you outsource goods or widgets, you can be held accountable for your vendors' unethical behaviors.

One of the best tools you can use to identify which current and future workplace and supplier policies to report and how, is to look at your competitors. Understand how they report their data—whether in a dedicated sustainability report, or as part of their 10K. Review topics they call out in their reports, including quantitative metrics (e.g. numbers of workplace injuries, numbers of senior leaders from underrepresented groups) and qualitative insights (e.g. description of how suppliers will be engaged to eliminate child labor at their plant). Also, look at progress competitors made on those issues over the years, through year-by-year trend analysis that may be offered in their reports. See what they are doing correctly and build from there.

Appendix: ESG Analysis for Beginners

If you want to stay in business, and even be competitive as a top employer for the best candidates, then regularly re-assessed and improved worker and supplier policies are a good way to future-proof your business.

The purpose of the chart on the following pages is to detail just a few of the many worker and supplier issues that can affect your reputation and revenues. Use these as prompts for corporate reporting, to consider whether you are adhering to rules already in place, or what you intend to put in place to improve worker and supplier experience. This information shouldn't replace formal standards and frameworks (e.g. Value Reporting Foundation, Global Reporting Initiative); rather, it can complement and help validate the importance of these workplace topics to your business.

The worker- and supplier-issue list below is neither exhaustive, nor industry specific. In fact, as you take next steps in building worker and supplier policies and corporate reporting around them, you should view these issues in context of your specific industry. The way a particular issue plays out, in terms of reputational and revenue risk or opportunity for your firm, may vary from industry to industry and sometimes region by region (depending on regional regulations, economic environment, and so on).

This list compiles only some of worker and supplier topics that are likely to grow in importance. These issues can be critical to attracting the best talent, getting financing from investors, and maintaining social license to operate with the public. We'll explore those issues in context of three items:

1. *Risks* associated with these issues

2. *Opportunities* associated with these issues

3. *Interventions* your firm can take to ensure your practices align with best worker, supplier, and societal outcomes

Issue: Worker safety: COVID-19 safety

Risks:

- As of early 2022, OSHA is working on a COVID-19 healthcare standard, thus there is no clear guidance to be followed in the U.S. Lack of standards present a wild west scenario where each entity is on its own to develop guidance
- Because no framework exists, employees may suffer from severe illness, ruined lives, long-lasting personal harm, and even death; business outcomes include sizable lawsuits and reputational catastrophe
- Pressure from the public and negative media could require expensive marketing efforts to improve public sentiment and entice customers and employees back to your firm

Opportunities:

- Tightening worker health and protection efforts—especially when not litigated to do so—may improve investor and employee perception of the company
- Demonstrating this type of industry leadership, even at cost to your firm, reflects your company values; during public health crises, this can increase your company's intangible value (e.g. reputation) as well as financial value
- When workers feel a company is committed to their health and the health of their families, workers may feel a deeper commitment to the firm resulting in increased productivity

Interventions:

- Closely follow state regulations, as well as federal and OSHA regulations
- Companies with international suppliers or workers should look to ISO standards
- Discuss your plan with employee groups to understand worker health concerns so they can be addressed
- Engage industry organizations to identify measures taken by others in your industry to support worker health

Appendix: ESG Analysis for Beginners

Issue: Supplier standards and oversight

Risks:

- Supplier oversight and due diligence poses challenges for large firms that rely on hundreds or even thousands of vendors; even mid-sized firms should ensure they also have rigorous policies and enforcements around their vendors
- US Foreign Corrupt Practices Act (FCPA), the UK Bribery Act (UKBA), and the Canadian Corruption of Foreign Public Officials Act (CFPOA) are just a few laws that business should be aware of and should ensure their suppliers follow
- Steep fines (and sometimes prison time) aren't the only consequences for bribery and corruption for business and or government officials who participate; reputational damage can flow from vendors to larger companies that bring them into their supply chain

Opportunities:

- Work with compliance team to identify regulations from all the regions where you have vendors, and use those regulations as a basis for your internal policies
- Partner with existing vendors to build a plan to ensure zero tolerance for bribery, corruption, human trafficking, and other illegal conduct
- Use due diligence and vendor screening solutions that exist in the marketplace when onboarding new vendors; ensure you are clear about any red-flag conduct from their past and understand measures they are taking to ensure their compliance

Interventions:

- Despite the need to bring new vendors on quickly—especially during the supply-chain crunch after the pandemic—be vigilant about proper screening when onboarding. Pay now with a bit more time or risk paying later if you onboard a vendor who engages in illegal activity
- Include in your contract with suppliers the right to audit all vendors, ongoing reporting measures, and even discontinue the contract immediately upon revelations of violating human trafficking policy
- Align with industry groups or directly with other firms in your industry to identify gaps and how you can better integrate your principles and policies throughout your value chain

263

Appendix: ESG Analysis for Beginners

Issue: Gender pay parity

Risks:

- Countries can have a variety of minimum wage rates according to geography and sector, and these may change

- Gender pay gaps are pervasive. Across the world, women still get paid 23% less than men, but there still is no universal solution or regulation around gender pay gaps

- There are business consequences to ignorance around regional laws and regulations ensuring equal pay. Some of these include: Lilly Ledbetter Fair Pay Act/US (2009), Equality Act/UK (2010), Article 20 of Labor Contract Act extension to include Part-Time and Fixed-Term Work/Japan (2020)

Opportunities:

- Aligning with the UN's Sustainable Development Goals, especially goals of gender equality and reduced inequalities within and among countries, may introduce regional partnership opportunities (e.g. governmental) that can give your business an edge on attracting top tier talent that leads to innovation

- Ensuring pay equity across various communities inside your organization, including part-time workers, is one important aspect to improving morale and delivering competitive compensation, both of which are needed for a sustainable business

- Delivering on fair and equitable pay metrics will support your firm in attracting and retaining top talent

Interventions:

- Identify what industry standards are for various roles, and determine where your company falls short in the area of parity (gender, regionally, in specific role. etc.)

- Devise a plan to achieve parity and ensure accountability throughout the organization

- Share clear quantitative commitments with employees and engage the board on your strategy and time frames for completion

- Monitor your company's efforts to achieve pay parity, via internal surveys and mid-year and end-of-year check-ins on progressing parity agenda

Appendix: ESG Analysis for Beginners

Issue: Diversity, equity, inclusion and belonging in your workforce

Risks:
- Diversity looks different in different regions; be intentional about creating policies that are tailored for your business' various locations
- Microaggressions, unconscious bias, and inappropriate language are some of the most sinister practices because they may not fall under formal HR policies and those who commit them may do so unknowingly, while still having a detrimental impact on the business culture
- If workers don't feel valued, aren't treated and paid equally, and don't have chances of promotion, all promises of "diversity" are empty

Opportunities:
- Many investors in this space shared that diversity tops their list as important information to disclose externally for investing purposes
- Leveraging a D&I index can inform you of your company's performance alongside other similar companies in your industry
- When people outside your company (e.g. media, analysts etc.) share positive stories about your business, that resonates with customers and investors more than tooting your own horn

Interventions:
- Align management pay structures to reflect hiring and retaining diverse talent,
- Ensure diverse talent is promoted into senior roles
- Combat microaggressions by addressing inappropriate words, names, and references that should not be tolerated at the company. This could be as obvious as gender, religious, ethnic, and racial slurs, but can also be less obvious terms that may be offensive
- When deciding between different countries for expanding the business, let inclusive and protective policies (e.g. sexual orientation, gender) be a factor in your decision-making

265

Appendix: ESG Analysis for Beginners

Issue: Human Trafficking

Risks:

- Lack of awareness about regulations such as United Kingdom Modern Slavery Act and California Transparency in Supply Chains Act poses a huge business risk. Learn about relevant regulations for your business, and prepare to enforce them

- Large firms have been sued by trafficking survivors for benefiting from forced labor; this demonstrates that the social contract companies have doesn't just include their direct employees anymore

- It's risky to be lulled into thinking you know what a trafficking victim "looks like" or that there is no trafficking in your industry. Be alert and aware of the different ways trafficking plays outs in different industries

Opportunities:

- Investing in robust compliance measures today—to identify existing and upcoming regulations from regions where you have vendors—helps you get ahead of tomorrow's new regulations so your resources can be spent on developing new products and services, not playing catch up on compliance

- Becoming a leader in designing best practices, in building zero tolerance bribery, corruption, and human trafficking plans, which helps you stand out and attract positive attention from NGOs and other stakeholders

- Enforcing actions—not just creating policies—against human trafficking and forced labor attracts customers and investors who share your commitment to those values

Appendix: ESG Analysis for Beginners

Interventions:

• Read stories of human trafficking survivors and circulate them widely among enforcement staff. A UN report is a good place to start. Understanding the trauma they continue to face will support your efforts in ensuring your firm does not even unknowingly support it

• Include in your contract with suppliers the right to audit all vendors, ongoing reporting measures, and even discontinue the contract immediately upon revelations of violating human trafficking policy

• Align with industry groups or directly with other firms in your industry to identify gaps and how you can better integrate your principles and policies throughout your value chain. Consider hiring specialist consultants and researchers when additional expertise is necessary.

• Leverage due diligence and vendor screening solutions that exist in the marketplace when onboarding new vendors to ensure you are clear about red-flag conduct from their past and measures they are taking to ensure their compliance

Issue: Human rights and indigenous peoples' rights

Risks:

- Extracting natural resources from indigenous communities, without consent from the community and government, may threaten biodiversity of the land and health of the people who depend on the land for their livelihood
- Lack of governance—particularly in sectors that extract commodities like energy and metals from the environment—may result in bribery scandals
- When businesses don't recognize the land rights of indigenous people, they can be subject to litigation as well as public ire

Opportunities:

- Hire directly from the community. This allows your company and the community to innovate products that are additive to the environment, as well as profitable
- Consult with indigenous communities at each planning step, and ensure shared revenue approach for their insight and work. This makes you more sustainable and respected than large, established players who might have historically taken advantage of or taken for granted the opinions of people who live there
- Remember the people who live on the land know better than you about how to sow into and reap a profit from it. Taking counsel in their opinions may pose the biggest business opportunities

Interventions:

- When looking to these lands and regions for business purposes, make sure your manufacturing and operations do not result in environmental degradation
- Know when to say no to a project because there is no feasible way to carry it out in an ethical manner. Indigenous people should be able to have the final say where necessary
- Seek the community's advice as it relates to who should work in the business enterprise
- Partner with indigenous communities to establish policies around initial engagement and ongoing engagement of business

Appendix: ESG Analysis for Beginners

Index

Page numbers followed by *f* and *t* refer to figures and tables, respectively.

Black Americans:
  as business owners, 11–12
  "Buy Black" movement, 11
  Buy from a Black Woman (nonprofit
    organization), 184
  employment of, 9–10
BlackRock (investment firm),
    2, 158
Blood, Robert, 183
Bloom, Ellen, 24
Bloomberg, 60, 132
Bloomberg, Michael, 159
Bloomberg ESG Data, 129
Blue bonds, 76–78
Blumenthal, Heston, 186
BMO Wealth Management, 96
BMW, 24, 209–210
Boards of directors, 1–2, 56,
    136, 200, 217
Bombas, 180–182
Bonds, 71–90
  basics of, 71–74
  blue, 76–78
  for environmental and social
    progress, 74–76
  green, 74–76, 83f, 84–86
  infrastructure and sustaina-
    bility, 86–89
  municipal, 83–84
  social, 79–81
  sustainability-linked, 81–83
Boston Consulting Group, 190
Boycotts, 9–10, 27, 240. *See also*
    "Buycotting"
BP (British Petroleum), 215
Brazil, 156, 157
BRI (Belt and Road Initiative), 86–87
Bris, Arturo, 57
Britvic, 243
Brooklyn, N.Y., 37
Build Back Better World (B3W), 88
Burger King, 241
Businesses:
  Black-owned, 11–12
  loss of customers, 10
  size of, 250–251

South African, 10
white-owned, 9
Business school curricula, 191–192
"Buycotting," 11
Buy from a Black Woman (nonprofit
    organization), 184

Canada, 165, 231, 244
Canal Street (New Orleans), 9–10
Capitalism, 12, 55–56, 215–216
Carbon dioxide emissions, *see*
    CO_2 emissions
Carbon footprints, *see* CO_2 emissions
Carbon neutrality, 28
Carbon sequestration, 39
Cargill (food company), 117
Caribbean region, 157
Carney, Mark, 158–159
CDP (carbon disclosure system),
    31–32, 129, 211–212
CDSB (Climate Disclosure Standards
    Board), 203, 210–211
Center for American Progress, 162
Center for Science in the Public Interest
    (CSPI), 240, 242
CEO Water Mandate, 33
Ceres (nonprofit organization), 151
Cerrejón (coal mine), 230
Chicago Tribune, 24
Childbirth, safe, 180
Child labor, 12, 117–118, 245–247
Children:
  advertising to, 242
  disabled, 184
Chile, 157
China, 33, 76, 86–88, 119,
    237–238
China Securities Regulatory
    Commission, 105
Chinese railroad workers, 15
Chocolate industry, 117–118, 246.
    See also specific companies
Cholera, 12
Churchill Capital Corporation,
    60–61
Cigarettes, 240

270

271

Index

275

Index

MSCI (country-risk ranking provider), 97–98, 98*t*, 130, 139–140
Müller, Matthias, 25
Municipal bonds, 83–84

NAACP (National Association for the Advancement of Colored People), 9
Narratives, explanatory, 217
National Association for the Advancement of Colored People (NAACP), 9
National Greenhouse and Energy Reporting Act (Australia), 105
National Grid, 36–37
National Grid Renewables, 36
Native Americans, 15, 27
Natural disasters, 118
Natural gas pipeline, 37
Nestlé, 56, 117, 226, 246–247
NetZero by 2050 Plan, 36
Net-zero goals, 36, 159
Neuberger Berman, 54
Nevsun Resources, 244
New business models, 21–41
  empty promises, 22–28
  successful goals and plans, 29–37
  supply chains, 37–41
New England Journal of Medicine, 26
New Orleans, La., 9–10
New Plastics Economy Initiative, 189
New York City, 241
New York City Board of Health, 241
New York Court of Appeals, 241
New York Times, 26, 27, 241
NGOs (non-governmental organizations), 171–172
Nicaragua, 157
Nigeria, 179, 213
Nike, 164
Non-Financial Reporting Directive, 103, 104, 113, 211
Non-governmental organizations (NGOs), 171–172
Non-profit organization, 172–173
North Dakota, 226
Norway, 115

Nova Scotia, 165
Nuveen, 56, 64–66, 83, 214

Obama, Barack, and administration, 221
Official Journal of the European Union, 103
Oil and gas industries, 1, 15, 224, 226, 231. *See also specific companies.*
One for One® giving model, 180
"One Planet, One Health," 55
Online shopping, 233
Operational costs, reducing, 46
Oscar Meyer, 186
O'Shea, Virginie, 143–144
OxyContin, 25–26

Pacific countries, 245
Packaging, *see* Product packaging
Palm oil industry, 225
Pandemics, 253. *See also* COVID-19 pandemic
Paraguay, 213
Paris Climate Accord, 160
Partnerships. *See also* Investor-corporate partnerships; Public-private partnerships
  academia and business, 191–193
  business-organization, 174–180
  DSM-Meatable, 51
Patagonia (clothing company), 247
"People and Planet Positive" strategy, 34
PepsiCo, 241
Pershing Capital, 59
Personal Information Protection Law (China), 238
Peru, 230
PetSmart, 60
PGIM Real Estate, 61
PHE (Public Health England), 242
Philanthropy, 12, 171–194
  academia and business, 191–193
  business-organization partnerships, 174–180
  controversies, 182–184
  and product packaging, 189–191
  responsible investing, 187–189

280

Index

281

Index